W9-ARG-109

HISTORY
OF RUSSIA

Sergei Mikhailovich Soloviev

The
Academic International Press
Edition
of
Sergei M. Soloviev
History of Russia From Earliest Times

G. EDWARD ORCHARD
General Editor

Contributing Editors
HUGH F. GRAHAM
JOHN D. WINDHAUSEN
ALEXANDER V. MULLER
K.A. PAPMEHL
RICHARD HANTULA
WALTER J. GLEASON, JR.
WILLIAM H. HILL
G. EDWARD ORCHARD
LINDSEY A.J. HUGHES
NICKOLAS LUPININ
GEORGE E. MUNRO
DANIEL L. SCHLAFLY, JR.
ANTHONY L.H. RHINELANDER
PATRICK J. O'MEARA
PETER C. STUPPLES
T. ALLAN SMITH
MARTHA L. LAHANA
ANTHONY V. KNOWLES
HELEN Y. PROCHAZKA
GEORGE S. PAHOMOV
GARY J. MARKER

SERGEI M. SOLOVIEV

History of Russia

Volume 32

Peter's Last Years

Foreign and Domestic Affairs, 1722-1725

Edited and Translated

By

Gary J. Marker

Academic International Press

2001

The Academic International Press Edition of S.M. Soloviev's
History of Russia From Earliest Times in fifty volumes.

Volume 32. *Peter's Last Years.*
Foreign and Domestic Affairs, 1722-1725.
Unabridged translation of the text of Volume18, Chapters 2-3 as
contained in Volume IX of S.M. Soloviev's *Istoria Rossii s
drevneishikh vremen* published in Moscow in 1959-1966, with
added annotation by Gary J. Marker.

ISBN: 0-87569-230-3

Composition by Llano F. McCowen

Printed in the United States of America

A list of Academic International Press publications is found at
the end of this volume.

ACADEMIC INTERNATIONAL PRESS
Box 1111 • Gulf Breeze FL 32562-1111 • USA

www.ai-press.com

CONTENTS

WEIGHTS AND MEASURES

Linear and Surface Measure

Arshin: 16 vershoks, 28 in. (diuims) 72.12 cm
Chetvert (quarter): 1/4 arshin, 1/2 desiatina, 1.35 acres (sometimes 1.5 desiatinas or c. 4.1 acres)
Desiatina: 2,400 square sazhens, 2.7 acres, 1.025 hectares
Diuim: 1 inch, 2.54 cm
Fut: 12 diuims, 1 foot, 30.48 cm

Obza (areal): c. 10 chetverts, 13–15 acres
Osmina: 1/4 desiatina, 600 sq. sazhens, .256 hectare
Sazhen: 3 arshins, 7 feet, 2.133 m
Vershok: 1.75 in., 4.445 cm, 1/16 arshin
Verst: 500 sazhens, 1,166 yards and 2 feet, .663 miles, 1.0668 km
Voloka (plowland): 19 desiatinas, 20 hectares, 49 acres

Liquid Measure

Bochka (barrel): 40 vedros, 121 gallons, 492 liters
Chetvert (quarter): 1.4 bochkas, 32.5 gallons
Korchago (wine): Rus, unknown

Kufa: 30 stofy
Stof: Kruzhka (cup), 1/10 vedro, c. 1.3 quarts, 1.23 liters
Vedro (pail): 3.25 gallons, 12.3 liters, 10 stofy

Weights

Berkovets: 361 lbs., 10 puds
Bezmen: c. 1 kg, 2.2 lbs.
Chetverik (grain measure dating from 16th century): 1/8 chetvert, 15.8 lbs.
Chetvert (grain measure): 1/4 rad, 3.5 puds, 126.39 lbs., c. 8 bushels
Funt: 96 zolotniks, .903 lbs., 14.4 oz., 408.24 kg
Grivenka: 205 grams
Kad: 4 chetverts, 14 puds, 505.56 lbs.
Kadka malenkaia: 12th-century, small measure

Kamen (stone): 32 funt
Korob (basket): 7 puds, 252 lbs.
Osmina (eighth): 2 osmina to a chetvert (dry measure)
Polbezmen: c. 500 g, 1 lb.
Polosmina (sixteenth): 1/2 osmina
Pud: 40 funts, 36.113 lbs. (US), 40 lbs. (Russian), 16.38 kg
Rad: 14 puds, 505.58 lbs.
Zolotnik: 1/96 lbs., 4.26 grams

Money

Altyn: 6 Muscovite dengas, 3 copecks
Bel: Rus, pure silver coin
Chervonets (chervonnyi): gold coin of first half of 18th century worth c. 3 rubles
Chetvertak: silver coin equal to 25 copecks or 1/4 ruble (18–19th centuries)
Copeck: two Muscovite dengas
Denga: 1/2 copeck
Grivna: 20 Muscovite dengas, 100 grivnas equals 1 ruble, 10 copecks
Grosh: 10 peniaz
Grosh litovsky (Lithuanian grosh): 5 silver copecks
Kopa grosh: 60 groshas, one Muscovite poltina, 1/2 ruble
Kuna: 12th-century Rus coin comparable to Westerns denarii or Eastern dirhems. Varied in value by region. Replaced late 14th century by the denga or serebro (silver). Also a marten skin.
Moskovka: 1/2 copeck
Muscovite denga: 200 equals 1 ruble
Novgorod denga: 100 equals 1 ruble
Novgorodka: 1 copeck

Peniaz: 10 equals one grosh (Lithuania)
Poltina (poltinnik): 50 copecks, 100 dengas, 1 ruble
Poltora: 1 1/2 rubles
Polupoltina (-nik): 25 copecks, 50 dengas
Rezan: 12th century Rus coin. 50 rezan equals one grivna kuna
Ruble: 100 copecks, 200 dengas
Shiroky grosh (large silver coin): 20 Muscovite copecks
Veksa: 12th-century Rus small coin equal to one squirrel pelt (belka)

Foreign Denominations
Chervonnyi: c. 3 rubles
Ducat: c. 3 rubles
Dutch efimok: "lion dollar" or levok, 1 thaler, 2.5 guilders
Efimok: foreign currency, 1 thaler, .75-1 ruble, 1 chervonets or chervonnyi
Levok: Dutch silver lion dollar
Thaler (Joachimsthaler): c. 1 ruble, 1/3 chervonets or chervonnyi

Note: Weights and measures often changed values over time and sometimes held more than one value at the same time. For details consult Sergei G. Pushkarev, *Dictionary of Russian Historical Terms from the Eleventh Century to 1917* (Yale, 1970).

PREFACE

This book is an unabridged translation of Volume 18, Chapters 2 and 3, which are pp. 407-533 in Book IX of the multi-volume edition of Soloviev's *Istoriia Rossii s drevenishikh vremen* (History of Russia from Earliest Times, 29 volumes, St. Petersburg, 1851-1879) published from 1959 through 1966 in Moscow. Soloviev's original long chapters have been subdivided and in some cases given new titles and section headings. Thus Chapters I and II of this volume coincide with his Chapter II, Chapters III-VII with his Chapter III.

The present translation endeavors to render the text and Soloviev's thought as accurately as possible. No attempt has been made to reproduce his style and text word for word, for this would have yielded a bizarre Russianized text. The main consideration has been to make his history as readable as possible in contemporary English consistent with accuracy while retaining at least something of the flavor of the language of that era. An effort has been made to find English language equivalents for all technical terms Soloviev employs (ranks, offices, titles, legal, administrative and so forth) in the belief that English is no less rich in such terms than other languages. This is intended to smooth the flow of the narrative for the reader and to avoid marring the pages with annoying untranslated words. The exception involves Russian words which have become common in English—boyar, tsar, cossack, and others.

Soloviev's prose follows the tradition of grand historical narrative that was common in the nineteenth century. The sentences tend to be long, complex and loosely structured. Paragraphs typically go on for pages, and transitions from one topic to the next are made abruptly with little attempt at transition. To make the text easier to follow for contemporary readers, long paragraphs and sentences have been broken into shorter ones. Most of the subtitles are based on the descriptive topic headings clustered at the beginnings of the chapters in the Russian edition. These headings have been moved into the body of the text as subtitles to mark and ease for the reader the transition from one subject to another. In some cases, to even the frequency of breaks in the text or to show topics not listed by Soloviev at the beginning of chapters, new subtitles have been added. Soloviev's arrangement of the material has been followed strictly.

Brief explanatory or interpretive materials have been inserted into the text enclosed in brackets, or added as footnotes to each chapter at the end of the book. All material enclosed in brackets has been added by the present editor and all material in parentheses is the author's. Emphasized words or phrases in italics are the author's.

The general policy followed in annotating has been to indentify prominent personalities at first mention, and to give explanation and elucidations of less common or obscure terms and passages, assuming the typical reader to have relatively little familiarity with Russian history. If brief, these have been included in the text in brackets, otherwise they appear as numbered footnotes at the back of the book by chapters. Most of the author's own notes are not included because their highly specialized archival, documentary and bibliographic nature is of value solely to specialists who in any case will prefer to consult the original Russian text. In addition, most of the notes added by the editors of the edition published in Moscow between 1959 and 1966 which are also technical in nature—fuller bibliographic citations than those in Soloviev's notes—have not been included. When the author's notes are included, or those of subsequent editors, they are so designated. All other notes are those of the present editor.

Russian personal names are preserved in their Russian form except for Alexander, Alexis, Catherine, Peter and others which English usage has made familiar with respect to Russian historical figures, and for important ecclesiastics whose names have been recast into Latin or Greek equivalents, especially for the earlier period of Russian history. This applies to prominent individuals. Russian forms usually are used for the less prominent. Certain other names and terms have been anglicized for the sake of clarity and because they are used widely, among them Courland, boyar, rubles, versts, Dnieper river and others.

The editors of the Moscow edition of 1959-1966 frequently added patronymics and other names, and these have been retained without brackets. Patronymics appearing in the original edition also have been included. Plural forms for names and terms which might be confusing have been anglicized—the Dolgorukys, not Dolgorukie, and so forth.

Even so, in a few cases the Russian plural form is used when this form is common. Most Slavic surnames show gender, and this has been preserved. Since an "a" at the word end usually signifies a female, Golovkin would have a wife or daughter called Golovkina. The final "iia" in feminine personal names has been shortened to "ia"—"Maria" and "Evdokia" instead of "Mariia" and "Evdokiia."

Non-Russian names, locations, terms, ranks and so on are spelled according to the language of the person or particular to the city, region or culture when this can be determined. Confusion arises at times because the text is not clear about nationalities. Two excruciating examples are Lithuania, where at least three languages intermingled, and the Black Sea region where several languages and alphabets coexisted. In such cases the context is the guide used and as a last resort the Russian spelling in the text is accepted. Individuals whose names were once non-Russian but were in Russian service for generations are named by the original spelling of the family name. Turkish, Tatar, Persian, Polish and other names are spelled in the original according to accepted forms in scholarly books. In some instances, if not otherwise ascertainable they are transliterated from the Russian as given by Soloviev. The names of geographical locations conform to commonly accepted English usage—Podolia, Moscow, Copenhagen, Saxony and so forth.

Finally, with respect to transliteration, this translation follows a modified Library of Congress system omitting diacritical marks and ligatures, and rendering the initial "Ia" and "Iu" as "Ya" and "Yu" ("Yasnaia" and "Yury"), and occasionally the initial "E" as "Ye" ("Yermak," "Yevlev," etc.), the suffixes "ii", "skii," "skaia" and "skoe" as "Dmitry Poliansky," "Polianskaia," "Polianskoe," and the form "oi" has been replaced by "oy" ("Donskoy," not "Donskoi") for certain names familiar in this form in English. In some cases "i" has been inserted in place of hard and soft signs, or apostrophes indicating these signs. Hence "Soloviev," not "Solov'ev." The soft sign is not indicated by an apostrophe, as in some transliteration systems, but is dropped completely.

All dates, as in the original, except where otherwise specified, are according to the Julian calendar ("Old Style"), that is, for the seventeenth century ten days, and for the eighteenth century eleven days, behind the Gregorian calendar used in the West. A table of weights and measures is included at the front of this volume for the convenience of the reader, as are a table of Muscovite court and service ranks and the Table of Ranks of the Petrine and post-Petrine era in the Appendices. In preparing the present volume I wish the thank Ketty Karamzin and Anastasia Korzukhina, who helped decode some particularly arcane terminology, Professors Daniel Kaiser, Valerie Kivelson and Richard Hellie, for their explanations of Muscovite legal terminology, and Professor G.E. Orchard, the General Editor of this series, who applied both the expert eye of the historian and a discreet editorial red pen, as well as the sympathetic attention of a fellow contributor. Errors which remain are, of course, my own.

Gary J. Marker

INTRODUCTION

Sergei Soloviev afforded Peter the Great far more space in his scholarship than to any other dynasts. All or part of five books (Volumes XIV-XVIII) in the original *History of Russia* were devoted to Peter and his times, and Soloviev wrote extensively about Peter in other venues. For example, a series of twelve semi-public lectures presented in 1872 in Moscow as part of the bicentennial celebration of Peter's birth immediately were published under the title *Publichnye chteniia o Petre Velikom* (Public Readings on Peter the Great. Moscow, 1872). Soloviev wrote several other essays on Peter, and a number of his synthetic and more popularized publications, such as the *Obshchedostupnye chteniia o russkoi istorii* (Readings on Russian History for the General Public. Moscow, 1874), gave Peter pride of place in the narrative. This attention alone conveys Peter's centrality to Soloviev's characterization of the transition from ancient Rus to modern Russia.

Previous volumes of the *History* have gone into exhaustive detail about Peter's reforms, his ambitions and the barriers he confronted along the way. This installment extends the threads of foreign affairs, international intrigue, and foreign policy from the end of the Northern War to the last years of Peter's life. As the concluding volume of the Petrine section it contains lengthy editorial passages in which Soloviev indulged in impassioned and dramatic phraseology, much of which is quite revealing of Soloviev's own predilections and political preferences. Interestingly, for all the space given over to tracing the intricate and consequential machinations of foreign affairs, Soloviev often characterized diplomacy as a "game." Thus "Dolgoruky played the very same game, and he spread word of the Russian forces in Persia," or "The year 1723 brought this game to an end."

In this vein Soloviev recapitulated the complex political negotiations through which Peter's envoys prevailed upon the rest of Europe to accept the imperial title which the Russian tsar embraced in 1721. These negotiations took place mostly with representatives of the leading crowned heads of Europe, though the affected populations typically lived in the smaller states contiguous to Russia. The disposition of Poland and the Orthodox populations living there loom large in this account, as do the duchies of Courland and Holstein. Through these discussions Soloviev sketched something of an ethnic and religious landscape of Russia's new empire, albeit filtered through his own deeply-held Orthodoxy, national and occasionally ethnic consciousness, and celebration of the great-power status which empire brought with it. Thus Soloviev celebrated Russia's emergence as a European power, asserting that "one of the greatest acts in European and world history had been completed. The eastern half of Europe had entered into a common existence with the western half..., [The West] feared that the great tsar, having concluded the Northern War with such uncommon success, and possessing an unheard-of energy, would not leave Europe alone." "Western nations...have been obliged to turn their attention to...the decisive influence which Russia had on the fate of Europe, consequently of the entire world. Moreover they have had to recognize Russia as representative of the Slavic tribe, by which the monopoly of the Germanic tribe was destroyed."

This tone of mastery recurs wherever Soloviev underscored the Russianness of the new imperial order, specifically in juxtaposing the circumstances of Russian/Orthodox populations to the fates of other people within the empire. Polish Catholics as a collective body "persecuted" the Orthodox and forcibly obliged some to accept the Uniate faith, whereas the Russian abuse of Catholics, although frankly acknowledged, is almost invariably ascribed to the cruelty of specific individuals. Thus Ignaty Rudakovsky may have behaved with excessive force as the tsar's representative, but he was carrying out Peter's otherwise virtuous policy of returning to the Orthodox populations those churches seized by Uniates. At times Soloviev virtually exulted at the righteous exercise of imperial power over vanquished malefactors. "The Roman Catholics and Uniates wailed in vain, as if in a frenzy, 'Woe to us! Our doom is at hand! We would be better off seeing Turks or Jews in these churches than these damned schismatics....'"

The passing reference to "Turks or Jews," Soloviev's own interpolation, by the way, provides further insight into the multiple layers of marginality by which non-Russian and non-Christian peoples were identified. Did Soloviev embrace these particular implications of empire? Individual readers can draw their own conclusions, though later historians including Kliuchevsky, Miliukov and Liubavsky did criticize him for what they took to be his ethnic and religious chauvinism. In this particular volume Jews and Muslims are virtually invisible as religiously-defined peoples.

Extensive discussions of religious persecution and conflict in Mogilev, which had perhaps the strongest concentration of Jewish population within the Russian empire, and elsewhere in the territories between Poland and Russia where Jews lived in large numbers, refer to Orthodox, Catholics, Uniates and even Lutherans, but pass over Jews in silence. When individuals are identified in the text as Jews their identity becomes essential and explicitly non-Russian. "The chief procurator," Soloviev writes, "responded to this far-fetched suggestion, saying 'Mikhail Shafirov is not a foreigner but a Jew, the son of a boyar's bondsman, with the nickname of Shaiushka, and his father Shaiushkin was a driver in Orsha for a schoolboy whose relative even now resides in Orsha, the Jew Zelman....'"

Further east and south, Muslims are not mentioned at all in spite of the many passages dealing with the Persian campaign and the peoples on the lower Volga, especially the Bashkirs. Tatars are mentioned only in passing, and the sole reference to Kalmyks comes in a quote regarding V.N. Tatishchev from William (Vilim) Gennin, sent to Olonetsk to investigate the disorderly state of mining. "Personally, I do not like his ugly Kalmyk countenance, even though I see he is completely in the right on this matter...." By contrast, local cossacks are mentioned frequently both in official documents, which Soloviev quotes at length, and in his own commentary.

The very seamlessness which typifies the *History*'s prose enabled Soloviev to shift effortlessly back and forth between quotation and commentary. This narrative strategy effectively embedded Soloviev's own persona as scholar-narrator within the events he recounted, except during those pauses when he steps outside the narrative to explain to readers what we are to make of what we have just read. Such a strategy renders Soloviev's stated approval or disapproval largely irrelevant to our reading because of the matter-of-fact way in which characterizations of non-Russian peoples make their way into the text. If Shafirov was "not a foreigner, but a Jew" and if Tatishchev had an "ugly Kalmyk countenance" well, this is what empire was all about, both in Peter's time and in Soloviev's.

Although he never highlighted it in his analysis Soloviev displayed sensitivity to the nuances of diplomatic language, the encoded and euphemistic turns of phrase by which laws and communiqués so frequently conveyed messages other than their nominal meanings. Private communications in 1718 about the disposition of Courland and the political fate of his niece Anna Ivanovna between Peter and his aide in Courland, General Peter Bestuzhev, dwelt on strategies for strengthening the hand of Anna and the Russian party. Yet within a single paragraph this hardheaded *Realpolitik* is juxtaposed to Peter's public pronouncements on the same subject which adopt instead the language of brotherhood and respect for the ancient rights of a small state. "His majesty the tsar is informing the king and the Polish Commonwealth that he will not permit any division of Courland into provinces. He is doing this not for his niece alone, but also for the noble knights and landed governments of his Courland neighbors. He does not want to allow the destruction of Courland's ancient rights. He has no wish to obtain for himself either all of Courland or any part of it, nor can he permit anyone else to do so."

Here, as in almost everything else, the subject is not so much diplomacy but Peter himself. Soloviev, the quintessential Hegelian, imagined Peter as Minerva's Owl, soaring at the dusk of Muscovy, glimpsing a future which he struggled to accelerate but with only the most modest success. Believing in the primacy of law and governing institutions, Soloviev painted Peter in mosaic and, as we shall discuss below, mosaic tones, grappling to lead his tribe to a higher order of civilization, a historicized promised land of reason, order, greatness and civility, ultimately sacrificing his own life in the process. Peter emerges in the end as the quintessential lawgiver to the lawless. Hardly a paragraph goes by without reference to a decree or manifesto Peter issued to deal with a particular contingency. Law, then, functioned simultaneously as the embodiment and the agency of improvement, the vehicle by which the Petrine state came into being and brought the nation forward.

"The Russian people understood that knowledge of the laws of the land should serve as a counterweight to all those impudent acts, as the only means possible for living *as other educated nations did.*" [italics added] "The nation was passing through a difficult school…learning civic responsibilities and civic activity. In the process of publishing every important regulation and introducing important reform, the *legislator* [italics added] was explaining why he was doing so, and why the new was better than the old. A Russian was receiving instruction of this kind *for the first time.* [italics added] …For the first time the thinking of the Russian individual was aroused, and his attention was directed to important questions of state and social structure…. Peter's entire system was directed against the basic ills from which ancient Russia had suffered, namely the dispersal of forces, the unaccustomedness to consider matters in their totality, the absence of self-reliance, the lack of initiative.

"A large portion of what had been accomplished stood only at an initial stage, other portions existed in rough outline, and for much of the rest only materials had been readied, only instructions had been drawn up. For this reason we have termed the activities of the reform era 'a program' which Russia is still fulfilling even now and will continue to fulfill, and deviation from which always leads to unhappy consequences."

Still, a close reading reveals a distinction between the law as a civilizing and epoch-making spiritual force, and individual *laws*, which are consistently violated and ignored by the backward but crafty Russian people, or which deliberately obscure a very different, murkier and far less progressive reality than the grand theory of history would suggest. Indeed, were we to excise the lengthy reflective passages which didactically inform the reader of Soloviev's outlook, it would be difficult to distill the march of progress and reason from the narrative. Episode after episode is marked by an overt hostility to specific laws and to codes of conduct which, in Soloviev's view, ought to characterize a state governed by laws and civilization.

"If trade were to be strengthened...and if the concerns of a government which well understood their significance were to be addressed, the old ways of doing things, *which no government was in a position to undo* [italics added], raised some horrendous barriers to the hope of strengthening trade." "Commissioned Officer Volkov, ordered to become the ambassador to Persia, sent a dragoon to the magistrate. They brought the town councillor Tikhon Bocharnikov to Volkov, showering the former with profanities. Volkov commanded the dragoon, who had thrown the town councillor to the ground, to grab him by the hair and arms, and then Volkov began to beat him with his staff...." "Members of the highest institutions feuded, and they insulted one another in the crudest manner. Bribery was as strong as ever. As before, the weak were subjugated to the strong."

This tension between the law as the preeminent, if impersonal, metahistoric force, and Russia's dispiriting legal culture vividly emerges in this volume precisely because Soloviev was so determined to show Peter as the Herculean lawgiver who obliges a scornful culture to acknowledge, however grudgingly, that the rule of law marked the road to a higher stage of civilization. Thus the antinomy of the transcendent power of the law and the ineffectuality of the laws constitutes an ongoing tension throughout the text. "Peter's immense activities were not directed at foreign relations but to waging war...for him only a means for carrying on domestic activities. Here he faced a wider, more multi-faceted, and more difficult theater of action, more formidable barriers, more numerous enemies, more secretive and dangerous, losses were frequent and heavy, successes slower and far in the future." "We have seen how old Russia had passed on to the new a monastic clergy which was in most unsatisfactory condition.... Measures which the Reformer undertook to alleviate this harmful state of affairs proved unsuccessful, and simply exacerbated the problem. They evoked powerful hostility against the Reformer who, understandably, responded in kind."

Soloviev, of course, was far from the first writer to employ the metaphor of war in describing Peter's relationship with Ancient Rus. Yet the imagery is so stark here, the opposition of Peter vs. Russia is so absolute and so frequently repeated ("by incredible effort and frightful sufferings the nation yielded to Peter's demands") that Peter, as often as not, is portrayed as Russia's antithesis rather than its embodiment and logical product, as Soloviev's philosophy of history insisted he was. This opposition is not always conveyed in militant or military language, but the dichotomy is nevertheless ubiquitous in the text. Several passages draw Peter as a veritable life force—active, virile, male—energizing and possessing a passive and recumbent land. "Thus were the Russian people reared in the harsh school of reform! The horrific burdens and deprivations all served a purpose. A general program had been traced out for very many years to come, traced not on paper but on the soil, which now was compelled to open its riches before the Russian man whose learning had endowed him with the full right to possess it. This on the sea, where a Russian navy took shape, and on the rivers, which had been linked by canals. It was traced on the state by new institutions and regulations. It was traced on the nation by means of education which broadened its intellectual horizons, enriching its storehouse with a diet of knowledge... thrown open to them, and a new world now established within Russia itself."

The undertones of this passage ("compelled to open up its riches before the Russian man") seem oddly out of place in Soloviev's linear and document-rich exposition. In fact this particular volume, so pivotal in explicating the transition from ancient to modern Russia offers extensive commentary about Peter's, and Russia's, bodily strengths and weaknesses and his place in human history. In the process it exposes a passionate side to Soloviev's prose. As in previous volumes most of the narrative is set within the familiar polarities of the reforming state as opposed to a resistant and backward society, an emergent powerful Russia as opposed to an older, more established, and arrogant Europe, a visionary, energetic, irrepressible ruler contending with a primordial, landed, recumbent people. Here these themes become brutally explicit, even visceral, as Soloviev endeavors to come to terms with what was for him the unavoidably painful birth of Russian modernity. "The favorable conditions abroad in which the state currently found itself was bought by imposing a severe strain on the nation's forces, but this strain could not be diminished very much. So now, in order to preserve this prominence and advantages, he had to employ the very means that enabled Russia to obtain such prominence in the first place. Peter thus affirmed to the Russian people that, having been pleased with what had been obtained, they were not about to fold their hands." "Storms do clear the air, but the devastation they leave behind shows that this cleansing is bought at a heavy price. Severe illnesses call for strong medicine. We know that pre-Petrine Russia suffered from many illnesses, and particular contours of the reform era reflect this fact even more. The *body politic* [italics added] recovered, it gained the means to extend its life, and that life proved rich in powerful endeavors. The historian would fall into an indefensible one-sidedness were he not to acknowledge that these strong means usually leave behind unwelcome consequences for the organism."

Side by side with the theme proclaiming the epochal dawn of modernity Soloviev narrated a sharply different everyday existence built upon clan, patronage, bribery, lawlessness, superstition, backwardness, hidebound tradition and violence. This was the resilient Muscovite culture which remained largely scornful of the spirit of the law, playing out its politics through intrigue, personal intervention and brute force. Time and again he proclaimed that the rule of law and respect for the dignity of the individual were taking hold in Peter's wake. Yet these assurances often sound more like pleas rather than convictions born of scholarly dispassion and the laws of history. "A new state of affairs is expressed here in that Dolgoruky protested in the name of the law of the land against a public affront.... We ought to welcome this new way of doing things for by this path, namely, powerful people turning more and more attention to the laws of the land, a society gradually comes to guard the security of a person as a person, and not only as a chancellery councillor." "This is how development gets started, and it then proceeds in the large towns to a very high degree. This law of development is general in a nation's life, and it brings good to those states which do not violate it, know how to manage development correctly, while fearing to push it along too quickly. Such an undeveloped Russia as existed in the first quarter of the eighteenth century could be satisfied with an institution which was obliged to be an academy of sciences, university, pedagogical institute and gymnasium all in one, obligated to become the seed out of which all these institutions ultimately would develop."

Subsequent scholars, commenting on Soloviev's characterization of Peter, largely have assimilated the major features of Soloviev's statism and historicism, although several noted historians rejected outright his political and normative gloss on the Petrine era. An essay by V. I. Gerie (Guerrier) published in *Istoricheskii vestnik* (The Herald of History) in 1880 shortly after Soloviev's death proclaimed Soloviev as Russia's "national historian," more important than Guizot, Ranke or any other leading historians from other cultures. "If history expresses within itself the self-consciousness of the nation the historian, through whom that self-consciousness is completed, should relate with empathy to the substantive features and aspects of the historical development of his own nation. It is precisely those conditions which are combined at the highest level in S. M. Soloviev."[1] For Gerie who, for all of his Russocentric sentiments, was of not-so-distant French ancestry, Soloviev had perceived Peter exactly right, asserting that the organic unity of Russian history ("united by the laws of history ") produced Peter as the negation of all that was backward and unworthy in Muscovy. "All the preceding history made the reforms a necessity...."[2]

Gerie was personally close to the Soloviev family and he became a major influence upon Soloviev's son Vladimir Sergeevich, the future philosopher.[3] His unrestrained adulation thus needs to be read with considerable qualifications. A more cautious defender, the historian and liberal politician Paul Miliukov, and an outright opponent, the Slavophile Konstantin Aksakov, both of whom adopted a less hagiographic and deterministic tone than Gerie, also accepted the fundamentals of Soloviev's rigid paradigm. The dialectic of old and new Russia, Peter's personal agency in creating this division and Soloviev's emphases on the state and law as the institutional instruments of modernity, all reappear in their respective works. Both identified Soloviev as a founding father of the historical-juridical school, the tendencies of which both expressed considerable discomfort. Yet both recognized along with Gerie that Soloviev's massive text demanded center stage in the competition to preside over the grand narrative of Russian history.[4] All subsequent histories had to be contrasted to Soloviev's, a circumstance which virtually everyone conceded and one which essentially substantiated Gerie's bold ascription of "national historian."

Soloviev emerges in the essays of these authors as a generative presence, or father, of Russian scientific historiography, a position much like that which Soloviev granted Peter within Russian history. At times it appears that Soloviev understood and embraced this affinity, almost to the point of reproducing in his own life the outlooks about work and responsibility that he ascribed to Peter in his *History*. In this context it is interesting to contrast the extended and searching reflections on Soloviev as a historian penned by most of his professional heirs to the more understated and carefully-worded reactions to Soloviev penned by his own offspring, and to the excruciatingly proper encomia offered by his most famous student and successor at Moscow University, V. O. Kliuchevsky, with whom his relations were often quite uncomfortable.[5]

Soloviev fathered a dozen children, eight of whom lived into adulthood, and his sons Vsevolod and Vladimir and his daughters Poliksena and Maria left behind letters and reminiscences which commented on their father, if only in passing.[6] With the exception of Vsevolod, all expressed respect and appreciation of their father, yet extremely sparingly, almost in passing. They depicted a calm and wise paternal presence, sitting at the head of the table and offering sage and tolerant counsel amid what was otherwise described as a lively, cohesive, playful and affectionate family who put on plays and dramatic performances for each others' amusement. Everyone else in the family was described by one another as participating actively in these activities. The many letters back and forth among them confirm that impression. Only Sergei Mikhailovich stood apart, joining the ambience of the family exclusively during those moments when the family daily gathered to eat and converse, and then for slightly longer periods during summers in the countryside.

Rarely did any offer so much as an anecdote, a hint of playfulness or informality, or any tale suggesting that the father was an active presence or participant in the life of the family, except as a transcendently benign paterfamilias. We learn that Sergei Mikhailovich once advised Vladimir to read whatever he wished, even if some of what he read ran counter to the strongly Orthodox moral tone of the household. Similarly, we are told that Sergei Mikhailovich stubbornly refused to concede to death until the very end because he was determined to complete his *History* through the beginning of the nineteenth century. Yet these comments express esteem more than affection.

This respectful aloofness emerges more starkly in the family's letters and almost formulaic reminiscences of him. Vladimir Sergeevich, a prolific and emotive letter writer who corresponded voluminously with his mother, siblings, and friends, wrote only rarely and tersely to his father. In discussing his father's illness and ultimate death from liver cancer he wrote to his close friend D.N. Tsertelev only the following on July 1, 1879. "I am going through a very sad time, my dear friend Dmitry. My father apparently will not be getting any better. The tumor near his heart apparently has regenerated—an untreatable illness from which Alexis Tolstoy died."[7] When Vladimir republished selected passages from his father's memoirs in 1886 he worried that people who had not known his father personally would have gained an inaccurate impression of him from previous essays without having read these memoirs. "Perhaps someone will find it inappropriate for a son to speak in print about his father. First of all, in the present instance I will not so much be speaking about father as pointing out and summarizing what he said about himself and about his own life during frank conversations with his children. Secondly, everyone would surely agree that for every general rule there may be special circumstances on the force of which a public reconstruction of the moral figure of a father is not only permissible for a son as an indulgence, but is even demanded of him as a moral debt."[8]

All of this sounds noble, and vaguely touching. Yet throughout the rest of these commentaries Vladimir shifts to a more formal voice by referring to his father as "the author of the memoirs," or simply "the author." Maria's memoirs mention her father only as he lay dying, and even then the focus lay on the rest of the family, particularly Vladimir who was known to go in and out of dark depressions, rather than on their father or their feelings for him.[9] Poliksena began her own memoir with the words "My father was the historian S.M. Soloviev," and then made no mention of him again. Only Vsevolod, the eldest son, let slip any public emotion toward his father. It was Vsevolod who went through his father's papers after he died and uncovered the five notebooks containing the memoirs. "Father did not like medical attention and he did not like to speak about his own health. I nevertheless tried to prevail upon him a few times to go to Carlsbad by pointing out examples of the success that

Carlsbad had in treating liver ailments, but all my suasion and proofs shattered against the single word 'Some day.'

"I somehow managed to ask him 'When will that time be?' 'When I finish the *History*,' he responded. 'When I have approached the end of that burden, if God will let me live that long, I shall rest! I'll take a big trip around Russia, and then shall write my memoirs.' I inquired whether he had not prepared something, whether he had begun. His words were 'I have made a beginning, and at various times over the past fifteen or sixteen years I've jotted things down. When I have some free time I'll look it over, make some corrections and continue it.'"[10]

Standing between the professional and the personal was V.O. Kliuchevsky, Soloviev's student, his begrudged successor at Moscow University, and in many ways the heir apparent to Soloviev's vaunted standing as national historian. Kliuchevsky composed his own multi-volume history of Russia, which built upon Soloviev's work but diverged sharply from his emphasis on state structures and politics. Kliuchevsky wrote several essays on Soloviev as scholar and teacher, the tone of which carefully straddled the impassioned engagement of Soloviev's colleagues and the cool distancing of kin.

Several scholars have commented upon the formal and cool relations between the two men, an unstated reality which nevertheless shaped Kliuchevsky's essays.[11] In the absence of affection, Kliuchevsky wrote "In the life of a scholar and writer the main biographical facts—books, the most important events—are ideas. In the history of our scholarship and literature there have been few lives so rich in facts and events as Soloviev's."[12] Kliuchevsky praises Soloviev as a lecturer for speaking and not reading his lectures and for his ability to impart complex ideas and information.[13] "The harmony of thought and word! How easy it is to pronounce these well-formed words, and how difficult it is to execute them in teaching!"[14]

Writing specifically about Soloviev's Peter, Kliuchevsky endeavored to convince his readers of the relevance and topicality of Soloviev's work. "In the five volumes devoted substantially to Peter's activities, and then in all of the subsequent ones, the reader confronts the full elaboration of the reform with its multi-dimensional consequences and connections.... All of this on the basis of very broad study, in large measure of previously untouched historical material, a study which not a single Russian scholar before Soloviev had undertaken."[15] Kliuchevsky maintained that Soloviev's study of Peter's reforms reflected a broader concern

with reform and civilization in general, in particular with the great reforms of Alexander II. Thus Kliuchevsky's public homages to his mentor painted a picture of a scholarly giant, for whom scholarship became
a subtle means of intervention in the larger political issues of his own day.

Nevertheless it is worth noting that Soloviev wrote little about contemporary affairs. Most of what he did write was virtually forced out of him
by higher authorities. Vsevolod recounts that in May 1879 his father was
instructed by Tsarevich Alexander Alexandrovich to write something
about the contemporary situation in Russia. Although reluctant to do so,
Sergei Mikhailovich did begin such an essay, which his son Vsevolod
discovered among his father's papers and subsequently published. The
reader is struck by its pessimism, its lack of enthusiasm for the very spirit
of reform and emancipation, as if nothing which happened in his lifetime
fulfilled the hopes he inscribed so passionately on the Petrine era. "Domestic disorders, revolutionary phenomena, derive from the weakening
of the state's moral authority. The nation cannot rise up against that which
it respects.... Primarily from the nineteenth century Russia begins to fall
ever more powerfully under the influence of Western European life. The
starts and stops, the reactions in its domestic life, reflect developments
in the West. Two French revolutions, overflowing into virtually all of
Europe (1830 and 1848), were reflected in Russia by measures of con-
servatism, especially in the latter years of Emperor Nicholas's reign...."
"Thus, the younger generation emerged from school into life with a lack
of moral discipline, with a loss of authority, regard for their elders. This
was the preparation it received by the time of the most important domestic reforms [the Great Reforms of Alexander II's reign]." "These reforms
irrevitably generated profound vacillation within a society which must
grapple with its political, moral and economic interests. Emancipating the
peasantry was entirely necessary, timely for political and moral reasons
...." "[But] Russia has not yet matured sufficiently for the emancipation
of work, and the very suddenness of the shift from servile to free labor
in such a very expansive country has threatened it with great disorders."[16]

Soloviev's memoirs ("for my children, and perhaps for others as
well") adopted an even more dour tone when he characterized the peasantry as having been completely unprepared for emancipation, as a result
of which they transformed their new status into a freedom to get drunk,
brawl and not work. Soloviev decried the state of the countryside in his
latter years, convinced that moral turpitude developed at the expense of
the land and the nation. "Until this time a laborer lived under protection.

The guardian required him to work and, not surprisingly, occasionally demanded more than was his due. This evil side of guardianship, the evil of serfdom, now has been done away with. Yet one must keep in mind another evil, the evil of freedom, when someone freed from obligations begins to work less than he should.... For this striving [for freedom] to be forceful a well-known development is required, a familiarity with the demands which it is very desirable to satisfy, becoming accustomed to freedom and to orderly work, the moral influence of the family, and so forth. To what extent can all of this be expected from a Russian peasant placed in a very dangerous position, a transitional status from unfreedom to freedom, when the necessary striving is experienced as an absence of necessity and the possibility of working less.... With total senselessness, in the absence of any careful attitude on this matter, literature poured forth in a campaign against tax farmers, with the demand that good vodka be made less expensive for the simple folk, demanding for them the easiest and most active poison.... So drunkenness quickly spread in horrifying dimensions. Someone for whom the worthy exercise of freedom should be the realization of his physical and moral powers simply became drunk. The peasant economy received a severe blow, for drunkenness merged into merrymaking.... A drunken father could hardly forbid his own sons, wife, daughters-in-law and daughters to drink. Young people of both sexes began drinking before they had emerged from childhood...."[17]

After this dispiriting diatribe written, let us keep in mind, contemporaneously with much of his writing on Peter, we are left to wonder how Soloviev was so approving of Peter's reforms and so disappointed in the reforms and people of his own day. What sort of modernity was achieved if, a century and a half after Peter, Soloviev characterized his own nation as immature, unschooled in civil authority, the overwhelming majority of its people seemingly so child-like, so untouched by civil society that they reduced freedom to drinking, the very essence of incivility! These issues almost certainly were in the back of Soloviev's mind as he wrote his chapters on Peter. It can only be wondered how he reconciled the qualified optimism of the *History* with the gloomy pessimism of the memoirs.

We are left to ponder how great Soloviev's faith in the power of history and reason really was. Did Soloviev's Peter truly inaugurate a progress which *very gradually* took root in Russia or, as Soloviev's memoirs hint, was deliverance unto civility still a distant dream in the 1870s, a century and a half after Peter's death?

As in other volumes Soloviev's underlying source base comes from the laws, regulations and the attendant commentary in Polnoe sobranie zakonov Rossiiskoi imperii (Complete Collection of Laws of the Russian Empire), published during the 1830s. It often has been noted that Peter changed the nature of legal texts by personalizing them and by adding extensive commentary explaining the rationale for the law and its connections or break with existing practice. Peter was a voluminous legislator, issuing literally hundreds of decrees in his reign, most of which were published individually and subsequently included in the Collection. They provide a wealth of information about Peter's thinking, his expectations and prejudices, and his vision of empire. Soloviev augmented this legal framework with extensive archival research, mostly in the Kabinet Petra I (Peter I's private papers) and those of the newly-founded Senate.

On foreign policy Soloviev relied primarily on the archival documents from the College of Foreign Affairs, currently housed in the Archive of Russian Foreign Policy. These documents consist mostly of official and confidential correspondence from Russian diplomats in Poland, Sweden, Austria, France, England, Denmark and Prussia. Occasionally Soloviev augmented these institutional materials with diaries and other personalia, such as the diary of Duke Frederick-William von Bergholz, who served as ambassador of Holstein to St. Petersburg, published as *The Diary of Chamberlain Bergholz, Kept by Him in Russia in the Reign of Peter the Great from 1721 to 1725* (Moscow, 1858). As in earlier volumes, his anecdotes rely heavily on Ivan Golikov's multi-volume *Acts of Peter the Great*, albeit with a good deal less reverence than Golikov conveyed.

The discussions of religion and state institutions rely heavily upon Senatorial documents as well as the archive of the chancellery of the newly-established Holy Synod. Very few of these documents were published in Soloviev's day, and this remains true today. An exception, upon which Soloviev relied rather heavily, is G. V. Esipov, *Schismatic Affairs in the Eighteenth Century Extracted from the Preobrazhensky Chancellery and the Chancellery of Secret Investigations* (St. Petersburg, 1861).

Readers of this series will have become accustomed to testimony to the voluminous and ever-growing scholarship on Peter and his reign. For a listing of the basic English-language scholarship readers are advised to consult the admirable list compiled by Professor Lindsey Hughes for Volume 26 of this *History* (pp. xxi-xxiii). On religious reform see James Cracraft, *The Church Reform of Peter the Great* (Stanford, Cal., 1971);

Gregory Freeze, *The Russian Levites. Parish Clergy in the Eighteenth Century* (Cambridge, Mass., 1977); and *The Spiritual Regulation of Peter the Great.* Ed. and trans. by Alexander V. Muller (Seattle, Wash., 1972). A fine recent synthetic study, which modifies many of the standard interpretations of the old Soviet historiography, is Evgenii V. Anisimov, *The Reforms of Peter the Great. Progress Through Coercion in Russia* (Armonk, N.Y., 1993). On economic history see Arcadius Kahan, *The Plow, the Hammer, and the Knout. An Economic History of Eighteenth-Century Russia* (Chicago, 1985). Finally, on the legacy and reputation of Peter see Nicholas Riasanovsky, *The Image of Peter the Great in Russian History and Thought* (New York, 1985).

HISTORY OF RUSSIA

Volume 32

Peter's Last Years

Foreign and Domestic Affairs

1722-1725

RELATIONS WITH POLAND

COMPLAINTS BY BISHOP CHETVERINSKY

If, when referring to the Armenians, Peter declared that "Christianity forbids denial of protection to fellow Christians," it is understandable that he hardly could refuse to extend that protection to those Russians who consistently requested assistance against persecution by Polish Catholics and Uniates.[1] In January 1722 when the emperor was in Moscow the Belorussian Bishop Sylvester, in secular life Prince Chetverinsky,[2] "having been insulted and exiled by the papists and the Uniates," travelled there to meet with him. Sylvester presented to the College of Foreign Affairs a long list of offenses and oppressions the Orthodox clergy had suffered from the Polish nobility. The bishop himself bore a scar on his arm which he had received under the following circumstances. In Orshansk the nobleman Swiatzki[3] sought to force an Orthodox priest on his estate to become a Uniate. The priest refused and for this transgression received several hundred blows with a cane from the nobleman. Sylvester came upon Swiatzki on the road near Mogilev and reproached him for this incident with the priest. Instead of responding, Swiatzki drew his sabre and struck the bishop twice on the arm. He and his companions bound the priests with four neck bands and beat them until they cried out that they would consent to become Uniates. The Polish lord tied a priest behind his horse and then rode off, forcing the priest to walk three versts.[4] The bishop of Wilno then banned, under threat of death, building any new Orthodox churches.

RUDAKOVSKY AND RUDINSKY HEAD INVESTIGATION

Receiving these reports Peter wrote to the king "The one and only way to end the complaints of clergy and laity of the Greek confession is to investigate the offenses. The only means of receiving satisfaction consists of expeditiously appointing a commission, with members chosen by us. To that end we have assigned a translator, Ignaty Rudakovsky, to the embassy in Warsaw. Along with him we have sent a monk, a teacher at the Savior monastery behind the Icon-Painters' Row[5] (Yustin Rudinsky), whom we have commanded to live in Mogilev to conduct a detailed study of the offenses perpetrated upon people of the Greek confession, and to present this report to the court of your royal highness with the demand that the abuses be resolved in accordance with the treaty of eternal peace of 1686,[6] on the basis of both their rights and privileges. If these satisfactions are not carried out according to the letter of the treaty and in line with the expectations of our representation and request, we will be obliged to pursue satisfaction on our own."

PRUSSIAN KING INTERCEDES FOR POLISH PROTESTANTS

At this very time the matter of the Orthodox Russians was linked to that of the oppression of Protestants, also by Polish Catholics. Thus the entire affair assumed the character of a question of religious dissent. The Polish Protestants already had requested assistance from Peter. During the time in question the Prussian court turned to the Russian emperor with a request to intervene on behalf of the Evangelicals, who also suffered persecution in Poland.

SEJM OF 1722 AND THE IMPERIAL TITLE

Prince Sergei Grigorievich Dolgoruky[7] continued to serve as Russian ambassador at the court of Augustus II.[8] At the beginning of 1722 he went to considerable lengths to persuade the king to recognize the Russian sovereign's imperial title.[9] When he approached some sympathetic senators concerning this matter, they responded that the Polish Commonwealth[10] would accede unless the king stood in its way. There remained only one issue in doubt, whether the title provided a pretext for future Russian sovereigns to interfere in those Rus districts currently under Polish control. "Would it not be all the same," answered Dolgoruky, "whether he were the tsar or emperor of All Russia?" Nevertheless the Polish nobles persisted in their interpretation, maintaining that they could grant the imperial title only if they were given written assurance that the emperor and his successors would not lay claim to the Rus districts under Polish sovereignty. They perceived a danger in the title, but they found none in other instructions which Peter sent Dolgoruky. "Present all the Polish senators and ministers with a clear account of the contents of our charter to the king, which concludes that if satisfaction is not forthcoming we will be obliged to seek it unilaterally. Be extremely diligent to see to it that commissioners are named expeditiously, among whom Rudakovsky should be included as our commissioner. Send Rudakovsky from Warsaw to Mogilev at once, before the commissioners from the Polish side are appointed. Have him stay at the residence of the bishop, Prince Chetverinsky, there to compile a list of all the offenses perpetrated against individuals of the Greek confession. Tell him to ensure that there be no further persecution of people of the Greek confession. You may notify the Prussian ambassador in Poland that you have received an order to intervene on behalf of the Evangelicals. If you deem it in our interest you may make a representation about this matter to the Polish court, demanding in return that the Prussian ambassador assist you on behalf of the issues involving those of the Greek confession."

The Sejm convened in September, during which a prior initiative to secure the inheritance of the Polish throne for the son of Augustus II[11] was advanced on behalf of the court. Knowing that the Russian ambassador would do everything in his power to prevent this, the court party circulated a rumor that the Russians had suffered major losses in Persia. They also spread word that Dolgoruky would use threats to force the Sejm to recognize the imperial title for his sovereign. If the Sejm refused, sixty thousand Russian troops would invade Poland. They further suggested to the Sejm's deputies that if the Polish Commonwealth agreed to grant the imperial title to the tsar, basing himself on that title Peter would withdraw all Rus provinces from the Polish crown. Under these circumstances the king could be expected to come to the defense of the Commonwealth. Therefore he must be assured that his son will succeed to the Polish throne.

DOLGORUKY AND THE SEJM

Dolgoruky played the very same game, spreading word of the successes of the Russian forces in Persia. The Russian ambassador was fully confident that the king could never resolve the succession through the Sejm, that is, he could not force the Poles to agree to recognize his son as heir to the throne. Therefore Dolgoruky was surprised that the court in Berlin feared just such an outcome. In Dolgoruky's opinion, Augustus II could achieve his end only through intrigues and unrest. "If concerning the succession the court makes to the Sejm a recommendation contrary to our expectations," said Dolgoruky, "I will issue a protest and refuse to enter the Sejm until the matter is concluded."

Inside the Sejm an old arrangement was revived whereby Fleming would turn command of the Polish forces to a native Pole.[12] As before the court opposed this but, by bribing the delegates to the Sejm, Dolgoruky prevailed upon them to demand that Fleming turn over command. Although the Sejm's delegates submitted to the influence of the Russian ambassador, virtually all Polish magnates sided with the court, prepared to carry out August's wish to keep Fleming in command and to reinforce the regular army. This stance offered the king the surest means of achieving his goal relative to the succession, especially given Austria's assistance and the Russian tsar's absence on distant campaign.

Under these circumstances Dolgoruky deemed it necessary to dissolve the Sejm over the matter of Fleming's command in order to "suppress the court's reprehensible design." The danger of having Dolgoruky begin these actions compelled the court to concede on the matter of Fleming's command so that the Russians would agree to allow the Sejm to continue, if only for three more days. At that time the court served notice that once the Saxon field marshal was relieved of his command the king no longer could consider himself secure. He therefore demanded other measures to guarantee his security, in particular a mutual defense treaty with Austria. The "virtuous" delegates, as Dolgoruky termed them, refused to go along with extending the Sejm, which consequently was dissolved at the end of its legal term without coming to any decision.

Moreover Ignaty Rudakovsky, named as a commissioner by the Russian side, wrote to the emperor that the Roman Catholic clergy was firmly opposed to his membership in the commission. The clergy suggested that this was a matter extraordinarily harmful to the realm. As if this were something new, that the Russian sovereign wanted to reign as a despot in a free country! "The Roman clergy," wrote Rudakovsky, "will attempt in every way possible to harm me or to lure me from loyalty to your majesty's court. Seeing my unflagging efforts they suppose that were I to remain in Lithuania their entire fond hopes of converting the Orthodox to the Uniate faith would disappear. Perhaps they can even induce our own people to do me harm, in particular those opposed to our pious faith. All Roman Catholics imagine that providing this small satisfaction to your demands will lull your majesty's court to sleep and allow them to root out the Greek confession even more easily from these areas." The king did indeed write to Peter that he would appoint the commission as demanded. After a complaint from the monks of Pinsk about Uniate seizure of Orthodox monasteries and churches the matter was remanded to the courts, which ordered the churches and monasteries returned to the Orthodox, despite the strenuous opposition of the Catholic clergy.

This unique affair brought the year 1722 to an end in Poland. At the beginning of 1723 King Augustus departed Warsaw for Dresden. Dolgoruky left after him, receiving an audience in Breslau with Prince Konstantin, son of the former king Jan Sobieski.[13] Dolgoruky informed him of the emperor's will, suggesting that the prince pursue his own interests concerning how to gain the Polish throne within the time demanded. Konstantin responded that Poland hoped above all for the family line of the Wiśniowiecki princes,[14] and he obediently placed himself under the emperor's protection. Those hostile to Russia in both Saxony and Poland also were cheered by the news that Turkey immediately would declare war on Russia if Peter continued his incursions into Persia.[15]

Fleming deliberately allowed Dolgoruky to see a letter from Hetman Siniawski,[16] who wrote that the Turks were on the verge of declaring war on Russia, and that Sweden, England and Denmark also would combine their fleets against Russia. Since in Siniawski's opinion the Russian forces would pass through Poland, the hetman demanded that an extraordinary Sejm be convened to seek a way of forestalling this possibility. "At the Russian court," said Fleming, "Saxon ambassadors are customarily upbraided in a less than kindly manner. Now you see just how well disposed the Poles are towards you!"

At this point Fleming also passed along a rumor that at the previous Sejm the Prussian ambassador Schwerin gave Dolgoruky three thousand ducats for expenses.[17] "I neither demanded nor received such money from Schwerin," answered Dolgoruky. "I am very surprised," he wrote to the emperor, "that the honorable Prussian ambassadors who reside at the Polish court could keep nothing confidential, for all their activities were well known at the court here." According to the budget which Dolgoruky presented to his own court for expenses connected with the Sejm, only two thousand ducats were received from Schwerin. Altogether 2,590 ducats were distributed, of which eight hundred went to the Lithuanian hetman Denhof, the rest being spread among the Sejm delegates.

RUDAKOVSKY INTERCEDES FOR POLISH ORTHODOXY

While all of this was taking place Rudakovsky was busy in Western Rus. In Pinsk he carried out the royal decree with a flourish, ordering the return to the Orthodox population of the churches taken from them by the

Uniates. The Roman Catholics and Uniates wailed in vain, as if in a frenzy. "Woe to us! Our doom is at hand! We are better off seeing Turks or Jews in these churches than these damned schismatics!"[18] The Catholic bishop of Lutsk vainly threatened damnation to all Catholics present when the churches were taken back, wishing by this threat to inflame the Catholics against the Orthodox. In Minsk Rudakovsky rescued one townsman converted to Catholicism by force, who upon returning to the faith of his fathers was nearly burned.

When he arrived in Mogilev and observed what was taking place Rudakovsky wrote to Peter "To put an end to the persecution of the Eastern churches two simple steps are required. First, the nobleman Sokoliński,[19] the most ferocious persecutor of the Eastern church, who lives within two miles of the Russian border, must be apprehended and brought to Russia under the pretext that he took the title of archbishop of Smolensk and Severia illegally. Secondly, apprehend Lindorf, the elder of Mstislavl, who also lives close to the border, and spirit him to Russia on the pretext that in previous years he plundered your majesty's treasury near Borisov. Otherwise the Eastern church cannot be free of these terrible persecutors. All the others, once they see this, will go into hiding, and their memory will vanish with a bang. The Poles will weep and wail, as they usually do. Then they will just as quickly grow silent.

"If we fail to intimidate them with this bugbear it will become difficult to set matters right. So even if in Pinsk I have taken back the churches what should I confiscate to compensate for the losses and destruction? Do I turn to Rome, where there is no law? It would be easier to drink water from the sea than to seek justice in Rome. We will be left seeking justice on our own, the enemies of our church elsewhere will plunder, and the matter won't end. On the other hand, once these two individuals are seized all offenses will cease immediately. The bishop of Belorussia then will report all of the truths to your majesty that he somehow forgot to write concerning the persecution of the Eastern church."

At the very moment Rudakovsky proposed these measures against the persecutors of the Eastern church he himself, along with the bishop of Belorussia, was subjected to a horrific insult from his own Orthodox monks. The bishop, Prince Chetverinsky, invited him along to the Kutein monastery near Orsha[20] for the purpose of investigating the lives of its monks, about whom much that was not good was reported. When the monks met with the bishop, they assaulted his retinue. When he ordered them to hand over the instigators of the riot so that they could be placed under guard, the abbot jumped on his horse, sped to the town of Orsha, commanded its inhabitants to sound the tocsin, and roused a large number of nobles and common people with the cry that thieves and bandits were laying siege to the monastery.

A crowd gathered shouting "Beat, slash the Muscovites and their schismatic priest!" They threw themselves upon the bishop and Rudakovsky, assaulted them, pillaged and held them under guard, while the local authorities declined to intervene. In his report to the emperor concerning this "tragedy," Rudakovsky wrote "The Russian clergy are completely culpable because they interfered in the life of this diocese with their letters of benediction, thereby freeing the local monks from obeying the bishop of Belorussia. Could anyone imagine the bishop of Rostov interfering in the diocese of Kiev, or the Kievan archbishop interfering in the affairs of the diocese of Novgorod? This is impermissible. Only in the diocese of Belorussia do all the bishops interfere through their letters of benediction.[21]

"Our Orthodox faith must bear the consequences, for once the monks have the letters of benediction in hand they live undisturbed in drunkenness and every sort of depravity. When the Belorussian bishop wishes to humble them, they serve notice that they are subject to the diocese of Kiev. The only things that rouse them from their shiftless existence are the taunts of the enemies of the church, who were scared to death after the churches in Pinsk were taken away, but now hold their heads high. It has been ordered, my sovereign, that the Kievan clerics not interfere in this diocese, that the Holy Synod annul all letters of benediction previously issued.

"In truth, my lord, affairs here are troublesome even without these letters of benediction because everyone to a man wishes to eradicate the pious faith. The Orthodox here find themselves more demeaned than the Jews. Yet the letters of benediction set spiritual children against their own pastor. In this atmosphere of discord our faith emerges the poorer. The bishop, Prince Chetverinsky, beseeches your majesty with lamentations to permit him to act solely upon the authority of the Holy Synod."

In Mogilev, too, where Rudakovsky resided, Catholics did not miss the opportunity to heap insults upon the Orthodox. During their celebration of Corpus Christi[22] they demanded that bells be rung by the Orthodox churches. When the bishop refused the Catholics sent their own people and rang the bells. In other places more remote to the Catholics, the popular will held firm. According to Rudakovsky this stoutness enabled them to restrain those who believed they could save their souls by heaping offenses on Orthodox or Protestants! Rudakovsky suggested to his own superiors that one means of restraining Poles who were particularly zealous in their persecution of the Orthodox would be to seize their wares in Riga. The most prominent representatives of the Rus clergy in Belorussia suggested another course of action to Rudakovsky, namely to mobilize the common folk and set them against the Catholics and Uniates because, they said, *all* the common folk would follow them, not just those who remained Orthodox but even those converted to the Uniates by force. Rudakovsky told them to forget this and await the protection of the Russian emperor who already had dispatched Rudakovsky to defend the Eastern church. The clergy responded by lamenting that they could not live under such hellish tyranny unless assistance from his imperial majesty arrived soon.

Rudakovsky's own position as "the most accursed Muscovite schismatic" was hardly enviable. A certain Carmelite monk had already broken into his house, threatening to murder him and announcing that he was a hired assassin.

CLASH BETWEEN RUDAKOVSKY AND DOLGORUKY

Rudakovsky's predicament was made still worse by the malevolence of Prince Dolgoruky, who apparently was furious at the commissioner for having sent a report to his own superiors about these matters, some which did not relate at all to the clash between the Rus people and the Catholics and Uniates. In the matter of the Kutein monastery Dolgoruky had not sought the help of Rudakovsky and the bishop. On the contrary, he wrote to the emperor that Prince Chetverinsky had acted improperly because the Kutein monastery in fact fell under the authority of the Kievan hierarchy. Rudakovsky, moreover, had received an order from Petersburg to limit himself to observing that the Catholics and Uniates did not oppress the Orthodox, without interfering in the affairs of the Orthodox clergy.

Even into 1724 Dolgoruky continued to regard Rudakovsky with hostility. "Here," he wrote to Peter, "complaints are made to Rudakovsky's translator incessantly. I think that there will emerge significant dissatisfaction and complaints within the Sejm about his indiscretions. He interferes in matters beyond his authority. May it please you to forbid this with your imperial order instructing him to conduct himself discreetly with the local citizenry. Otherwise they may behave indiscreetly with him in a manner offensive to the high honor of your imperial majesty, for already they have discussed his violent and disreputable actions in a dishonorable way."

As a consequence of this report Rudakovsky was reprimanded anew for his tactless behavior, and rebuked for the bad language contained in his report. "Your written accounts employ a great many Polish and other foreign words and expressions which make it impossible to understand the actual state of affairs. Henceforth compose all your missives to us in plain Russian, without employing any foreign words and terms." "The enemies of the church," Rudakovsky responded, "are marshalling their forces to harm and besmirch me, who am blameless, before your majesty (and neither I nor the bishop received any satisfaction from Prince Sergei Grigorievich Dolgoruky for the offenses perpetrated against us). My unflagging effort on behalf of the interests I represent make these two very uncomfortable when these outrages take place in their districts.

"Thus in response to a request from residents of the counties of Mozyr, Piotrków and Rechitsa we have just now dispatched two clergymen who, with fifty churches currently under the yoke of the Uniates, returned to the bosom of the Eastern church. They reported to me that the entire population of the Kiev military command and others favor the Orthodox faith and dearly wish to leave the Uniates, but they need some help at the next Sejm. Being steadfast in the faith, I am greatly embittered over these accusations, of which I am in no sense guilty. It is very painful to me that your majesty's ambassador in Warsaw, knowing full well the oppression suffered by the Orthodox population here, prefers to believe false reports, does not believe what we say, and then proceeds to write ill of me. I have received news from Warsaw that the entire Roman clergy and the laity who fall under their laws (which includes one of our own men) have gone to immense efforts to undercut me and my authority in this matter."

PRINCE VASILY LUKICH DOLGORUKY IN POLAND

A rumor circulated in the Western Rus regions that the next Sejm would have an important bearing upon the fate of the Orthodox residents. Either their fate would improve or the Russian sovereign would place them resolutely under his own protection. Failing this, the Poles would take decisive measures against the Eastern church. Peter deemed it necessary to assist Prince Sergei Dolgoruky by recalling his more experienced and skillful relative Prince Vasily Lukich[23] from Paris and dispatching him to Warsaw. Prince Vasily was granted two accreditations, one as ambassador plenipotentiary, the other as extraordinary and plenipotentiary envoy.

The first was to be presented to the king upon his arrival in Warsaw, the second to be made public only if absolutely necessary. Dolgoruky was supposed to arrive in Poland prior to the preliminary selection of representatives to the Sejm. He was instructed to sway delegates to the general Sejm so that they would be well disposed towards the Russian emperor and towards the Polish Commonwealth. He also was expected to attempt to make certain that the man chosen as marshal (chairman) at the general Sejm was well disposed to Russia, to obtain an agreement from the Sejm that the residents of the Greek confession would receive satisfaction for offenses, and a guarantee that the residents of the Russian empire living abroad receive due satisfaction for their sufferings at the hands of the Poles. He was ordered to attempt to remove command of the armed forces from Fleming and return it to the hetmen, and to bring the Prussian ambassador under his influence. If out of fear the Poles failed to grant the title of All-Russian emperor to the sovereign, the lands of Old Rus that currently fall under Polish sovereignty should be compelled to acknowledge that title, and they must agree to grant the title Emperor and Autocrat of all Great and Little and White Russia, an old title recognized by Poland which simply replaced the word "Tsar" with the word " Emperor." Lukich also was commanded to pursue the extradition of the Little Russian cossack, the traitor Nakhimovsky, who had fled with Mazepa, and who subsequently was with Orlik,[24] who employed him in his relations with the Porte and the Crimea, and now was sent to Poland by the Turks.[25] Under no circumstances was he to allow the inheritance of the Polish crown to go to the house of Saxony. He also was to make representations on behalf of the religious dissidents.

Prince Vasily Lukich began his reports from Warsaw on a sad note. The king's party was strong, and it included the Potockis, Czartoryskis and all the hetmen. These were inclined to side with the king, as did a large proportion of the nobility, as a consequence of which Potocki, the primate's brother, was elected unanimously as marshal of the Sejm. Potocki was totally under the king's influence. The issues which he believed the Sejm should address were very important. (1) Increasing the size of the army, towards which many are favorably disposed. "This is the most troublesome matter for us because our involvement is suspect because we are neighbors." (2) The question of Courland.[26] "It is widely stated that Courland belongs to the Polish Commonwealth, and that other powers have no right to interfere. This is a dangerous issue, though not as dangerous as the first." (3) Confirmation of the previous treaties with the tsar. "In view of these perils," wrote Dolgoruky, "and in anticipation of still more, without any hope of doing anything at this Sejm on behalf of your majesty I intend, if everything goes as the king wishes, to dissolve the Sejm as the best way of serving the interests of your imperial majesty."

KING'S FAILURE AT THE SEJM

With this aim the Dolgorukys commenced seeking out a few brave individuals among the delegates upon whom they might rely should the Sejm be dissolved. On this matter they and the Prussian ambassador were in accord. The primate Potocki, for his part, threatened the delegates with a Sejm on horseback, or a confederation, if they permitted the Sejm to be dissolved.[27] To eliminate any cause for dissatisfaction, Fleming handed over command of the armed forces to the hetmen. The Dolgorukys were not swayed, continuing to seek out courageous individuals to dissolve the Sejm. Notables and the wealthy delegates opted not to involve themselves in this dangerous venture. One notable promised to seek out two less well-off delegates who would agree to dissolution of the Sejm, but they demanded that the Dolgorukys tell them in advance how they would be rewarded. One of the delegates promised to dissolve the Sejm, others were sought. The Prussian ambassador sent word that he too hoped to find some stout souls. These labors and expenses proved superfluous when a basis for discord soon came to light. Since Fleming had yielded command, the king and his party demanded that the guards at least remain under the king's command. Other delegates disagreed. Amidst these arguments November 2 arrived, the date at which the Sejm's session was scheduled to end. The delegates departed without accomplishing anything. Under the most favorable circumstances possible the king had won nothing, nor had he gained any concessions against the fact that the Saxon field marshal lost his command of the Polish military forces.

After the Sejm ended Dolgoruky held a conference with the Polish ministers and senators, presenting them with his court's demands as detailed in his instructions. He received the following response. "The king wishes to preserve the friendship of his majesty the tsar without interruption. Consequently the issue of recognizing the imperial title will be delayed for a future Sejm. The subjects of the king and the Polish Commonwealth who follow the Greek dispensation have found that whenever they sought royal protection they were granted a hearing and received satisfaction. As proof, the churches were returned to them, after which they had no further complaints. The religious dissidents[28] in the crown estates had nothing to fear so long as they live peaceably."

On their part, the Polish ministers apprised Dolgoruky of the following points. "Riga and Lifland [Livonia] are to be returned at once in accordance with the treaty. Affairs in Courland and Semigallia are to be straightened out. Poland is to retain the towns of Chigirin, Kanev, Terekhtemirov, Cherkassy and other border towns without interference. The Polish and Lithuanian military forces shall be paid the millions specified in the treaty of alliance. Cannon shall be returned to Poland and Lithuania, as shall the prisoners."

Reference was made to the fact that during the two years Rudakovsky spent in Mogilev no one could understand why he was named commissioner for his majesty the tsar. He interfered in religious matters, disturbed the peace between the Catholic clergy and those of other religions with pronouncements both false and offensive, to provoke his majesty's wrath. "We therefore demand," wrote the Polish ministers, "that this envoy be recalled, for we cannot remember any time when such commissioners lived in our lands and interfered as he does in our religious affairs." Finally the Poles demanded that the [Orthodox] bishop of Pereiaslavl not send his agents to [interfere with] Polish priests in his districts.

II

RELATIONS WITH OTHER FOREIGN POWERS

THE PAPAL COURT AND ORTHODOX RUSSIANS

The matter of Orthodox Rus residing in Polish territories, an issue which so deeply concerned Peter, led him to cultivate relations with the head of Catholicism, who at times could restrain the zealotry of Polish fanatics. Even before the end of the Northern War Peter instructed his representative in Venice, Savva Raguzinsky,[1] to communicate with the court of Pope Clement XI[2] and advance the proposition that all Catholic clergy other than Jesuits be admitted into Russia so long as they did not engage

in improper correspondence or interfere in political matters. These were
the reasons the Jesuits were expelled.[3] Savva Vladislavich [Raguzinsky]
observed these orders and Cardinal Ottoboni[4] responded that the clergy
of various orders—Capuchins, Franciscans, Carmelites—would engage
only in religious teaching and worship. The Pope had ordered them under threat of severe punishment not to interfere in affairs of state or civil
society. Were the Pope to receive a charter from the Russian sovereign
that this was agreeable to the Catholic clergy in Russia, in gratitude he
would recognize the [imperial] titles. Moreover, another gift was in the
offing, a statue or some other antique.

The death of Clement XI broke up this relationship. In the spring of
1722 the Jesuit Niccolò Gianpriamo arrived in Russia on his way back
to Europe from China. Russia provided the Jesuit free passage, taking
advantage of the opportunity to send through him a letter to Cardinal
Spinoli,[5] composed by Chancellor [Gavrila Ivanovich] Golovkin,[6] complaining of the persecution suffered by the Orthodox population in Poland. "His majesty has ordered me," expressed Golovkin in this official
communiqué, "to write to your eminence to present this matter to the
supreme pontiff, prevailing upon him to send a strongly-worded decree
to Poland not to offend the people of the Greek confession, in contraven-
tion of the treaties, rather to provide them freedom of conscience because
God alone reigns over conscience. Unless Catholics, whether Polish or
Lithuanian, desisted from violating Christians of the Greek dispensation
and obscenely force them to become Uniates his imperial majesty will be
compelled, in retribution and against his wishes, to forbid the Latin clergy
from conducting worship in Russia."

The Jesuit responded to the Russian chancellor only at the beginning
of 1724 that Cardinal Spinoli had written to Santini, the papal nuncio in
Poland, demanding a detailed account of this matter. Santini answered
that Rome desired very detailed information, especially since Poland had
sent word that the Russian sovereign demanded it. Because of the many
inaccuracies in these demands, Rome required reliable information from
Poland to put this matter to rest.

AFFAIRS IN COURLAND

In addition to the problem of Orthodox believers the issue of Courland
loomed large in relations between Russia and Poland. This matter was
broached earlier at the death of Courland's young duke Friedrich

Wilhelm, husband of the Russian sovereign's niece. The widow, Duchess Anna Ivanovna, whose circumstances were provided for in the marriage contract, remained in Courland. To safeguard her and Russia's interests, Commissioner General Peter Bestuzhev, father of the noted diplomats Mikhail and Alexis, remained with her.[7]

Bestuzhev was kept very busy because the interests of Anna and her uncle were in conflict with those of Duke Ferdinand, who wished to remove his dangerous rival from Courland. The interests of the former also ran counter to the interests of the Courland nobility, which had no desire to satisfy Anna's demands in regard to property and income as set out in the marriage contract, not to mention those of the king of Poland, who wanted to reconcile the interests of Duke Ferdinand with those of his subjects. The king wanted to nullify the marriage contract of the late duke because Friedrich Wilhelm had not reached his majority, and thus eliminate the claims to rulership of his widow the duchess, or at least to pass her over in favor of his own candidacy.

The interests of Poland also ran contrary to Anna's because Poland did not want Anna to establish a new ruling house in Courland. Instead it desired that upon the death or removal of the old and childless Ferdinand, Courland be annexed to Poland and divided into provinces. Prussia instinctively kept its guard up with respect to Courland. Knowing that nothing could happen there without powerful Russia, the Prussians joined their interests with Russia's and went to great lengths to arrange a marriage between Anna and the margrave of Brandenburg-Schwedt,[8] a union hostile to the Polish king. In this clash of interests the Courland nobility naturally fractured into parties.

"Our local supporters," in 1718 Bestuzhev notified Peter, "have suggested to me that the sovereign tsarevna not depart the country prior to resolving the matter of the succession. In her absence several factions hostile to her might arise, which could display an undeserved courage in these matters, whereas those well disposed towards us might not display the most reliable courage. If her majesty remains in residence she can win the highest authority as the genuine sovereign of this land."

BESTUZHEV IN COURLAND

To strengthen the Russian party Bestuzhev took advantage of the Poles' stated intention of dividing Courland into provinces and made written representation to the noble lords, senior councillors and noble knights.

"You can judge," he wrote, "that in such circumstance all your freedoms, both civil and religious, would be eliminated, for it is well known that in Poland and Lithuania the Lutherans endure great persecution, none being allowed to hold any position in the government. Therefore his majesty the tsar will inform the king and Polish Commonwealth that he will not permit any division of Courland into provinces. This he does not for his niece alone, but also for the noble squires and assemblies of his Courland neighbors, nor does he want to allow the destruction of Courland's ancient rights. He has no wish to obtain for himself either all or any part of Courland, nor can he permit anyone else to do so."

At the Sejm of 1719 a mighty struggle ensued between the Russian and Polish parties. The Russian party insisted upon a resolution requesting that the king and Commonwealth leave Courland as it was under German and ducal administration. The leading personages of the ducal administration were Kosciuszko and Eden, who wanted to retain only the German administration, not the ducal. Finally the Russian party got the upper hand. Poland did not abandon its claims, whereupon in March 1723 Peter wrote to Bestuzhev "With regard to a candidate from our side we must act quickly, holding out as long as possible. If it is not harmful, select a few candidates who do not want to go forward on their own (for the time being we shall entrust the original plan to you) in order to bring the Poles into line one way or another." As a means of strengthening the candidacy of the widowed duchess Bestuzhev suggested that the Russian court hold in Anna's name the deeds to the ducal lands currently mortgaged by the nobility. Thereby, as is easily understood, great distress would be inflicted upon on Poland and on the Polish party in Courland.

In 1724 a judgment was pronounced in Poland about the Courland nobility, which had withheld the funds held in escrow from the widowed duchess. The judgment stated that the nobles must return the confiscated money and pay an additional fine for doing this deed contrary to the commission's decrees forbidding the mortgaging of ducal lands to powerful people and foreigners. The nobles then approached Bestuzhev, maintaining that they had taken the mortgage funds and passed the lands to the duchess, thereby satisfying the wishes of the Russian emperor. All things considered, they did not consider the duchess a foreigner but rather looked upon her as their sovereign. The nobles asked the emperor to intercede on their behalf with the king and Polish Commonwealth and not consign them to poverty. Peter ordered Bestuzhev to reassure the nobility that the Russian ambassador in Warsaw had received instructions to demand that the Polish government annul the decree placing blame on the emperor's niece. The redemption of the land was done under the terms of a marriage contract with the deceased duke.

The Courland nobility could rely upon Peter's word, for that word always was expressed with force. Thus when Bestuzhev complained that the Courland government acted contrary to Russia's interests the emperor quickly sent off a letter to the general in command of the Baltic region. "Peter Bestuzhev writes to us from Mitau that the Courland district councillors are responsible for actions hostile to our niece Tsarevna Anna Ivanovna. They pay her no heed at all. In particular they offer no quarters to her aides at court. They do not keep horses available for the post. Furthermore, when our ship *Foundling* was docked at Libau laden with hemp and lashed with ropes they extended no help to our men, nor did they offer them provisions. In light of this, make haste to Courland and inform the authorities not to engage in any actions offensive to our niece Tsarevna Anna Ivanovna. They must observe her wishes, as their sovereign, in all matters, nor should they disregard our interests. Should they fail to comply, notify them that you have a decree empowering you to call a dragoon regiment into Courland. If they still persist in their hostility and respond to your notice with hostility, you are to execute the order and march a regiment into Courland and quarter it there."

Concerned primarily with the interests of the widowed duchess, Bestuzhev was not in accord with her mother Tsaritsa Praskovia Fedorovna,[9] as is apparent from a letter to her from Tsaritsa Catherine Alekseevna. "Concerning sending your daughter Anna Ivanovna to Courland, his majesty the tsar already has sent sufficient word to his most illustrious Prince Alexander Danilovich [Menshikov], and I of course hope that he supplies the money and service for this journey, for his illustriousness has been sent a decree on this matter. When, God willing, her grace arrives in Courland, your majesty no longer must worry about maintaining her at your expense since the maintenance of her home has been arranged already. For this purpose Peter Bestuzhev remains there with orders to collect funds forthwith for this purpose in the best towns, especially in Libau, Vindau and Mitau. Beyond this, your majesty, be advised that I will not look kindly upon your taking the entire sum needed for your rooms for all of next year, or imposing all your expenses in Courland upon those who live there. I hope that her grace your daughter can reside there without such great costs.

"Regarding Bestuzhev, he has been detached to Courland to oversee several matters most vital to his majesty the tsar, other than merely to attend your daughter's court. If he is dispatched from Courland simply for this one matter only, it will harm all of his majesty's other affairs there. I am surprised that your majesty has harbored such anger against him for so long. This saddens him and he seeks an explanation of why you bear this temper against him because in no way did he bring about this situation deliberately, being concerned for the honor of your children. Please keep in mind that either Andrei Artamonovich (Matveev)[10] or Lvov[11] are there with Tsarevna Anna Ivanovna, and both are obliged to tend to all of his majesty's necessary and eminent concerns. Regarding the court pages, please instruct that the best Russian schoolboys be found, and I advise you to be pleased to direct that they be chosen from among the Courlanders, for those Russians, Chemisov and others in the company of Tsarevna Catherine Ivanovna, are much worse."

AUSTRIA

Preoccupied with domestic matters, indeed ill with a severe internal disease, Poland simply could not turn its attention to Eastern affairs, which in the period under discussion so preoccupied Peter. The situation was different in Austria. In June 1722 Lanczyński[12] wrote from Vienna that the main topic of conversation there was the military activities of the Russians in Persia. The Austrians considered the situation from a variety of perspectives. They made particular mention of the fact that Peter, having occupied the most significant sites on the Caspian Sea, would establish communications with India by way of the Persian Gulf. This step would make it easy for him to become involved in the turmoil in Persia. Rare is the official in Vienna who does not have a map of Asia on his desk to observe the course of events. The English party suggested that the Austrian government acted imprudently in not concluding an alliance with England against Russia prior to the Treaty of Nystadt [1721]. By making war in Persia the tsar now might establish a state more powerful than Rome.

By autumn Lanczyński's attention was diverted from affairs in the East by a communiqué received from his court. "The Prussian king has notified us of disagreements arising there with the court of the Holy Roman emperor, requesting our cooperation in bringing them to an end. We therefore instruct you to notify the ambassador of the Holy Roman empire that previous disagreements between Austria and Prussia hitherto not only have not been put to rest, they have intensified. Since we have the good fortune to be on friendly terms with both courts, if his majesty the emperor is amenable, we are prepared to use our good offices to bring these discords to an end. You are to offer this suggestion delicately so as not to lead the Holy Roman court to suspect that we intend to intercede in this matter on behalf of the Prussian king."

Lanczyński made this offer on the Prussian situation in a conversation with Count Schönborn[13] about affairs in Poland. Schönborn thanked him and responded that it was necessary above all to know in which direction the Russian sovereign was leaning. If he was inclined towards the Holy Roman empire, matters should be left to take their course. The source of the disagreement between the two courts was well known. The Prussian chargé d'affaires was denied access to the Holy Roman court, and a courier was dispatched to Berlin announcing that the fault lay with the local chargé d'affaires. The Prussian king did not wait for the courier and barred from his court the Holy Roman chargé d'affaires, who had done nothing wrong. Had not the Prussian king been one of the more powerful rulers within the empire, unquestionably the Holy Roman emperor would not have allowed such an insult to pass. The emperor acted with great patience, as a father would with his son, merely demanding that the king again receive his ambassador at court. Were the Russian court to suggest to the Prussians the unfairness of their behavior, the emperor would be pleased.

Russia earlier was worried whether the court in Vienna would assist the Saxon prince[14] who was betrothed to the emperor's niece to lay claim to the Polish crown. Lanczyński was reassuring on this account when he wrote that the Viennese court considered this contrary to the interests of Austria and the private interests of the [Austrian] empress's daughters. Why would the court wish to strengthen a house certain to call into question the right of [Peter's] daughters to rule in Russia?

Therefore Vienna chose not to refuse the Saxons outright. Instead it avoided giving a decisive response. With regard to the unfriendly behavior of the Austrian chargé d'affaires in Constantinople, Lanczyński also offered the calming reassurances of the emperor's diplomats that there could be no clashes between Russia and Austria. Vienna did not covet Russia's acquisitions on the Baltic Sea because Sweden always was the enemy of the Austrian house. Consequently, Austria's interests required the pacification of Sweden. In regard to the East, Austria was motivated by a wish to see the expansion of Russian trade. There existed no causes for war between Russia and Austria at a time when other states, having grown rich from the Eastern trade, employed their wealth in war against Austria. In a word, there were no other two courts on the face of the earth whose interests were as closely linked as the Russian and the Austrian.

At these assurances the Prussian ministers' fears that Russia might move closer to France and Spain began to surface. Yaguzhinsky's[15] visit to Berlin deeply alarmed Vienna, where Prince Eugene[16] had become noticeably cool to Lanczyński. This coolness intensified when a rumor circulated that Yaguzhinsky had visited Paris for negotiations about obtaining the Polish throne for the duke of Chartres, son of the regent duke of Orleans, and to conclude a marriage alliance with the house of Bourbon.[17]

Peter demanded that the Viennese court use its good offices in Constantinople to ameliorate the discord between Russia and the Porte over affairs in Persia. The Viennese court promised to do so, but at that very time news arrived that the French ambassador in Constantinople was interceding over this matter. The Viennese court reproached Lanczyński, saying "If you trust us and consider our credit with the Porte strong, why did you turn to France? If you think that France can serve you better there, why turn to us?"

At the beginning of 1723 the court in Vienna was in a troubled state. Some sort of détente was emerging between Russia, Prussia, France and Spain. Austria's lone ally, the king of England, was in conflict with the Holy Roman emperor over religious matters. As guardian of Catholicism in Germany the emperor could not give way to the protector of Protestantism, the elector of Hanover, who as king of England took advantage of the opportunity and boldly announced his demands. In a secret council Count Schönborn, a consistent foe of the English party, demanded that the Holy Roman emperor express his dissatisfaction with the king of England, as was the emperor's right in dealing with an elector. This was a sensitive matter. Such a gesture would make the emperor the accepted mentor of the king of England.

Count Zinzendorf[18] advised moderation, recognizing that without England's friendship the emperor in Vienna could not be secure in Italy if war broke out with Spain. Count Schönborn demurred, arguing that it would be preferable to push matters to the limit than to bear such insults. Moreover it was essential to know with whom Spain would willingly go to war, the emperor or England? Who had done greater harm to Spain, the emperor or England? Since there was no possibility of reaching an accommodation with Spain, the king of England would see himself prevailing.

Prince Eugene shared Schönborn's opinion, forcefully saying so to the English ambassador, apprising him that the emperor might make war and conclude peace without the king of England. The ambassador grew silent. The Austrian side decided that this step sufficed, choosing not to push matters to the limit. Relations of this sort made it impossible for the Viennese court to grow too cool towards Russia. The English, Saxon and Danish ambassadors warned the Austrian ministers that aggravating Russia would have frightful consequences, for the Russian tsar intended to seize Danzig. They received a reply that, as matters came to a head, the emperor would take all necessary measures.

THE MECKLENBURG AFFAIR

Between the courts in Petersburg and Vienna there existed one additional point of contention, namely Mecklenburg.[19] In May 1723 Count Schönborn notified Lanczyński that the emperor, out of the special esteem and friendship in which he held the Russian sovereign, turned a blind eye to the disobedient and offensive behavior of the duke of Mecklenburg, which he could tolerate no longer. Both conscience and the imperial title demanded that the emperor put an end to it. The duke had abandoned the empire and refused to acknowledge imperial decrees, thus behaving like a veritable rebel. In spite of all of his illegal actions the emperor had left him an annual income of a hundred thousand thalers.[20] Were the duke to appear before a commission of the imperial court the emperor willingly would assist him in bringing all of these matters and trials to an end in the most favorable manner possible. The duke disdained this kind offer of the emperor, who no longer could permit Mecklenburg to fall into such extreme ruin. The duke had left in charge of the duchy's administration the worst and most insolent of men, who said right to the faces of the emperor's commissioners that they did not recognize the emperor's authority. When they received the emperor's decrees they treated them with complete contumacy, tearing them to pieces. Out of respect for the Russian sovereign, the emperor as the last means at his disposal wished to send the duke a communiqué in which, as father of the empire, he granted him three more months to return to his allegiance to the empire. Should he fail to return in that time the emperor would be obliged to appoint a government in Mecklenburg and end the current state of affairs there by his own authority.

After this communication Lanczyński found an opportunity to visit someone skilled in the affairs of the Holy Roman empire, from whom he sought the reason behind this decision on Mecklenburg's account. This expert responded that, as a consequence of the duke's absence, the Hanoverians had demonstrated their intent to gain influence in Mecklenburg, something deeply offensive to the Viennese court and the entire Holy Roman empire. Lanczyński understood the sense of what Schönborn meant when he maintained that the Holy Roman emperor could not allow Mecklenburg to fall into such extreme ruin. Peter directed him to request that the emperor delay acting on this decision, thus granting him some time to convince the duke to heed the warning. This request was accepted with great pleasure, although Schönborn told Lanczyński that the time limit could be extended only if the duke took the first step. He must send the emperor a formal letter in respectful language requesting an extension. This was sent, yet the duke also dispatched letters to the princes of the empire complaining that he was oppressed, and about everything that had not transpired in Germany, a course of action which greatly annoyed the Viennese court.

When Lanczyński inquired of Prince Eugene about removing the military force from Mecklenburg, he learned that it could not march so long as the duke did not return, and none of the other issues could be resolved either. At this point Eugene grew indignant and, raising his voice, continued "To what end would an armed detachment be dispatched? To give the court in Mecklenburg the freedom to chop off heads, to hang people, or break them on the wheel, just as the duke directed not so long ago? You speak about a letter which the duke sent to the emperor. The duke also sent other letters to the princes of the empire which railed against the emperor in the harshest tones. To make matters worse, he ordered a paper read from the pulpits of all the churches in which he covered with shame everything done according to imperial decrees. He forbade obedience to these decrees under threat of severe punishment. Is this really a sign of the genuine obedience and good will to which we should return?"

Lanczyński countered that the duke wished to return to Mecklenburg, to administer it responsibly. How could he return when an armed detachment was there? It would mean that he had handed authority to his enemies. If the duke punished some of his subjects this was consistent with justice, for every imperial prince has the right of the sword. "I have already clarified this matter satisfactorily," replied Eugene. "The court here has completely different information about the duke's executions. Concerning the right of the sword, there remains one question. May an imperial prince, who currently resides outside the empire in flagrant disregard of the emperor's decrees, exercise his rights within the empire? You hold out hope that the duke will return, but we know very well that this will not happen. We have seen him here, we have come to understand his ways completely, we know that he since has grown even worse." Schönborn came to Lanczyński's aid. "The guilt," he responded, "for spilling the blood of innocent people executed by the duke rests with the emperor for delaying so long. Your sovereign's intention to assist his relative is laudable, although you cannot be certain the duke will not show contempt. We have no wish for contempt, nor shall we continue to play this game any longer."

This game brought the year 1723 to a close. Lanczyński began the new year of 1724 with a report that the Mecklenburg affair had reached a crucial point at the Viennese court, none of Russia's representations having had any effect. "Who is to blame that the Mecklenburg court does not prepare to offer assistance to your imperial majesty and, contemptuous of all good counsel, rushes headlong to its own demise?" Nevertheless Lanczyński obtained a two-month extension for the duke. In regard to the Austrian ministry's views on the Eastern affair Lanczyński reported that Russia's favorable settlement with the Porte was not acceptable to the Viennese court. The thinking there was "Better peace than the warring to which we somehow have become accustomed. At the same time, the enemies of the Austrian house could ensnare us."

"Yet with all this," continued Lanczyński, "they proceed with their malicious suggestions that once your imperial majesty brings this matter to a favorable conclusion, you might instigate something else against Europe. Here they respond to this suggestion as follows. 'It is not our affair who controls the Caspian Sea, which is very far away. If the Russian sovereign wishes to be involved in yet another matter, we can find the means to resist him. This sovereign knows very well the difference between a European and an Asiatic war. It is one thing to act in the Eastern theater, where you need only appear to take over towns and regions. It is quite another to act in European regions where everywhere you turn there is someone with whom to negotiate."

PRUSSIA

Vienna had little concern for the spread of Russia's authority in the East. It was much more concerned about the relations of the powerful new empire with the European powers. Prussia was closer in its relations to Russia than the others, there having been trouble between Prussia and

Austria for some time. Prussia acted in concert with Russia in Poland in its rivalry with Saxony, whose strengthening at Poland's expense it in no way wished to permit.

At the beginning of 1722 the Saxon court tried to determine whether it could drive a wedge between Prussia and Russia in Polish affairs. Baron Ilgen[21] informed Count Alexander Golovkin[22] that Fleming had expressed his readiness through the Prussian representative in Dresden to cooperate in arranging a rapprochement between Prussia and Austria. He hoped to use his credit in Vienna to facilitate this matter, but Prussia must become a party to the well-known Viennese treaty which brought about the alliance between Austria and Saxony.[23] Ilgen assured Golovkin that Prussia would not join this treaty, nor would it entertain any hypocritical suggestions. Ilgen maintained that the main culprit in this matter was the Hanoverian ambassador Bernstorff.[24] Whitworth, the English ambassador in Berlin,[25] according to Golovkin's observations also pursued rapprochement between Prussia and Austria, although in Golovkin's opinion even if this rapprochement came about there would be no greater accord or trust between them.

Prussia's interests demanded above all an alignment with Russia, although it made sense that Prussia could not disturb the closeness of the two powerful empires without English involvement. That is why it hastened to establish a strong toehold in Courland as a means of countering Russia's influence there. King Frederick William[26] deemed it necessary to apprise the Russian emperor that it would be dangerous for Russia to undertake anything against Europe. "I will not," he told Golovkin, "renew the treaty with Denmark guaranteeing Schleswig's security unless I receive word of what is happening at your court with the duke of Holstein,[27] for I do not want to take any step offensive to your imperial majesty. Still, I do not think that his majesty, upon concluding such a glorious and beneficial peace [Nystad, 1721], would want to be involved in some new venture. If this is not the case, I should inform you in the utmost confidence that all of Europe will grow very suspicious."

The Russian side hastened to reassure the king. Thus when Russia demanded that its ships have free passage through the Sound [the Oresund, between Denmark and Sweden] without paying tolls to the Danish government, Golovkin forewarned the Prussian ministry that the emperor would employ only proper and friendly means in this matter, taking no measures that might be cause for war. Those in Berlin who were well-disposed towards Russia, among whom was the prince of

Anhalt, informed Golovkin that the king must be reassured with regard to Courland. At the first convenient moment the ambassador informed the king that this was a delicate matter which would not soon be resolved. Haste would be dangerous in that it risked alienating the Poles and estranging them from Russia and Prussia.

The king, so it would appear, was satisfied with this explanation. Yet he wondered whether it might not be preferable to reach an accord over Courland in advance, as in all affairs connected with Poland. The response was that the emperor stood firmly behind the treaty of 1718 about the betrothal of the duchess Anna with Karl, [cousin of the] margrave of Brandenburg-Schwedt.[28] Moving quickly to put this treaty into effect would be contrary to Russia's interests. The Polish Sejm required support for its opposition to the emperor of Austria. If Russia established its dominance in Courland the Sejm would be irritated and the king's position strengthened. In October 1722 Golovkin informed the king of Prussia that the emperor had directed his ambassador in Warsaw, Prince Dolgoruky, to oppose Saxony's plans as described by the Prussian ambassador Schwerin.[29] He requested that the king instruct Schwerin to give Dolgoruky funds necessary to finance the entire matter. The king agreed to transfer the money by voucher. The ambassador [Dolgoruky] added that the money must be transferred quickly because Schwerin himself needed it for bribes.

The Polish Sejm dispersed, whereupon all attention in Berlin turned once again to Courland, where success depended on Russia. At the beginning of 1723 Frederick William told Golovkin "If the Viennese court really wishes to pursue my friendship there can be only two reasons. Either it wants incite me against France, or it wants to conclude some sort of alliance utterly unacceptable to your emperor. I am allied with the Russian emperor, not the Holy Roman emperor, and refuse to pursue any advantage for myself against him.

"Regarding an alliance against France, little profit can be expected because the [Holy Roman] emperor will not, and indeed cannot, grant me even a small district in the German lands. He cannot win me over with money because I have enough of my own. General Seckendorf of Saxony visited me. Discussing these important matters, he suggested that the Russian emperor holds a position of great strength. This arouses suspicion among the other powers, although this strength is most dangerous for me as your closest neighbor. He also suggested that the Polish court has extensive information that an alliance is forming between Russia and

France, from which no small measure of concern will arise among the other powers.

"Therefore Vienna, London and Dresden have agreed about measures needed to maintain their security. In this Seckendorf was suggesting in every way possible that I too enter into this alliance. I answered that the Russian emperor and I are on friendly terms, and I see no danger to myself from him whatsoever. Above all I wish his strength to grow especially great so as to compel the Viennese court to behave with greater moderation, displaying greater respect for others. At that point Seckendorf noted that I tried to dissolve the last Sejm in Poland, that I spent a lot of money for that purpose. We [Prussia and Saxony] could avoid all these expenses and receive no small profit were I to align closely with the Polish king. Thus, were I to help the king secure the Polish throne for his son he could secure for me the bishopric of Warmia and Pomerania. I asked him when the Polish king would give this to me. 'When,' Seckendorf responded, 'everything is carried out according to the wishes of my sovereign.'"

Golovkin observed to the king that the Saxons were behaving insidiously, that they urged a risky venture while insisting that how long they waited and what they gave did not depend on them. Were they to achieve their aim, upon receiving the inheritance they might introduce autocracy into Poland as well. As an autocracy the Saxons could choose to do whatever they wished, and they might also seize Prussian lands. "This is true," the king replied. "I am of the same opinion. Therefore both your emperor and I need to act with great caution, refusing Saxony's observations. The Saxon court previously disavowed the Jew Leman's project to divide Poland.[30] Now they seek to revive it."

This was a curious discussion. The king and the Russian ambassador represented each other as seeing no advantage in the Saxon suggestion. It was as if they had forgotten completely that a binding agreement on this subject existed between Russia and Prussia since February 1720. Both powers obligated themselves to see to it that the Polish Commonwealth retain its rights and privileges. If the Polish royal court displayed any intention of subverting the Commonwealth's freedoms, or began to influence it to accept the alliance concluded in Vienna between the Holy Roman emperor and the kings of Great Britain and Poland, Russia and Prussia through counsel and deed must oppose it. They must assist the Polish Commonwealth to remain as it was and especially not allow the crown prince of Saxony to ascend the Polish throne while his father was alive or after his death. These treaty document held very little significance whereas according to the expression of the day "the political state of affairs" had a great deal.

Rapprochement finally was arranged between Prussia and Austria. Simultaneously Frederick William concluded a treaty with George of England and Hanover for common action in defense of the interests of the Protestant population in Germany. At the beginning of 1724 the Prussian king told Golovkin "I shall never exchange your emperor for anyone else because I do not have such friendship with anyone else. Although I am at peace with the Holy Roman emperor I have little confidence that this will continue. We cannot have such a close friendship with the king of Poland. I shall enter no agreement, nor did I oppose your emperor's military actions in the latest war against the Swedes. I was not opposed to the rights of the duke of Holstein to the Swedish throne,[31] nor did I oppose the return of Schleswig to him. I wish him to regain Schleswig, and under the circumstances I shall not refuse to assist him. I shall, however, expect congenial company. I will not enter this matter alone, nor will I initiate anything else."

The Prussian ministers complained to Golovkin about the Saxon court. It appeared to be attempting to engage in Italy and the empire among the Catholic princes to form a Catholic alliance to prevent the large Protestant territorial princes from becoming powerful. The Saxon court wished to bring Poland into an alliance between Austria, Bavaria and Saxony. If successful, the ministers said, this would merge two alliances into one. Religion would be the pretext, although the primary goal was to establish the Saxon dynasty on the Polish throne. The Saxons also wished to hand over Courland to the prince of Saxony-Neustadt.

Saxony's failure in Poland somewhat diminished these perils. The court in Petersburg wanted the court in Berlin to enter into the alliance concluded between Russia and Sweden. In Berlin the question was raised unceremoniously about what Prussia would receive in return. Petersburg could not supply a satisfactory response. A certain cooling of relations ensued between the two courts, the first cause of which was Courland, the marriage contract concerning which had been rewritten. Prince Karl of Brandenburg-Schwedt was named instead of Margrave Friedrich, but the old contract remained on paper. When in July 1724 Peter was informed that the Prussian court demanded quick resolution of the Courland matter because the death of Count Ferdinand was imminent, the emperor directed "in accordance with earlier decrees they should continue to shun such resolution." The Berlin cabinet persisted in asking its counterpart in Petersburg when the Courland matter would be resolved. Petersburg persisted in answering "Wait!" "How long must we wait?" people were saying in Berlin, growing increasingly angry.

The other cause for chilled relations, if hardly the most important, consisted in the fact that Peter, as a way of showing his appreciation of Frederick William, a passionate collector of towering soldiers, sent him some Russian giants. The king was very pleased, thinking that the giants were given as a gift. Peter did not deem it permissible to give these soldiers as gifts, and requested the return of the giants, promising to send others in return. Frederick William parted with the giants reluctantly, but a frightful shock was being prepared for him. The new soldiers sent from Russia were not as large as the first! The king could not forget this for a long time. When Golovkin had to speak with him about important matters people well disposed to Russia informed the ambassador that it was not a good time because the wound in the king's heart over the giants was still too fresh.

DENMARK

Denmark held on to Schleswig once it left the Northern War although this plunder was not secure because the duke of Holstein did not renounce his claim. The opposition of this weak-willed princeling could have been disregarded, except that he had claims to the Swedish throne. Moreover he was at that very time staying in Petersburg seeking the hand of the tsar's daughter. In the event of such a wedding Denmark must deal not with the duke of Holstein, but with a powerful Russia whose assistance could secure the Swedish throne for the duke. Alexis Bestuzhev[32] wrote from Copenhagen in 1722 that the Danish court recognized Peter as the All-Russian emperor on condition that he guarantee Schleswig's security, or at least expel the duke of Holstein from Russia. "In my opinion," wrote Bestuzhev, "we need to keep the duke in Russia so long as the court here fails to observe your majesty's wishes because everything is done from fear, not in goodwill. I am already quite familiar with the Danish court. Successful negotiations can be concluded with them only so long as the duke remains in Petersburg. Were he to leave, immediately the Danes would lift their heads and the Hanoverian ambassador, Bothmer, would place impediments before all your interests."

RUSSIA DEMANDS EXEMPTION FROM THE SOUND TOLLS

Russia's demands involved not just the imperial title. According to Bestuzhev's reasoning, the Russian court demanded from the Danes free passage through Oresund for all ships departing Russian harbors and all those returning. When Bestuzhev informed the Danish ministers of this demand in a meeting, both the chancellor, Count Holst, and the privy councillor, also named Holst, blanched. Reporting to his own court about the evasive responses of the Danish government regarding the Sound tolls, Bestuzhev wrote that the Hanoverian ambassador Bothmer supported them in their stubbornness. Bothmer governed Denmark through the two Holsts, who received annual pensions from Hanover. Since native Danes found themselves removed from managing their own affairs, they expressed their deep indignation at this situation. Bothmer assured the Danish government that in the event of hostilities by Russia an English squadron would sail to the Sound. Bestuzhev wrote Peter that Russia need not declare war, although it would be worthwhile to place the army and navy on a war footing. The English nation was impatient to sail its fleet, and the king of Denmark was needful of much, for he would have to outfit a fleet in great need of money. Native Danes and Norwegians said openly that an English fleet would lead their governments to tremendous losses and could offer no more assistance than Sweden had earlier.[33]

By spring a rumor swept Denmark that Peter was giving the duke of Holstein between thirty and forty thousand soldiers and thirty ships of the line, exclusive of frigates and galleys. The Danish government believed the rumor, and hastened to arm its fleet. Yet while the Danes awaited the arrival of the Russian ships with trepidation Russia was constructing vessels and sailing them down the Volga for the Caspian campaign. Peter wrote to Bestuzhev that by subtle exercise of external pressure, without making threats, he must prevail upon the Danish government to cancel the Sound tolls. "There is no need," answered Bestuzhev, "to threaten the court here, because every threat sets off an indescribable panic about the presence of the duke of Holstein in Russia, about the fact that the duke of Mecklenburg is travelling there, and about your majesty's negotiations with France and Spain." Fear began to dissipate when word arrived that Peter was marching to Astrakhan.

In Russia, by contrast, there was growing uneasiness upon news that Denmark was giving considerable effort toward a mutual defense alliance with Sweden against Russia. Bestuzhev was instructed to request an explanation of this matter from the ministers or from the king himself.

Bestuzhev answered that he saw no need to hurry, since the Danish court would ascribe haste to fear and grow still bolder. On the contrary, it must be demonstrated that the Russian court was not devoting much attention to this alliance, certain that Denmark, England and Sweden together could not harm Russia. This all the more so because everyone in Denmark fervently wished for an alliance with Russia except for the two Holsts, who acted at Hanover's direction. Bothmer, however, needed to use Russia to frighten the Danish court and induce it everywhere to look to its interests and depend upon its alliances. Thus not long ago a rumor circulated that the Russian sovereign was on his way not to Astrakhan, but to Archangel, and that the Russian fleet under the command of Vice Admiral Gordon[34] was already on the Baltic Sea. Once again panic gripped the Danish court. Soon Bestuzhev had the pleasure of reporting that the Danish court, seeing Sweden's disinclination to form an alliance, denied in every way possible that it had pursued a Swedish alliance. Incessantly it averred (rather like the fox in the fables) that it had no wish to form such an alliance. Bestuzhev advised against expelling the duke of Holstein from Russia, for otherwise the Danish court would grow bolder and ignore Russia's demands.

Once Peter returned from the Persian campaign, Bothmer assured the Danish court that it had nothing to fear from Russia. The tsar had retreated with significant losses because of a storm on the Caspian Sea. He also lost his horses in this arduous campaign. According to Bothmer the Porte was well fortified against Russia, thus preventing the tsar from turning north towards the Baltic.

Bestuzhev reported that under current circumstances renewing the suggestion on the Sound tolls would be inadvisable. Better for the time being just to renew the demand over the imperial title. To assure success in the matter of the imperial title, Chancellor Holst must be given ten thousand ducats, Privy Councillor Holst six thousand, Privy Councillor Lent six thousand, and von Galen three thousand for favorably orchestrating foreign affairs. This was precisely what the Hanoverian court would do to woo Denmark away from an alliance with Russia. Bestuzhev hoped that he could have the Holsts, Lent and Hagen on his side for twenty-five thousand ducats. Already he had on his side an individual who was influential with the king, Secretary of State Habel, who on March 10, 1723 arranged a private audience for him, bringing him to the king by a secret route.

Bestuzhev began his speech with a request that his majesty not credit the malicious insinuations circulated by the criminal plots of the emperor's enemies. On the contrary, the emperor had every intention of sustaining their existing friendship, securing it and making it much closer, were the king immediately to enter into a treaty which, as a sign of friendship and respect, recognized him as All-Russian emperor and freed Russian ships from the Sound tolls.

"I never gave credence to those malicious rumors against your sovereign before," the king responded, "and I will not now. Sweden has been trying to convince me to enter into an alliance against his majesty, but I have declined. Were King George to attempt to lead me to join an alliance harmful to your sovereign, I still would refuse, preferring the friendship and alliance of your sovereign and wishing to oblige him in all matters. Report to his majesty privately that, were I to receive a guarantee from Russia regarding Schleswig, and if the duke of Holstein gives assurances for himself and his heirs that he cedes Schleswig to Denmark, renouncing any future claims, I shall grant the duke the title of royal majesty and help him gain the Swedish crown.

"What is more, if your sovereign takes up arms against King George on behalf of a pretender to the throne, or seizes Bremen and Verden for the duke of Holstein, or if he sends armed forces into Mecklenburg, I will not remain neutral. I will feel obliged to provide every assistance. In particular the Russian fleet will find free anchorage in all my harbors. Should your sovereign reject the friendship which I have conveyed through these arrangements and profitable proposals, of course his majesty will not be surprised that I will find it necessary to enter into an alliance with King George. Again I want to emphasize that you must report my words only to his majesty so that my ambassador at the Russian court, Westphalen, knows nothing about it. Since I would like the treaty to be negotiated through Habel alone, and my privy council to be unaware of it, let his majesty grant you complete authority to conclude this treaty."

Bestuzhev commented that in addition to conveying this suggestion from the king he was supposed to report to the emperor on developments regarding the imperial title and the Sound tolls. "Upon concluding the treaties," answered the king, "I shall recognize willingly the imperial title for your sovereign. Yet if his majesty demands [recognition] before a treaty is signed, without offering any incentive and while keeping my opponent the duke of Holstein at his court, I cannot consider this a sign of friendship. As regards exempting Russian ships from the Sound tolls, this I cannot do, inasmuch as the Swedes, English, Dutch and other nations immediately will demand the same concession, which I could not refuse. Still, I can observe his majesty's wish on condition that he consent to an annual delivery, free of charge, of an agreed quantity of hemp, resin and tar to Denmark. On that basis concessions to other nations could be avoided." In his report on this conversation Bestuzhev wrote that he must have three thousand ducats immediately for bribing Habel.

Russia, not surprisingly, did not consider it appropriate or profitable to deprive the duke of Holstein of his hopes of returning to Schleswig or to remain neutral in the event of war between Denmark and King George, a war which Peter did not wish to initiate. Thus the year 1723 passed in fruitless negotiations over the Sound tolls. Everyone in Denmark comforted themselves by hoping for war between Russia and Turkey over events in Persia.

In March 1724 the king fell ill. Bestuzhev wrote to Petersburg that the cause of the illness was news of the alliance between Russia and Sweden. Should the Danish court receive further word of rapprochement between Russia and the king of England, it would grow more frightened, all the more so since the Danish court tended to be less brave in spring than in winter. They were fearful not just about Schleswig, but also about Norway.

Soon an additional piece of bad news arrived. Turkey entered into an agreement with Russia over Persia. So there would be no war! The king of Denmark then went to great lengths to arrange a meeting with the kings of England and Prussia to create a triple alliance of Denmark, England and Prussia against Russia and Sweden. The Prussian king declined this overture because he did not wish to arouse the suspicion of the Russian court. At that point Copenhagen was plunged into despair. The possibility was broached among ambassadors at the courts of Denmark's allies of an alliance with Russia. The tsar had proposed to Denmark that he guarantee Schleswig, that he expel the duke of Holstein from Russia within four weeks should the king accord the tsar the imperial title and free Russia's ships from tolls at the Sound. This arrangement would have brought the Danes no benefits for they already considered Schleswig lost. Let us now turn to Sweden and observe how the alliance, which so frightened Denmark, was concluded with Russia.

ALLIANCE WITH SWEDEN

After the peace at Nystadt, Mikhail Petrovich Bestuzhev-Riumin,[35] brother of the chargé d'affaires in Denmark, was dispatched as chargé d'affaires in Sweden. He began his reports about Sweden with these words. "As I see it, matters here are just as they are in Poland. Every nobleman is out for himself, paying no attention to the senior status of his own superiors, neither is there any order whatsoever."

The first order of business for Bestuzhev was to offer Russia's good offices in arranging a rapprochement between the king of Sweden and the duke of Holstein. The chargé d'affaires "took some notice" that the king found this suggestion very offensive. In May 1722 Bestuzhev reported that a rumor was going around Stockholm that Tsarevna Elizabeth Petrovna was engaged to the Holstein duke. This rumor provoked great anxiety at court and immense joy among the Holstein party.

It is curious to note how these talented Russians, sought out by Peter and sent by him to diplomatic posts, attempted to grasp not only the current situation of states and the reciprocal relations among them. They also studied their history and drew their own conclusions about contemporary interests on the basis of historical considerations. Bestuzhev was suspicious of the frequent consultations between the Holy Roman emperor's ambassador Freitag, the Hanover ambassador, and four Swedish senators (Counts Horn, Duecker, Tessin and de la Gardie)[36] whom he called republicans, in other words proponents of the form of government introduced in Sweden upon the death of Karl XII.[37] How then did Bestuzhev explain these frequent consultations and close friendships? "I think," he wrote to Peter, "that they want to unite Denmark, Sweden and Norway under one king, just as it was under the so-called Union of Kalmar at the time of the Danish Queen Marguerite, and that both the Holy Roman and Hanoverian courts would support this project. This is just my opinion."[38]

Bestuzhev's understanding was too far-reaching in that there were no plans to reconstitute the Union of Kalmar. Baron Sparre,[39] Swedish ambassador at the English court, presented to his king the project of a triple alliance between Sweden, Denmark and England, adding that the king of England promised to convince Holland to join. The king showered flattery upon the English ambassador, with whom he regularly had supper along with the ambassador from [Hesse-]Cassel.[40] Sometimes the Danish ambassador joined them at these suppers, but no one else. Above all, the king wanted to arrange for the inheritance of the Swedish throne to be transferred to his own house of Cassel. He believed that the only way of accomplishing this was to reestablish autocracy, and throughout winter and summer the king travelled through the provinces cajoling and bribing people of influence so aggressively that the aristocracy grew upset with him. The senators told Bestuzhev that they clearly understood that the king intended to abrogate the constitution. They placed all their hopes on the Russian sovereign, who [they hoped] would not permit this. "It is very surprising," wrote Bestuzhev, "that the king's private council consists of non-notable and discredited individuals. One of them is Neugebauer,[41] formerly tutor of the late Tsarevich Alexis Petrovich,[42] and the others are just like him."

Fearing most of all the duke of Holstein and his connections with Russia, the king wrote to the French ambassador at the Russian court, Campredon,[43] that he was prepared to accord Peter the imperial title so long as the tsar entered into no arrangements with the duke of Holstein and removed the duke from his court. Acting on instructions, Bestuzhev apprised the king that the emperor would not enter any arrangement with the duke of Holstein which might be harmful to his royal majesty. Surely the king must recognize that removing the duke would offend the honor and word of the emperor, who wished to see rapprochement between the duke and the king. Only in this way might they ensure that the duke would not be a part of any enterprises hostile to the king. Once a rapprochement was concluded, the duke would depart Russia.

The king responded that he did not oppose rapprochement with the duke. The duke need merely send his own ambassador to Sweden and make amends for his previous deeds. The Holstein ambassador must not visit Stockholm until the Riksdag meeting concluded. This would avoid intrigues while it was still in session. "The Holstein ambassador," Bestuzhev replied, "will come at a time convenient to your majesty. May it only please your majesty to move towards rapprochement, assuring me that when the duke takes the first step, through his ambassador recognizing and acclaiming your majesty as king, that your majesty will grant the duke the title of royal majesty." The king did not like this suggestion at all, and immediately changed the subject.

The Riksdag opened in January 1723. It chose as its marshal the president of the Treasury College, Lagerberg, "the best patriot, an opponent of the court's intentions, well disposed towards the duke of Holstein," according to Bestuzhev's account. "This demonstrates," wrote the chargé d'affaires, "that the court party is utterly powerless in relation to the others, even though a large proportion have been paid off. I earnestly hope that the king does not increase his power and authority during this Riksdag, even less that he succeeds in passing the inheritance of the throne to the house of Cassel. The royal party dare not mention anything about this." The king's party somehow also suffered a defeat in the elections to the Secret Committee, whose hundred members conducted confidential activities such as concluding alliances and so forth. It appears that of those chosen ninety-eight were patriots, in other words opponents of the king's intentions, and only two belonged to the king's own party.

Although the king notified Bestuzhev that the Holstein ambassador was to arrive after the Riksdag was over, a man already familiar to us, Bassewitz,[44] appeared at the very start of the Riksdag in his capacity as ambassador extraordinary of the duke. The king sent instructions to Finland to detain Bassewitz, but public opinion obliged him to retract the order. Bassewitz brought Bestuzhev one thousand ducats for essential expenses at the Riksdag. Shortly thereafter the king's party endured a third setback.

From among the peasant deputies appeared a proposal to strengthen the king's authority. The deputies from the urban estates informed the noble deputies about this, and then the deputies from three estates—noble, clerical, and urban—unanimously rejected the proposal. They resolved to seek out the instigators of this business from among the peasant deputies, to punish them as traitors. This decision elicited loud applause from among the noble deputies, and great joy spread throughout the city. Several of the most eminent noble deputies told Bestuzhev that had the deputies of the clergy and towns approved the peasant proposal, the nobles would have dissolved the Riksdag and sent a deputation to the Russian emperor requesting protection. This was because in the seventh paragraph of the Nystadt accord the emperor was obligated to support the present form of administration in Sweden. "I know," wrote Bestuzhev, "that the Swedish nobility intimidated the clerical and urban deputies with this seventh paragraph, frightening them with the specter that it demanded an army and galleys from the Russian emperor in defense of their freedom. This threat kept many of them in line. Thus all the king's trouble was for nothing, his travel around the provinces paying out money all in vain. Your majesty, take advantage of the great regard in which you are held here. So long as the current form of administration persists, I have nothing at all to fear from the Swedes."

Whereas Bestuzhev wrote that Russia had nothing to fear from the king of Sweden, others wrote the king that he indeed had something to fear from Russia. At the beginning of March Bassewitz visited Bestuzhev to show him a letter he received from Campredon, the French ambassador in Russia. The letter said that the emperor had begun to treat the duke of Holstein very coolly, and that Russia was in dire straits. It had no money, anticipated famine, its army was in the most pathetic state, a third of its fifty thousand horses lost in the Persian campaign and, finally, expected war with Turkey. Bestuzhev learned that Campredon dispatched the same news to the king of Sweden through the Cassel chancellery, and that this news was circulated, as if it were secret, to certain individuals.

These pieces of information had no effect. The notice delivered by Bestuzhev in the emperor's name made a powerful impact upon its recipient, Count Horn, president of the College of Foreign Affairs and the most influential figure in Sweden at that time. The notice said the following. "Since word has reached his imperial majesty that the king is attempting to dissolve the current form of government and replace it with autocracy, his imperial majesty has directed me in the strongest way possible to assure all true patriots that he is obligated by the peace treaty to offer his assistance and not countenance any change in the present form of government."

This notice greatly distressed Horn, who asked the chargé d'affaires to come the next day to see Count de la Gardie. Bestuzhev found Horn at de la Gardie's, along with two patriots. All requested that Bestuzhev convey their appreciation to the emperor for his great kindness. At the insistence of the Riksdag, Bassewitz finally received an audience with the king, who had been putting it off, hoping to delay until the Riksdag closed. "The affairs of the duke of Holstein are currently in the best possible state," wrote Bestuzhev, "and it would be possible at this Riksdag to confirm his inheritance of the Swedish throne, but we need more money. Although the duke has many well wishers, they do not want to do anything in vain. The people here have an interest in the outcome, including the poor folk, and it is fair to say that money will achieve everything."

Bassewitz delivered a formal speech with the demand that the duke receive the title "his royal highness." The Riksdag agreed, at the same session resolving to recognize the imperial title for the Russian sovereign. The news that the elected Riksdag members had resolved to grant the title of royal highness to the duke of Holstein deeply saddened the king. His supporters grew timid "and his closest partisans appeared with gloomy faces as if great misfortune had befallen them," in Bestuzhev's words. It was generally thought that the king approved the resolution of the Riksdag while clutching his heart, then stated that he was very displeased with this resolution, delivering a protest written in his own hand. The queen also issued a handwritten protest. Both stated that recognizing the duke as royal highness affronted the crown, that it was equivalent to recognizing the duke's right to the Swedish crown.

At the next session of the Riksdag the court party endorsed the royal protests. The Holstein and patriotic parties, being ten times larger, overruled the court party. The Riksdag served notice that it would not alter its resolution. The actions of the king and queen distressed the crown officials even more, a situation from which the duke of Holstein benefited. Friends secretly informed Bestuzhev that the protocol of the Secret Committee included a plan whereby the king would become an autocrat and consolidate the inheritance of the Swedish crown in the house of Cassel, for which he promised the Prussian king the remainder of Pomerania in return for his help.

Peter was very pleased. He bestowed the title of lord-in-waiting upon Bestuzhev and granted him the title of ambassador extraordinary. At the same time he directed him to determine whether the Holstein party needed the assistance of the Russian fleet to proclaim at the Riksdag that the duke of Holstein was heir to the Swedish throne. To this question the Holstein well-wishers unanimously responded that although they thanked the emperor for his kind intentions and wholeheartedly wished to secure the inheritance for the duke at the current Riksdag, they could not. Against expectations the king had agreed to everything that the crown officials demanded of him. Therefore they must hold back rather than pursue these ultimate intentions, thereby not to spoil relations, introduce suspicion, or harm the trust the nation had in the Russian emperor. Those covertly in the duke's service who sat on the Secret Committee also advised against raising the issue of the inheritance, which would not pass to the duke so long as he continued to conduct himself as he had hitherto.

Once this news was received the duke was obliged to settle for a pension, which the Riksdag duly granted him. Moreover Bestuzhev immediately suggested a mutual defense alliance between Russia and Sweden, a recommendation accepted in spite of the efforts of the English and Danish ambassadors to interfere. Once the Riksdag had concluded its session the Senate gave Bestuzhev full authority to negotiate a treaty, which was done on February 22, 1724. It resolved that were one of the signatories attacked by any *European, Christian* state, the other must use its good offices to halt hostilities. Were these efforts fruitless, the other power must declare war against the aggressor. Russia would commit twelve thousand infantry, four thousand cavalry, nine ships of the line and three frigates. Sweden would commit eight thousand infantry, two thousand cavalry, six ships of the line and two frigates. The state receiving assistance would pay the military forces of the power rendering aid and also furnish provisions, forage and quarters. General command would be exercised by the assisted state and every important impending action discussed in council in the presence of a general from the assisting side.

The signatories stipulated that they would form no alliances conflicting with that just concluded. If another power wished to enter the alliance it could do so only with the approval of both signatories. A commercial treaty was to be signed as soon as possible. The defensive alliance was to last for twelve years. To these formal terms were appended two secret articles, and another separate one. "Since the reigning duke of Schleswig-Holstein," the first secret article stated, "has been deprived of the principality of Schleswig for many years, and since both the all-Russian emperor and the king of Sweden consider it vital that this ruler, who is close to both of them, receive what is rightly his and be reinstated in the North in a timely fashion, Russia and Sweden commit themselves to assisting him in the strongest possible way, both at the Danish and other courts. If unable to achieve a resolution, Russia and Sweden will seek the advice and counsel of other powers, especially the Holy Roman emperor, that this matter be brought safely to a successful conclusion."

The second secret article concluded with the following obligation. "Since their Russian and Swedish majesties aver that the goal of the defense alliance, especially the security of their realms and subjects, is unattainable so long as disorder prevails in the Polish kingdom, either because of domestic causes or external instigation, their majesties firmly agree to avert and subdue such disorder, particularly endeavoring to preserve the Polish Commonwealth's ancient freedoms, privileges, the Pacta Conventa[45] and other rights belonging to it." In the separate article Sweden was granted the right for twelve years, namely the term of the defensive alliance, to import goods tax-free from Russia in the amount of a hundred thousand rubles annually.

In June Bestuzhev sent word of the engagement of Grand Duchess Anna Petrovna to the duke of Holstein, taking the occasion to write to the emperor "I cannot convey adequately to you the universal joy here among the highest, middling and common people. This betrothal is accepted as the basis for a true, unbreakable and eternal friendship between Russia and Sweden. It is true that the court and its party are not at all pleased, but in the nation itself joy truly reigns. It is said that, although all the dukes have left, the most exalted of them did not depart, finding himself a great and merciful guardian. Day by day the court party diminishes. Both its members and those of the republicans begin to walk the true path."

Concluding the alliance with Russia, the Swedish ministers proposed to the ambassadors from England and Hanover that they serve as mediators in pursuit of a rapprochement with the Russian emperor. In response to this offer England sent word that the French government was conducting such an effort, and that soon it should be brought to conclusion.

FRANCE

In 1721, at the time of the peace of Nystadt, Prince Vasily Lukich Dolgoruky was in Paris in place of Schleinitz,[46] on whom suspicion of arrogance had fallen. Once peace was reached Peter ordered Dolgoruky to visit Dubois and thank him for the assistance France had proffered in the peace negotiations. With this expression of appreciation Dolgoruky then went to meet with the regent himself, after which he wrote to his court that the king of England was furious at Dubois for not including him in the peace treaty between Russia and Sweden.

Fearing the indignation of the king of England, Dubois wished to arrange peace between George and Peter. "Now is the time," Dubois told Dolgoruky, "to give center stage to relations between Russia and France. To arrange between them a glorious and advantageous peace such as Russia has just received, certain guarantees are needed, guarantees to the kings of France and Spain. Were Russia to enter an alliance with France and Spain, the king of England as elector of Hanover must be included, otherwise the king of England would ally with the Holy Roman emperor and others. I do not think that your sovereign, even though wishing revenge against the king of England, would lose sight of the advantage of reconciling with him. If the king of England agrees to assist the duke of Holstein in recovering Schleswig, your sovereign's glory will wax still greater. I know that the king of England desires reconciliation with your sovereign."

At the outset Dubois requested that Dolgoruky inform his court about this conversation. Then he immediately sent a letter requesting that nothing be said. He was deeply concerned whether he was too late, whether

Dolgoruky already had sent his report to Petersburg. "In which case," said Dubois, "I would be obliged to direct Campredon at your court to retract everything I wrote."

Dubois attributed this turnabout to the fact that the English had made no commitment to reconciliation with Russia. For him to commence talking about this would annoy the king of England, in which case it would be more difficult to bring reconciliation to a successful conclusion. Therefore he wanted to wait while the English mulled over rapprochement.

Dolgoruky believed that there was another explanation, namely that Dubois wanted to demonstrate that the English were cool towards reconciliation with Russia, which should not demand so much. Regarding recognition of the imperial title for the Russian sovereign, the regent told Dolgoruky "If this matter depended only upon me, I would carry out his majesty's wish, but this is such an important issue that we need to think about it."

ELIZABETH PROPOSED AS BRIDE FOR LOUIS XV

In his dealings with France Peter had not abandoned his cherished idea of a relationship with Louis XV by marriage. On May 6, 1721 Dolgoruky received instructions from Peter to set about arranging a match between the king and Tsarevna Elizabeth Petrovna. At the end of the year Dolgoruky notified the emperor that the regent had grown close to Spain and had arranged a double marriage. The first was to be between the heir to the Spanish throne and the regent's daughter, the second between Louis XV and the Spanish infanta, who was in her fourth year, with the condition that she be brought to France and raised there until her majority.

OTHER FRENCH SUITORS

In 1722 other fiancées were found for the princes of France, brides who wanted to have Poland for their dowry. On January 5, 1722 Dolgoruky wrote from Paris "In an extract from Campredon's communiqué, which I saw, it was written that among those whom your imperial majesty counseled not to enter into consultations with Campredon, a certain someone suggested to him the possibility of a betrothal between the daughter of your imperial highness, Elizabeta (sic) Petrovna, and the duke of Chartres, son of the duke-regent. When this marriage occurs your imperial highness is to approve the duke of Chartres as king of Poland."

We have observed how Russia and other neighboring states dealt with the question of who should reign in Poland upon the death of Augustus

II. They did not want the succession to pass to his son, but who were the other candidates? On October 30, 1722, when Peter was away on the Persian campaign, the heads of the colleges[47] held a privy council. They began by reading a letter from the emperor to the chancellor dated October 16. "From the memoranda sent to us," this letter said, "it is rather evident that everyone is writing about King Augustus's weakened state, and that for this reason he is hastening to pass the inheritance to his son (about which a decree has been sent warning you of this). These memoranda also state that other courts are advancing candidates who would be under their thumb. We are asleep in this matter. Were something to happen soon, we would be left behind. For this reason it would be prudent for us to have a candidate at hand, to assure him that in the event we shall assist him. About the specific candidate, I do not know who is best, because I discussed this only just as I was about to depart."

The privy councillors recalled that Peter had spoken of Crown Prince Konstantin Sobieski,[48] and with that in mind they dispatched instructions to Prince Sergei Dolgoruky in Warsaw. Prince Vasily Lukich, however, wrote from Paris of other candidates. "As a rumor has arisen here that the king of Poland has grown ill and, based upon outward appearances, is not expected to live much longer, suggestions and negotiations have begun at this court concerning whom the current king will select for that throne. The English and Saxon ambassadors here are going to great lengths to see the son of the current king installed. I have been told this on good authority. I also have heard that the Holy Roman emperor is pursuing the same goal with the court here. The regent[49] and Cardinal Dubois[50] expressed little support for these aims. They considered it more desirable for France to have Rákóczi elevated to the throne, because he was an opponent of the Holy Roman emperor.[51] A short time later Count de la Marck[52] discussed with me in particular whether it would not be possible to arrange a marriage between your middle daughter[53] and the duke of Bourbon, whether you then would be willing to assist in installing the duke of Bourbon on the Polish throne. He said that France would attempt to accomplish this.

"I responded that I do not make your decisions for you, yet mentioned it would be more convenient for a marriage to be arranged between the duke of Bourbon and the younger daughter of Tsar Ivan Alekseevich (Praskovia),[54] and to betroth your middle daughter to the son of the duke-regent, the duke of Chartres. I deliberately went to Versailles on the thirteenth of this month. The cardinal told me that the ambassador at your court from the Holy Roman empire is attempting to forge an obligation between you and the Holy Roman emperor. The cardinal has every hope that you will not permit this to happen, for you allow it to be perceived with little difficulty that an alliance with the king of France is more advantageous for you than with the emperor.

"I answered that negotiations (with France) currently are not proceeding because Campredon has not yet received instructions to begin them. The cardinal promised to dispatch an official courier to Campredon with appropriate instructions. The cardinal said that the imperial title will be granted at once upon conclusion of an alliance. The cardinal continued that at the Porte certain powers were attempting to persuade the Turks to go to war against you. The moment he learned of this he dispatched an official courier to the French ambassador in Constantinople with a note ordering him to employ all possible means to dissuade the Porte from war with you. Then the cardinal took me by the hand, saying that he loved me as a brother. For that reason he would reveal a final important secret to me. The duke-regent can accept a marriage between your middle daughter and his son, the duke of Chartres. Thereupon you might see your way to assisting the duke of Chartres to ascend the Polish throne. The duke-regent holds both the daughter of the Holy Roman emperor and the daughter of the king of Portugal in poor regard, and intends to bind his own fate to yours."

None of these suitors pleased Peter, neither did the demands over Poland accompanying these proposed betrothals. In that same year, 1722, Prince Vasily Lukich was recalled from France, his position taken by the chamberlain Prince Alexander Kurakin,[55] the son of the well-known Prince Boris Ivanovich Kurakin.[56] The elderly father continued to serve as ambassador to The Hague where, among other things, he was obliged to observe that the press print nothing harmful to Russia, and to refute what was printed. Understandably it was difficult for Kurakin to carry out this responsibility in a republic with a free press. Kurakin, however, had received a direct rebuke from the emperor. "For some reason," it read, "he does not refute such false and malicious tales about Russia, and apparently freedom of the press is granted to the Couraniers (newspaper editors)." "The writings of the press are so painful for me that I am going out of my mind trying to resolve how to report about it to your majesty," responded Kurakin. "From my youngest days I have served and continue to serve your majesty with such a faithfulness and devotion, of which only the most loyal of subjects are capable. In all matters I have followed your majesty's decrees, carrying them out to the desired end. In regard to the journalists, to my own dismay I cannot achieve the desired aim.

"I am not the only ambassador to complain to them, but no one can warn them away from doing what they do. Refuting the news printed about Russia is very dangerous, for often I do not know the true state of affairs, so refutation risks causing harm to your majesty's interests, as for example with regard to the duke of Holstein. Perhaps I do not know of some obligations which really do exist that correspond with your majesty's interests. Thus some time ago General Weissbach was dispatched with an assignment to Vienna. In accordance with your highness's orders I divulged his journey here and published word in the newspapers that the general visited Vienna on personal business, without any assignment from the government. Then Weissbach writes to me with harsh denunciations that I am harming your majesty's interests."

When the younger Prince Kurakin (Alexander) was appointed to France his father travelled there in the autumn of 1722 and instructed him to notify Cardinal Dubois that he would remain for a short time, first to recommend his son to him, second to consult a skilled physician concerning his own unsettled health. "I have no assignment from my court." Dubois then ordered that the elder Kurakin be informed that he would treat him like an old acquaintance and friend, and would chat with him at length.

Indeed within a few days, after dinner, the cardinal invited Kurakin into his study and they had a long conversation. "I can assure you that the duke-regent has deep respect for his majesty the tsar, and intends to join France and Russia in a close alliance. Although this intention has been clear on our part, the response emanating from your court was less than effusive. It is true that in the tsar's absence not much can be done. We await his happy return, whereupon Campredon will turn to this matter so that I can apprise you of our views. His majesty the tsar is a great monarch, who by his deeds has gained great glory. He has expanded his realm, bringing it to such strength that it enjoys universal esteem in Europe. I do not believe his majesty wishes to expand his borders any further, but simply to preserve what has been won.

"Towards this end there can be no better means than to enter into a close alliance with France, which also has no intention of any further expansion. France strives only to assure its security and ensure that other states respect it. When France and Russia enter into close alliance they can hold the balance of European interests in their hands, sway other powers, and remain forever in friendship without jealousy.

"The main problem in Europe calling for action is that of the Austrian succession,[57] compounded by the problem of succession in the empire should the emperor die without male heir. As a consequence of marriage ties with the Austrian ruling house the two closest heirs are the electors of Saxony and Bavaria, while the current Holy Roman emperor has only a daughter. We must think in advance about which potential candidate to support. Allied with one another, we will accomplish what we wish. Moreover it is evident that sooner or later war will break out in the Germanies over the religious situation, and the interests of France and Germany demand attention to this matter. Therefore I believe that his majesty the tsar should keep his forces at the ready for some future emergency. He should not undertake initiatives which could alarm many states, prompting them to form alliances.

"This past spring, when it was learned that his majesty the tsar intended to become involved in the Holy Roman empire on behalf of the dukes of Holstein and Mecklenburg, the [Holy Roman] emperor promised to make thirty thousand troops available to the king of England [as elector of Hanover]. The kings of Denmark and Sweden and all the petty rulers in the empire also leaned towards making a commitment to him. I am letting you know that presently our plan consists of isolating the Holy Roman emperor by not allowing him to enter into close alliances with other powers.

"We therefore endeavor in every way possible to restrain England from renewing its earlier friendship with the emperor because England is strong and important in its standing and wealth. Were it to split from us now the balance could tilt against us and impede our intentions. I would like, we must attempt, to end all disagreements between his majesty the tsar and England. Should it prove impossible to reconcile them because of various difficulties, at least we must not alienate the English or drive them into the arms of the emperor, who could cause considerable difficulties for our common interests.

"There is absolutely no need to intimate any of this to the Prussian court, which lacks fortitude. In the event of danger it will strive to remain neutral. I know that reports have reached his majesty the tsar to the effect that we have no direct intention of seeking his friendship. This is completely unfounded. I can assure you that we wish for nothing more than to strengthen our friendship with his majesty, in which we see our own interests. Let me remind you of Sweden, how useful its friendship was to us, and what advantages Gustavus Adolphus provided for France.[58] Now

Sweden has fallen so low that we have no hope for it. In its place we wish to establish friendly relations with his majesty the tsar, which would be ten times more profitable for us, both because of his great power and because of Russia's position."

During his brief stay in France the elder Kurakin received suggestions from the other side as well. Marshal Tessé[59] inquired whether a marriage could be arranged between the duke of Bourbon and one of the tsar's daughters, and in such an eventuality to make him the king of Poland. Kurakin inquired whether the marshal were speaking on his own behalf or on orders from the duke. Tessé responded that he was speaking for himself, as a friend, and insisted on an opinion from Kurakin. What did he think, would the tsar agree? Kurakin said that without instructions he could not speak knowledgeably about whether his sovereign would agree. Then he asked Tessé to negotiate first with the duke of Bourbon, subsequently to notify him directly so that he could write an authoritative report back to Russia. Tessé answered that under current circumstances the matter was extraordinarily delicate. Were Campredon to learn about this from the Russian court and apprise the duke of Orleans and Cardinal Dubois, this would be deeply harmful to the marshal, as well as to the duke of Bourbon himself. The duke of Orleans and Cardinal Dubois would not permit this affair to prosper, deeming it better to wait for a more propitious time.

In 1723 Cardinal Dubois died, as did the duke of Orleans shortly thereafter, and the duke of Bourbon-Condé became first minister.[60] These changes at the French court demanded the presence of an experienced diplomat. Peter ordered the elder Kurakin, Boris Ivanovich, to go to France once again. Prior to his departure from The Hague Kurakin wrote to the emperor that Marshal Tessé, having seen his importance elevated thanks to his closeness to the duke of Bourbon, had visited his son. During conversation he underscored "Concerning what I told your father, write to him that so far things remain as they were." "Now that I am about to depart for France," wrote the elder Kurakin, "I request that your majesty direct that I, as well as the duke of Bourbon, be apprised of what your majesty will say now that the duke of Bourbon is prime minister. We need fear no danger, since he has always been well disposed toward me. On this matter let me advise your majesty that news has reached here through secret correspondence that the king of France is inclined never to marry the daughter of the Spanish king. At present he does not want her at all, and intends to send her back to Spain, forcing us now to seek another match."

As Kurakin was arriving in Paris (at the beginning of January, 1724) Tessé notified him that "the duke" now saw no danger from any quarter. As before, he wished to enter into marriage with one of the Russian grand duchesses in hopes that his father-in-law assist him in gaining the Polish throne upon the death of King Augustus. That crown "rests completely in the hands and will of the Russian sovereign, whose wishes in this matter will be decisive." "The duke in question," wrote Kurakin, "is very beholden to the interests of your majesty, as are all the ministers, especially the bishop of Fréjus (Fleury),[61] the king's tutor, and Marshal Devilliars. Everything now depends upon the bishop, who holds the king in the palm of his hands. When he was discussing the state of affairs in Europe with me, he said that the king of France, moved by his own conscience and the interests of France, sooner or later must intercede on behalf of the Chevalier St. Georges (a Stuart, and candidate for the English throne).[62] From this we can deduce that both he and the leading statesmen wish for nothing better than firm friendship with the king of Spain and close alliance with your majesty. If it is not profitable for your majesty to honor the duke of Bourbon's wishes relative to the marriage and Poland, at least dangle some hope before him and drag out the negotiations, just as England held the late duke of Orleans in bondage by dangling the French crown in front of him."[63]

Peter believed that it would not be profitable to follow the wishes of the duke of Bourbon. A powerful age-old wish [to marry his daughter to the French king] roused him only after Kurakin apprised him that Louis XV did not want to marry the Spanish princess. Peter immediately wrote his envoy "You write about two matters. First, that the duke of Bourbon would propose to our daughter, and second, that the king does not want the Spanish match. If all this is truly the case, we wish this [latter] suitor to become our son-in-law. I beseech you to use all available means to achieve that end. Your work is urgent, and at the first opportunity you might let slip a word with the pen or sensitively employ some other urgent method."

"Day and night I think about this," answered Kurakin. "I search for a method, and will continue to seek one to open effective channels through my friends, based upon the credit I have established here. I will inquire personally among the older people who surround the king, and my son will inquire among the younger. Contact with the king himself also is needed. This is such a delicate matter, as your majesty knows better than I, your slave, that I request that you deign for us to gather information and make plans. First we must make contact with the king in such a way that the duke and others who wish to support the Spanish connection do not learn about it in advance. Second, the suggestions must be made in the most delicate manner possible. Third, the greatest secrecy must be maintained.

"Let me report, for example, how such delicate matters are discovered. I know for certain that the Portuguese ambassador Dom Luis has instructions to devote attention to the matter of his king's daughter, and suggests that she replace the Spanish infanta, who lives here, the latter to marry the son of the king of Portugal, who has been estranged from him for years. Another, the duke of Lorraine, acts on behalf of his own daughter. The ambassadors of both courts have portraits of the entire family of their sovereigns. They distribute copies of the portraits of both princesses to many courtiers so that the king can see them. I offer for your majesty's wise consideration whether or not we need to do the same, though I do not have any portraits of the sovereign tsarevna at this time.

"Now I shall report briefly on the intrigues at the court here on this matter. There exists a large party of those who hover around the king for their own amusement, though they have no influence in matters of importance. Seeing that the king is disinclined to enter into a marriage with the infanta, they suggest that he tear up the conditions and marry a different princess. In this way they hope to take advantage of the king's favor to separate him from the enslavement of government officials and make themselves his people. The duke of Bourbon, on the contrary, strongly urges his supporters to have the king adhere to his former intention. Time will tell who wins this trial, although all opinions are that the anti-Bourbon party will triumph. Concerning the king's situation, I can report that at present he is as despotic as his great-grandfather. In truth he does not take the affairs of state upon himself. For his amusements he rules everything imperiously. No one dares to contradict him, not even the bishop of Fleury himself because, knowing his habits, he fears losing favor."

THE STUART PRETENDER

For purely political considerations the first order of business was reestablishment of diplomatic relations between Russia and England through the mediation of France. In the opinion of the elder Kurakin Russia's interests demanded acceding to France's wishes and reconciling with England, all the more so since reconciliation would be for appearance's sake only.

The duke of Bourbon also understood the matter in this way. In conversations with Kurakin he insisted upon reconciliation, suggesting that it would untie France's hands in entering into close alliance with Russia. Kurakin wrote to Peter that in his opinion it was necessary to reconcile with King George[64] without conditions and interpolations, to consign all that had transpired to oblivion, to exchange ambassadors and reopen diplomatic channels. Anticipating the objection that renewing diplomatic relations between Russia and England could weaken the Tory party and the Stuart pretender to the throne, whom Russia deemed it necessary to support, Kurakin wrote that when a Russian ambassador arrived in London, both parties [Stuarts and Hanoverians] would find support. It would be considerably more convenient to maintain contact with both parties directly through him than is the case now, with no representation in England.

The duke of Bourbon notified Kurakin personally that he was a true friend of the Stuart pretender, and would never stray from this friendship. He requested that Kurakin report to Peter that in *his own time* he would employ all means to further the interests of Chevalier St. Georges, as the pretender usually was called. The king and the entire court shared these feelings towards the chevalier. Because of the current state of affairs in Europe France could do nothing useful for him, and consequently must remain silent about its own good intentions towards him. France was obliged to attempt in every way possible to preserve peace in Europe. Towards that end it had to support friendship with King George of England although were that friendship in some way undone by the English side France would be obliged to act on its own and enter into an agreement with Russia for elevating the chevalier to the English throne, something which could be accomplished easily by these two powerful states. Before beginning a war in Europe King Louis XV must be afforded time to reach a sufficient age to be able to participate in such matters.

Peter wished to move closer to France, not to King George of England. The French government feared a break of Russia with England and proposed that prior to an alliance between Russia and France, Russia first must reconcile with the English king. At last Peter agreed to pursue reconciliation with the English king through French mediation, with the proviso that France accept Bestuzhev anew at its court in the capacity of Russia's ambassador. The French court referred this matter to the English, receiving the answer that King George accepted the Russian sovereign's wishes with great pleasure. He willingly would dispatch an ambassador to Petersburg and grant the tsar the imperial title. As regards Bestuzhev, some problems remained. Nevertheless authoritative sources in London notified Kurakin, through the French foreign minister Count Morville, that France was attempting to eliminate them.

This is where relations between Russia and France stood relative to England. The French government had made it clear that rapprochement with King George was to be a formality. The sympathy of both powers towards the pretender, or to Chevalier St. Georges as he was then called, was to be preserved in full. Meanwhile the pretender maintained his relations with Peter, upon whom the Stuart, or Jacobite, party placed its hopes more than upon any other sovereign in Europe as a consequence of his manifest hostility to King George.

In April 1722 a confidant of the pretender, Thomas Gordon, sent word to Peter that all news from England indicated that the English people endured greater burdens under the present ministry. All fervently wished to restore the lawful monarch to the throne. "I can honestly report," wrote Gordon, "that they seek the assistance of only six thousand armed men, with arms and munitions for an additional twenty thousand. If this undertaking succeeds with the assistance of your imperial majesty it will crown all the great deeds of your vaunted reign with eternal glory and eventually bring your subsequent enterprises to a happy conclusion. May it please your imperial majesty, if Russian troops are sent, to indicate in his exalted wisdom where the invasion might take place in the greatest secrecy. A felicitous outcome of this matter depends above all upon secrecy. For ships and transports to pass through the Sound they must proceed freely without boarding by Danish officials for inspection or collecting tolls. When the troops arrive in good condition at their appointed place in Britain the armed ships and transports must return, losing not a minute lest an unfriendly agent intercept them."

In June of that very year the pretender King James wrote to Peter that he lacked words to express his appreciation for the kind assistance the emperor had rendered him over so long a time. His favor, which so revealed his imperial majesty's virtue, could occasion him only new heavenly blessings and bring his name still greater glory in Europe. By supporting the just cause of the Stuarts he would secure a proper peace in Europe. James enclosed a plan for moving Russian troops to England, requesting that it be realized as soon as possible. This plan amounted to nothing more than relaying the contents of Gordon's letter.

Peter's Persian campaign revealed in the eyes of the pretender why his plans attracted no attention in Russia. At the beginning of 1723 he wrote another letter in which, while hailing the successes of the Persian war, expressed the hope that the emperor direct some attention to the communications on behalf of the pretender to the Russian ambassador in Paris. James assured Peter that the entire matter between them remained in the strictest secrecy. Never again would there be such propitious circumstances for sending troops to England as now.

The time for such propositions was chosen very infelicitously. Persian and even more Turkish affairs associated with them, occupied Peter's entire attention. Moreover, for all of his enmity towards King George, Peter could not imagine dispatching his troops on behalf of the pretender without the assistance of other powers, especially France. Yet the French stood firm on the necessity of coming to terms with the present government in England.

SPAIN

From 1723 onward Russia maintained a permanent embassy in Spain. Chamberlain Prince Sergei Dmitrievich Golitsyn[65] was sent to Madrid with the title of counsellor to the embassy. He was instructed to note everything occurring at the Spanish court, the military preparations, the armada, the friendships and obligations the Spanish king had assumed with other powers, especially with France. He was to learn whether the king intended to war in Italy against the Holy Roman emperor or with England as a way of regaining Gibraltar and Port-Mahon. Would it be desirable to send Golitsyn to the Spanish court to apprise the Spanish ministers of the emperor's desire to establish a firm trading relationship between Russia and Spain as a means of procuring goods first hand?

In response Golitsyn reported that the Spanish army, reduced from ninety to fifty thousand, was in a most pitiful condition. The officers were unpaid and the fleet in a dreadful state because there were virtually no capable officers or sailors. Very few ships were being built. The Spanish had no skill in seamanship and the foreign seamen, who were hated there, lacked the respect of the higher ranks. They obtained materials for constructing, outfitting and arming their ships from Northern Europe, even though Spain had everything in abundance and was capable even of supplying other countries. In these matters Spain lacked skilled individuals, an orderly admiralty or arsenal, and therefore was in no position to undertake anything. Not only this, it could not even defend itself against forays by Africans (Barbary corsairs). Consequently Russia could not rely upon Spain. The native merchantry in Spain was poor and commercially inept. Manufacturing did not exist.

While Prince Golitsyn reported from Madrid this sad news about Spain Father Arcelli, confidant of the duke of Parma, was in Russia to arrange a marriage between the Spanish infant Ferdinand and Peter's young daughter Tsarevna Natalia. This matter never amounted to anything.

III

STATE AND SOCIETY

One of the greatest acts in European and world history was completed. The eastern half of Europe entered into a common existence with the western. What did they think about this in the West, their gaze involuntarily turned to the East?[1] The smallest movement of Russian ships, of the Russian army, now evoked great disturbance in the cabinets of Europe. They apprehensively inquired about what any such movement meant. They feared that the great tsar, having concluded the Northern War with uncommon success, and possessing unheard-of energy, would interfere in Europe. They breathed easier once it was realized that he was occupied with affairs in the East.

In November 1723 Kurakin wrote to Peter from The Hague. "I cannot keep silent about all the discussions taking place here, to the personal glory of your imperial majesty, that the Persian war is progressing so well and so quickly. This surprises everyone utterly, all the more so at a time when affairs in Europe are following a similar course. Consequently no one can thwart your intentions. Thus the great glory of your name has risen higher than that attained by any monarch in several centuries. True, this enlarged power leaves their jealousy undiminished, it increases all the more because of your majesty's great potential, yet what can be done about it? Just have patience. All the jealous and malevolent forces opposing your majesty's power rejoice that your majesty is engaged in the Persian war. They wish it to continue for several more years to allow them to use that time to strengthen their positions."

Peter conducted the Persian war with economy and with the aim of not allowing Turkey to grow stronger at Persia's expense. When the course of the Turkish war threatened to produce such an outcome [the strengthening of Turkey], Peter struggled mightily to turn it around. This demonstrates that Peter's immense activities were not directed not to diplomacy but war, which was for him only a means of furthering domestic activities.[2] At home he faced a wider, more multi-faceted and more difficult theater of action, more formidable barriers, more numerous, secretive and dangerous enemies. Losses were frequent and heavy, successes slower and far in the future. Let us now survey the costs of reform, so burdensome to both tsar and nation, to which the Reformer turned with renewed vigor during the last years of his life.

PROCURATOR GENERAL

Above all Peter had to straighten the organization of the Senate which, in the words of its founder, would "hold everything in its hands." Once the colleges were established, their presidents entered the Senate. Peter soon perceived that this produced an awkward relationship between the Senate and the colleges, frankly conceding that this arrangement was imprudent. In a decree of January 12, 1722 he wrote "Even when direct instructions are lacking the administration of this state demands unceasing efforts from the Senate. The members of the Senate, however, virtually all of them, represent their own colleges, in whose interest they cannot handle further responsibilities. Even so, these obligations were imposed at the outset. Now it is incumbent upon us to correct this and other matters related to it in the following way. (1) To choose different presidents except at the War College and the College of Foreign Affairs, and add to the Senate some of the ambassadors at foreign courts. Members of the Senate thereby have no particular interests to pursue, rather they labor unceasingly for the good order and jurisprudence of the state and regard the colleges as free of selfish concerns. As it is now, how can members of colleges judge themselves? (2) The presidents of the War College, the College of Foreign Affairs and the College of Mines shall not attend the Senate except (a) when there is necessary information to convey; (b) when it is advisable to explain a new decree within the government; (c) when there is a general court; (d) when a new matter demands resolution; or (e) when I am present. Otherwise each shall tend to affairs in his own college. (3) The College of Audits shall reside at the Senate because its sole responsibility is a senatorial one, regardless of how things were done in the past."

Contemporaries speculated that the real reason behind Peter's removal of the collegiate presidents from the Senate was that the members of the colleges dared not contradict their presidents who as senators wrought numerous injustices. When complaints came to one of the colleges, that is, to its president who was a member of the Senate, other senators refused to undercut their colleague. Complaints simply lay there with no action taken. Consequently a decree appeared concerning the Senate's responsibilities. The Senate was to consist of senior privy and privy councillors appointed by the sovereign.[3] The Senate was instructed to resolve matters not decided in the colleges. All governors and military governors[4] were to report to the Senate about aggression by Russia's enemies, the plague, and all suspicious matters or other important events. In the absence of the sovereign the Senate resolved complaints about unjust decisions by the colleges and chancelleries, voted to select officials for its higher offices from collegiate councillors[5] and higher, excluding those serving at court, and to lesser offices without voting.

Not even these modifications afforded Peter any real hope that the Senate would proceed as he wished, and thus he could not bring himself to abandon the idea of appointing as senators men who would make certain that matters proceeded correctly. Earlier, in 1715, he had appointed an inspector general for the Senate, an official who presided over the publication and execution of decrees. The senators then began to select staff officers from the Guards who served for a month at the Senate with the title of overseers of decrees. Their responsibilities consisted of (1) assuring that the Senate reform its work to conform with the instructions of 1718; (2) improving actual execution of decrees as far as possible; (3) making certain that everything done in the Senate accorded with the second point, the responsibility of Senior Procurator Shchukin. Further, they were to guarantee that the Senate acted promptly and according to instructions.

If an official refused to make the necessary changes he was to be cautioned three times. If after the third notice he still failed to change, the matter was to be referred to the emperor, either verbally or in writing. If an official was quarrelsome or behaved impolitely he was to be arrested, sent to a fortress, and the emperor informed. This was to be pursued energetically and, were the culprit scornful, he was to lose everything he possessed and sentenced either to death or public defamation.

Even this form of supervision proved unsatisfactory. "Nothing is as essential to state administration," Peter continued to complain, "as the firm preservation of civil laws. Otherwise we are writing laws in vain when people fail to defend them or play cards with them, arranging them into suits. Nowhere else in the world have affairs been as bad as they were here, and in part still are. Most invidious is the fact that everyone takes pains to make certain that all documents appear to conform to the letter of the law."

As a way of lessening this harmful activity Peter in 1722 established "a public defender, that is, a senatorial overseer on behalf of the sovereign and the state."[6] Peter appointed Yaguzhinsky as his overseer. The official was obliged "to attend the Senate to ensure that it carries out its responsibilities in all matters which fall under the Senate's purview and authority, honestly, zealously and correctly, without wasting time, according to my regulations and decrees. He must ensure also that the Senate's business be resolved not just on the table, but carried out in deed and law.

"He must see to it that the Senate deals correctly and forthrightly with its charge. Should he observe something offensive, he must call this to the attention of the Senate immediately, clearly and with full explanation of how one or more members were not doing their duty, and must correct their behavior. If he is ignored he must protest forthwith and end the practice, informing us at once if it is absolutely necessary. Concerning other business of the Senate, he shall inform us either monthly or weekly, as our decree describes. Should he submit an inaccurate report in malice, he shall be punished according to the gravity of the matter.

"He shall oversee all procurators [Senate officials], making certain that they perform their calling honestly and zealously. He shall receive reports from the government inspectors,[7] make related suggestions to the Senate, and begin his own supervision procedures relating to the inspectors. If something improper is observed, he must notify the Senate immediately. The procurator general and senior procurators are beholden to no judgment other than ours. Concerning matters not clearly explained in our decrees, they shall recommend to the Senate that it issue clear decrees relating to them. The holder of this rank shall act as our eyes and ears, and as our legal expert in affairs of the state. In this light he shall behave honorably, otherwise he will be the first to be punished."

Wishing to reserve for the Senate the status of supreme governmental institution, wishing to teach the senators to consider important questions in national life, wishing them to be valued assistants and advisors, wishing not to have to decide important matters without prior discussion with capable men, Peter issued this pronouncement. "Should the Senate consider matters and find itself unable to make formal recommendations to the emperor, it shall discuss them first in the Senate and sign its opinions, then offer substantiation to his majesty because otherwise it would be difficult for his majesty to make a decision on his own."

MASTER OF HERALDRY[8]

Except in cases of "hypocritical judgment" and financial problems the Senate was obliged to make certain that young people not avoid service. Toward that end the position of master of heraldry was established in 1721, about which Peter wrote in his own hand. "The responsible figure (master of heraldry) shall keep three lists comprising all nobles in the entire realm: (1) those in active service, what they are doing, and where; (2) those not in service; (3) noble children who have not reached their majority, also all males who were born and have died. In addition, we do not yet have an understanding of civil affairs, and especially in economic affairs we respect almost nothing.

"Our academies now can remedy this by establishing a short curriculum and teaching economics and civics to representatives of every aristocratic and middle noble family. The master of heraldry further shall see to it that, above all else, the army and navy do not lack serving men from every family in society.[9] This office must detect those who conceal small children in their home or under a different name in the towns, and apprehend them. It shall not entrap anyone under the threat of civil or criminal punishment. Rather it shall maintain this information in the event such persons show up in civil matters." He then established the position of general master of petitions,[10] who was required to receive and review all allegations that one of the colleges acted slowly or made an unjust decision. He was to insist upon expeditious resolution, provide proof to the Senate about complaints with merit, intercede on behalf of petitioners, especially the voiceless, powerless or infirm, and represent them to the sovereign himself.

The Reformer's words about the responsibilities of the master of heraldry show that he was troubled by the condition of his servicemen. A realm such as Russia, open on all sides and surrounded by enemies, demanded an army and navy. The favorable situation abroad currently enjoyed by

Russia was bought by imposing a severe strain on the nation's resources. This strain still could not be eased very much. To preserve Russia's prominence and advantages the state now must employ the very means which enabled it to attain such prominence in the first place.

Peter conveyed to the Russian people that, if they were pleased with what was achieved, they were not about to fold their hands "and suffer the same fate as befell the Greek monarchy." Moreover, to have any chance of preserving the prominence and advantages which Russia had gained through force of arms, civil government must develop, above all, in financial administration. To this end learned and knowledgeable people were necessary. Where might they be obtained? They had to be groomed from among the servicemen. "The master of heraldry shall select them from among the servicemen and train them for civil service, though only a few, so as not to weaken the army and navy."

Peter felt more strongly than ever that the chronic failing of the Russian land, its shortage of people, was inappropriate for a population which occupied a huge country. It was always true [in Russia] that a development begun as a consequence of the activities of an epoch of reform was fated to deteriorate. From the middle of the ninth until the end of the seventeenth centuries Russia was a primitive state, the acute symbol of its lack of development being that the military was not separate from the civil service. Both in the time of St. Vladimir, and under Tsar Alexis Mikhailovich, armed retinues,[11] or serving men, divided into several ranks or grades, were soldiers. Upon concluding a campaign they then also took on civilian responsibilities.

TABLE OF RANKS

Not until Tsar Fedor Alekseevich's reign [1676-1682] did the idea emerge of separating civil from military responsibilities. Nevertheless this idea remained only on paper. Under Peter's rule affairs of state developed so extensively that differentiation of positions became a necessity. This principle was inscribed in the Table of Ranks, where all positions or grades were arranged according to classes. Civil and court ranks appeared side by side with military positions or grades.

Two senators, Golovkin and Bruce, and two major generals, Matiushkin and Dmitriev-Mamonov, *composed* the Table of Ranks in January 1722. In this table the grade of general of the cavalry or infantry is listed side by side that of senior privy councillor. This was not a grade in our

sense of the word. Senior privy councillors in fact were members of the
Privy Council, gathered usually to discuss important matters, above all
foreign affairs. Contemporaries relate that when Peter wanted to elevate
Count Bruce to privy councillor, Bruce himself declined the honor, asserting that although he was a loyal subject he was a foreigner. The appendices to the Table of Ranks said "To the sons of the Russian state,
princes, counts, barons, the most prominent nobility, as well as servitors[12]
of the most prominent rank. Although we may allow them free entry into
public gatherings at court, in recognition of their high breeding or that of
their fathers, before others of a lower grade, and although we openly wish
to see them distinguished from the others in all circumstances by their
dignity, we shall not make that rank available to anyone who does not
render service to us and the fatherland, neither shall they receive anything
to commend their character. Descendants of servitors of Russian origin
or foreigners of the first eight ranks are considered equivalent to the best
of the old nobility, even if they are of humble origin.

"Previously the civil grades were not so regarded. As a consequence
no one respected them. Servitors from the nobility considered such grades
beneath their proper station. Necessity now demands that the civil grades
be elevated. Towards that end we shall accept any fit candidate, even
though he may not have any grade. Since it would be insulting to military people in the ranks, who have endured such harsh service over many
years, to see people who have not put in the same amount of service
achieve the same or even a higher grade, anyone who is elevated to a
given rank will continue to merit that grade throughout his years."

An amendment was added to the Table of Ranks concerning the consequences of torture for the honor of a serviceman. "Many miscreants
exercise their spite against others by means of torture. Therefore, although someone who has been tortured without cause cannot on his own
redress his dishonor, he may provide us a formal statement detailing his
innocence." Thus Peter ordered a review of all instances in which torture
was employed, commanding that it be abolished in petty cases. As a
consequence torture was abolished specifically during investigations
concerning the theft of wood from a forest.

In the course of compiling the Table of Ranks the question of coats
of arms arose in the Senate, where and for what, and to whom they should
be granted. It was decided to research the issue and extract precedents
from Latin and Polish books.

THE SHAFIROV AFFAIR

Having appointed to the Senate an overseer for sovereign and state, Peter departed for the Persian campaign, while the Senate remained behind in Moscow. As the emperor was in transit to the campaign signs emerged of some extremely unpleasant clashes looming in the Senate in the sovereign's absence. While in Kolomna the senior procurator of the Senate, Skorniakov-Pisarev,[13] visited the empress to complain of his ongoing feuds with the procurator general. In the autumn of 1722 Peter himself received a letter from Skorniakov-Pisarev in which, after offering congratulations for his capture of Derbent,[14] the senior procurator added "in your majesty's absence life for us is poor and dull." These words contained more than just a simple expression of devotion.

In his letter to Catherine, Skorniakov-Pisarev explained the cause of his boredom. "Without you, life for us poor folk is very burdensome. I have already reported to your majesty in Kolomna about the causes of these woes. Rogues have turned Pavel Ivanovich (Yaguzhinsky) against me for my failure to cooperate with them, and I have witnessed some of the gentlemen in the Senate causing me offense. The lord Baron Shafirov[15] causes me particularly great offense in that he has shouted at me repeatedly in the Senate and then forbids me to talk with Pavel Ivanovich concerning your affairs.

"On the day we received word of your majesty's entry into Derbent I happened to be in Pavel Ivanovich's house. Upon seeing me he created a loud (drunken) disturbance, then attempted to stab me with a sword. Later in the Senate, in response to a suggestion I made to him in the course of debate he called me a liar, which is simply intolerable to a man such as I who hold a salaried position of responsibility to your majesty. I dare not report this to his imperial majesty because I do not want to trouble him, but I beseech you, most merciful sovereign, if Shafirov or someone else reports slanders against me, who am poor and without help other than you, (to convey) this my tearful petition at an appropriate time to his imperial majesty, so that I, a poor man, must not bear baseless calumnies from him and his confederates."

Soon the senior procurator lost his patience, sending a letter directly to Peter with complaints about his bitter life brought about by the depredations of Shafirov, whose attacks began when Skorniakov-Pisarev started feuding with the procurator general. "I live in such misery that I do not expect to live to see your majesty again. I fear that failure to rectify what has been done against me will take its toll. I do not have time for anything, especially on account of the harm Yaguzinsky has brought me. I am told openly that Shafirov and others of his ilk want me to say nothing in the presence of Pavel Ivanovich. Then they disingenuously suggest that I might lapse into words in front of him. Now Pavel Ivanovich causes me even more woes based on Shafirov's slander. He has shouted at me publicly in the Senate, threatening to bring a petition against me. Shafirov to flatter him wrote a report hostile to me which hypocritically commended him."

Ultimately the procurator general was obliged on orders from the emperor to leave Moscow, and Skorniakov-Pisarev had to put his affairs in order. Yaguzhinsky took this occasion to write to Peter, saying that so long as Skorniakov-Pisarev was present the Senate's discord could not be held in check. In fact the feuds and vulgar speech had increased. Skorniakov-Pisarev's departure raised the possibility that these dissensions might cease. Therefore Yaguzhinsky left behind in the Senate a written recommendation that these partisan quarrels and vulgarities cease pending the emperor's return. The procurator general explained to Peter that the entire quarrel derived from Prince Menshikov's Pochep affair, which arose out of a complaint from Hetman Skoropadsky[16] that near Pochep, which Menshikov owned, the most illustrious prince appropriated many unattached peasants and their lands.

Shafirov's own letter to Peter discussed the matter in greater detail. "I have worked in affairs of state for thirty-two years, twenty-five of which are known personally to your majesty. Till now I have suffered no offense or abuse from anyone such as I now endure from Senior Procurator Skorniakov-Pisarev. He has done me ill because when I was taking testimony and drafting the ruling on Prince Menshikov's affair about the boundaries of the Pochep lands, I refused to countenance anything which violated your decrees.

"Skorniakov-Pisarev labored with all his might to sway me to his side, first with blandishments, then with cries that he was terrified of Prince Menshikov's wrath. I remained unswayed. According to your majesty's decree, Prince Menshikov was ordered to receive only that land near Pochep which the hetman gave him after the battle of Poltava.[17] It was further ordered that the Pochep and other cossacks be freed from arrest and their rights and freedoms be restored. The Senate's written resolution stated that a special administrator was being sent to Little Russia to

investigate whether the towns of Baklan and Mglin belonged to the Pochep hundreds, but it said nothing about the cossacks.

"Once we saw that the resolution was composed improperly we turned
to the senior secretary to inquire why he had allowed such an error. At
this point the senior procurator leapt from his place and spoke instead of
the senior secretary, shouting that it was written that way for clarity's
sake, that it was not our place to encroach upon Prince Menshikov. In
response I said that I was addressing the senior secretary, not him. He
himself knew that the resolution was not composed in that way. He was
obliged to give way, and we rewrote the improper resolution virtually in
its entirety."

Shafirov may have triumphed over Skorniakov-Pisarev in this particular matter, just as the faction close to him led by Golitsyn and Dolgoruky
had triumphed over Menshikov. Shafirov, a man of low birth, was only
an instrument. In the atmosphere of generally lax morals which typified
service relations, Shafirov had given his enemies an opening to rehabili-
tate themselves by pursuing him aggressively. At one point he had used
his influence as a senator to secure a personal salary for his brother Mikhail while the latter was switching positions from one branch of service
to another.

At another time and under different circumstances this matter could
have been finessed with little difficulty. This time some very vigilant
eyes, those of his enemies, kept watch over Shafirov. Skorniakov-Pisarev
protested against the illegality of this act, and Shafirov was forced to
defend himself, which proved extremely difficult. He had to resort to
desperate means, demanding that a determination be made whether deductions were taken from the wages of foreigners released from service.
In this way he wished to count his own brother among the ranks of foreigners. The senior procurator responded negatively to this far-fetched
suggestion. "Mikhail Shafirov is not a foreigner, but a Jew, the son of a
boyar's bondsman, with the nickname of Shaiushka, and his father Shaiushkin once was a driver in Orsha for a schoolboy whose relative even
now resides in Orsha, the Jew Zelman."

Shafirov disagreed. "His majesty himself," said he, "deigned to know
and to grant payment to my father, who was not in indentured servitude
to anyone. Although in his early years he was held captive he was given
noble rank under Tsar Fedor Alekseevich which he retained until the end
of his days." "Shafirov's father," Skorniakov-Pisarev then wrote, "served

in the home of the boyar Bogdan Khitrovo, and prior to his death he sat in the rows of silk traders in a shop, which many Muscovites remember."

What worried Shafirov most was the thought that Peter, acting as the sovereign on behalf of the state, as the implacable emperor, must pronounce a stern judgement upon the senator, who then would have to be sacrificed in the interest of the state for intervening on behalf of his brother. In his letters to Peter, Shafirov called the matter trivial and commonplace. He attempted to lay the guilt onto Skorniakov-Pisarev by writing "When we were at the procurator general's home and heard the joyous news about your majesty's entry into the city of Derbent, we grew exultant. At that point Skorniakov-Pisarev began swearing and scuffling with Rzhevsky, procurator of the College of Justice, furiously beating him. Then he approached me for no reason, accusing me of stealing money from his own brother. I avoided him and suggested to the senators that it [this false accusation] was a lie. Although I made some noise, I twice turned away from him with civility. The third time he attacked me. Not content with profanity, he earnestly threatened that unless the procurator general ended things, repercussions were certain.

"I can swear that after the gentleman procurator general left not a single senatorial session went by in which the senior procurator did not offer some business and proposals in malice and contrary to your decrees. By shouting and swearing he compelled the senators to sign. Once your majesty arrives here safely, I can prove this clearly. In sheer malice he puts these trivial matters ahead of the most essential business, among which are some matters resolved while the procurator general was still present.

"All this spite directed against me originates from my opponents because, by my sworn duty, when I see things contrary to your interests, I do not keep silent. In this case I now report the following: (1) that I observed that the War College, when protesting nonpayment from the Bureau of State Accounts[18] based on the payment schedule of monies to other colleges, claimed that several regiments went a year or more without pay, leading many soldiers to desert. I suggested that the civil office be required to release the funds without delay to the army, square accounts with the Treasury College, and be then ordered to settle its accounts with the War College. Once the Bureau of State Accounts has settled accounts with these colleges, even if some payments remain outstanding because of insufficient funds, this matter will be resolved. In addition, the War College never again should be allowed to delay full payment of its obligations, because the army never has its full complement of soldiers.

"For officers receiving payment due to foreigners, money is currently available from the large deductions taken from the wages of officers sent home, fines, and salaries no longer due to the dead and deserters. The War College never counts any of these extra monies in its calculations, pretending that it has a full complement of troops. The Commissariat reports that the War College takes several hundred thousand rubles from it for unsanctioned expenses, for which it shows no receipts. Consequently there are insufficient funds for regular payments to soldiers and dragoons.

"I have remarked on several occasions to Prince Menshikov, or when he is not present to the senior procurator, that we must seize the original ledger of income and expenses from the War College if we are to know where this money is going. Instead of being allowed to institute this plan I am forced to bear even greater persecution from him and others.

"(2) A report from the War College to the Senate suggested sending a colonel and two companies, infantry and dragoons, for reconnaissance on the Yaik, and that we convey this intention to the cossacks. It further recommended that we evict all those new arrivals in the territory since the year [7] 203 [1695], and send them off in their own carts to Kazan. They were to be remanded there for disobedience. Then we were to send to them two regiments, infantry and cavalry. These regiments were to ensure that all this was completed, and to work this out with the Don Cossacks.

"I heard straight from the lips of Prince Menshikov himself that this deployment above all is because allegedly five hundred-odd of his peasants are there. I fear lest he propose this as a way of pushing the cossacks beyond endurance, as earlier, and as a pretext to use force. He did not report to your majesty what he was doing, sending the regiments without a direct order, which also concerns me. In order that their movement not be considered an offense, I would request that the troops be ordered to inform the cossacks when it is completed. They should not depart before receiving orders, and should notify to the Senate that this evil deed committed by Prince Menshikov and Skorniakov-Pisarev was an offense. To date the senators have been inclined against my opinion. Therefore they wrote the decision the way they did."

It must have been clear to Peter that Shafirov's blows were directed not so much against Skorniakov-Pisarev as against the men standing behind him, for whom the senior procurator was merely a loyal servant. The first point was directed against the War College, whose president was the most illustrious prince, the second point aimed directly at Menshikov.

Shafirov's enemies, rather than send letters directly, reached the emperor through the empress, through Makarov. They also acted against Yaguzhinsky, who did not side with the most illustrious prince.[19]

Yaguzhinsky's character was such that he refused to bow to or be dependent upon anyone. Peter probably appointed him procurator general with this quality in mind. "Previously," Skorniakov-Pisarev wrote to the privy cabinet secretary, "I sent you information concerning the first month of Pavel Ivanovich's (Yaguzhinsky's) Senate session. Now I am sending you news of what happened during the other three months. Permit me to observe that on some occasions he simply did not attend the Senate. On others he stayed for an hour or half an hour. At those times everything proceeded with his close companions, with cunning Shafirov and those like-minded. They forever suggested that he enjoy himself, that matters would work themselves out. Many told me that I would not be made to answer for these matters, that the entire business had all been brought about by Pavel Ivanovich. Then they spoke to him with cunning, so that he never said anything about this arrangement to me. In this manner they produced even more malice against me."

The matter of his brother's salary placed Shafirov in a compromising situation which deteriorated further because of a scene in the Senate on October 31. On that day a matter concerning the mail was being heard. This issue affected Shafirov personally since he was responsible for the mail. In the middle of the senators' discussion, in walked Shafirov. The senior procurator told him that the senators were hearing and discussing postal affairs, which related to him personally. Therefore he must leave because according to law it was inappropriate for him to be present. "In answer to your suggestion," retorted Shafirov, "I will not leave, and for you to expel me would be even more inappropriate."

The senior procurator then took a placard from a cabinet on which was glued the decree that judges must leave when matters concerning their relatives were heard. He read the decree aloud. "You tell me to depart as a senator," said Shafirov, "but this decree about leaving and the affairs of one's relatives is not pertinent." He insisted to the senators that he was charged by order of his imperial majesty to preside over the mails in everything just like Vinius and his son,[20] which Count Golovkin and Prince Menshikov knew full well. He further insisted that this matter could not be resolved without a personal decree [from the emperor].

The chancellor, Count Golovkin, long Shafirov's implacable foe, said that no such personal decree existed. To resolve the matter, Shafirov must leave. After lengthy discussions the senior procurator suggested that the senators order this issue settled as the decree mandated. "What you are proposing," cried Shafirov, "means that you are now my chief enemy. You are a thief, yet you call me a thief and have charged in writing that I deceived the sovereign."

At this point the most illustrious prince, along with Golovkin, said that were the senior procurator of the Senate a thief, how could they delegate work to him? Skorniakov-Pisarev made it clear that he could not stand any more of this. "There is no point," cried Shafirov, "in getting angry at me and sending me out! You and all the rest have become my chief opponents, including the most illustrious prince, because of the Pochep affair. I have several petitions in my possession to the sovereign himself, and registered in the Senate against Count Golovkin. For you to pass judgment over this would not be very fitting."

"Please don't kill me," Menshikov said to him. "I, kill you!? You are beating me!" responded Shafirov. Menshikov retorted that, according to Shafirov, he beats everyone. "I am not saying," answered Shafirov, "that you beat everybody, but rather you are capable of beating everybody. I did not involve you in the Pochep affair. Yet for that you have given me grief. Still, I am not fitting a noose around your neck like Volkonsky and Prince Matvey Gagarin have done." At this point Menshikov, Golovkin and Bruce walked out of the Senate. Dolgoruky, Golitsyn, Matveev and Shafirov stayed on and announced that they intended to hear the matter. The senior procurator informed them that he could not remain present, because Shafirov called him a thief.

On November 2, in Shafirov's absence, Menshikov handed down an opinion concluding that Shafirov must be suspended from the Senate for his illegal activities. The senators decided to accept this suggestion and put it in writing as the basis of a formal report when the sovereign returned. On the November 13 Shafirov appeared at the Senate to request that he be informed of the resolution to be adopted against him based on Menshikov's recommendation. The senior procurator answered that he would be informed when a decision was made. For the time being they must move on to other matters.

"Please do not speak to me in this way, I have a disagreement with you!" answered Shafirov. "We have to hear other business," repeated the senior procurator, "I am obliged to require this of you. Here is the decree!" "Merciful God! I truly must heed you!" said Shafirov.

On November 15 another squabble took place between Shafirov and Skorniakov-Pisarev. "Let it be known," Shafirov told the senators, "that the senior procurator never gives me opportunity to speak. Now he is angry with me for reminding him about the neglect of work at the municipal court." [21]"Also let it be known that the baron creates madness there practically every day," said the senior procurator. Shafirov suggested that they write or otherwise obtain formally Menshikov's opinion against him, and that they not change it one whit. He stood up and said, alluding to Menshikov, "I don't just happen to be here by a contract. I am not just some hired hand, and my sword will not be taken from me."

To resolve this matter they had to await the sovereign's return from the Persian campaign. On January 9, 1723 Peter sent a decree to the senators. "While returning home from the Persian campaign we received a written report from Senior Procurator Skorniakov-Pisarev against Baron Shafirov, alleging that while the Senate was considering his activities with respect to the mail, he did not leave the premises as the law required. Moreover Skorniakov-Pisarev claims that Shafirov called him a thief and behaved offensively in other ways. Baron Shafirov also offered written accusations against Skorniakov-Pisarev (and against others in the Senate), alleging that he acted illegally, and in passion. At this juncture I will look into this matter to determine an appropriate course of action for the Senate.

"In their respective accounts each has informed me about those hostile to them in the Senate. Shafirov identifies two—Prince Menshikov and Count Golovkin, with Skorniakov-Pisarev as a silent partner. Therefore we command that Shafirov's friends also be named so as to avoid any more offense from either party. Notify them that in this inquiry, both in their reports and in the responses, they shall write or speak only about the matter at hand, for which they will make a report or be held accountable on only that specific point into which we have inquired. Under no circumstances shall they make any references to other matters, under threat of harsh punishment. If either has need of sending lists of additional matters, this shall not be forbidden."

As requested by this decree Pisarev summoned Princes Grigory Fedorovich Dolgoruky and Dmitry Mikhailovich Golitsyn. The court, termed *Supreme,* was appointed from among senators—Bruce, Musin-Pushkin and Matveev, and generals—Buturlin, Golovin, Dmitriev-Mamonov, Brigadier Voeikov, Colonel Blakely, Guards Captains Bredikhin and Baskakov. Princes Dolgoruky and Golitsyn testified as defense witnesses. Menshikov,

Bruce, Golovkin, Musin-Pushkin and Matveev testified for Skorniakov-Pisarev and against Shafirov.

Among the witnesses, Dolgoruky and Golitsyn found themselves transformed into defendants because the two of them had signed the decree approving a personal salary for Mikhail Shafirov, and asserted that Shafirov might remain in the Senate during the hearing and deliberation of his affairs. Shafirov, seeing that he could not be vindicated, wrote a letter to the sovereign. "Throwing myself at the feet of your imperial majesty, I tearfully request forgiveness and mercy for my crime. Now I recognize that my vociferousness in this matter has angered your majesty by my refusal to leave the Senate when so ordered by the senior procurator, and that I dared on this question to order a decree attaching Kireev (the secretary) to the verdict relating to augmenting my brother's salary by a third, reasoning that a decree would enjoin them concerning this grant. I cannot offer any justification for this crime before your majesty, but I pray to cover my lawlessness with the blood of your mercy. I swear before this Supreme Court that I engaged in this without subterfuge. Have mercy on me, an orphan with no other help but your majesty himself."

"Regarding the decree," wrote Prince Golitsyn, "on excluding judges from the chamber when matters relating to their relatives are heard, I take full responsibility. I spoke with the senators only in private conversation and out of my own downright simplicity, not out of opposition to the decree. For this transgression I request your imperial majesty's merciful forgiveness." Prince Dolgoruky responded that he did not have an accurate understanding of the decree against being present when the affairs of kin were heard, He had not committed it to memory, and had not participated in the drafting of this decree. Had he been properly informed, he would have observed the decree.

While the hearing on the postal affair was taking place Dolgoruky could have absented himself to serve propriety, thus avoiding all of these difficulties, but the other senators had failed to send Shafirov out. Prince Dolgoruky offered this consideration not to justify his behavior, for he was supposed to be fully informed about this decree, and requested his majesty's merciful forgiveness, keeping in mind his prior devoted and humble service.

The court sentenced Shafirov to death based on its reading of a decree of April 17, 1722 which stated "Let no one dare in any way to organize or propose any activities contrary to regulations or excuse such behavior in any way or otherwise facilitate it. Let no one violate this decree under any pretext. Any violator of the laws of the state and enemy of authority shall be executed without mercy, allowing no one to entertain hopes for mercy based on his merits if he is guilty of such behavior." Besides his decree entered in the Senate and his grant of a personal salary to his brother, Shafirov was accused of spending state funds for personal expenses during an assignment to France. He had taken a village as a mortgage from Colonel Vorontsovsky as collateral for a personal loan, but he had not used his own money.

On February 15, early in the morning, the Kremlin was already filled with people. On that day the death penalty was to be carried out against Senator and Vice-Chancellor Shafirov. The condemned was brought from the Preobrazhensky Chancellery in a simple sleigh. Once the verdict was read they took from him a wig and an old fur coat and led him to the scaffold, where he crossed himself several times, knelt, and placed his head on the block. The executioner's axe was already raised in the air, then came down on wood. Privy Cabinet Secretary Makarov announced that the emperor, in recognition of Shafirov's service, commuted the death sentence to incarceration in Siberia.

Shafirov stood up and left the scaffold with tears in his eyes. In the Senate, to which he was sent, his old comrades clasped his hand and congratulated him on his pardon, but Shafirov remained in a gloomy state of mind. It is said that when a physician bled him, fearing the effect of such a powerful shock on his health, Shafirov told him "It would be better to open a large vein so I can be free of suffering once and for all." Many people, especially those from the court of the duke of Holstein and the foreign ministers, sincerely fretted over Shafirov, lavishing praise on his personal honor. "Though it is true," they said, "that he was a little hotheaded, he freely accepted all representations made to him, and his word always could be relied upon." Ultimately Peter freed Shafirov from Siberian exile and remanded him to Novgorod under such strict guard that he could not even attend church. His family went with him and were given thirty-three copecks a day for maintenance.

Skorniakov-Pisarev was in no position to exult. Peter found his behavior in the Senate illegal and unseemly, and reduced him to [serve in] the ranks with loss of his villages. Since Peter did not like losing capable servants he assigned the former senior procurator to oversee work on the Ladoga canal.[22] Even here Pisarev had the misfortune to earn the sovereign's opprobrium, which is apparent from Peter's resolution of May, 1724. "It might be said that he has been punished enough for daring to swear in the Senate that he deserved to be restored to his former grade. Yet he has met his responsibilities at the canal in a conniving and lax fashion. Accordingly I have judged him unworthy. Nevertheless in recognition of the celebration currently taking place (the coronation of the empress) and for the conviction of Shafirov he is granted the rank of colonel and may have half the confiscated villages back."

Dolgoruky and Golitsyn were stripped of their rank, placed by decree under house arrest, and fined 1,550 rubles each to go toward a hospital, for the fact that "(1) They had not heard the minutes dealing with the petition of Mikhail Shafirov. They were uninformed about the acceptability of granting the salary granted to the senior secretary at the request of his brother, Baron Shafirov, without the consent of other senators, only two of whom dared to sign the resolution granting this Shafirov a salary without deductions, and above and beyond that to add an extra third. (2) In their negligence they acted and spoke improperly, albeit without thinking, in allowing Shafirov to remain present when his affairs were discussed."

Dolgoruky and Golitsyn besought the empress to intercede. They were freed from arrest and reinstated in their former grades. It has been observed several times how the brave Prince Dmitry Mikhailovich prostrated himself on the ground before Catherine to thank her for her merciful intervention, but the fine was not rescinded. "I already have paid five hundred rubles, " wrote Golitsyn to Makarov, "but I do not have the rest. I took out a mortgage on my residence in Petersburg at a loss. I do not own a single plot of land, I have been living deep in debt and I maintain my household only through loans." Dolgoruky wrote about this as well. In January 1724, while presiding at the chancellery of the Supreme Court, Peter inscribed "overruled."

Peter explained in a decree of February 5, 1724 the basis for the strict punishment to which Shafirov was subjected. "Whoever brings about illegality in the court, or in some manner acts in counsel to one who does, or assists in some other capacity, and if he too engages in this illegality through some officiousness or willfulness, such violator of the laws of the state and of his own responsibilities is to be sentenced either to natural or political death based on the severity of the matter, and be deprived of all his property.

"Whoever violates his calling therein brings misfortune to the entire state in the following way. When a judge violates [his calling] regardless of whether he does so out of passion or material interest, or even more out of faintheartedness, he will try to lead his entire college to follow suit, lest they carry out reprisals [against him]. Once they go along with him, is the perpetrator at risk of dismissal? Will not the others be completely intimidated by the instigator, making punishment of the boastful ring-leader impossible? Should the ringleader realize that he alone is held ac-countable, brazenly he will conceal his crimes by reprimanding others, suggesting things they rather would not hear. Or someone will whisper in his ear or send instructions through a friend that if he cannot lure the other to his side, he will seek [a judge]. At this point the judge, even against his will, would be led to hush the matter, keep silent and let things pass.

"What follows from this? Nothing less than moral decline in the life of a subject, brazenness, ruin of individual lives, and still brasher suborn-ing of other judges. Moreover, seeing someone else enriched by unlaw-ful means and suffering no punishment, rare would be the person who is not tempted. Gradually everyone loses fear, causing ruin to those in state service. God will vent His wrath and thus, through this single act of trea-son, misfortune will gnaw away at the state, and even cause its ultimate downfall. Therefore it is fitting to punish severely those who violated their positions and engaged in such crimes as if they violated their respon-sibilities in battle, or were genuine traitors, for this crime is far greater than treason. We know that people are wary of treason, but not everyone is so wary of this greater evil. This evil may lie smoothly under wraps for a long period of time, yet ultimately it will lead to a bad end."

To make certain that unpleasant scenes like those which took place between Shafirov and Skorniakov-Pisarev were not repeated, Peter issued a decree in January 1724. "Those who act as judges in the Senate, the Synod, the colleges, the chancelleries, and in the courts of the entire state, and those who come before a court, shall behave decorously, as in the court of God. Those who treat God's business with negligence risk dam-nation from the Creator."

For swearing and shouting a fine of ten rubles was set, for a second offense, one hundred rubles and arrest. Whoever committed more than three offenses lost his rank and a third of his property. If that individual dared take matters into his own hands he was to suffer political death [loss of rank and office and possible exile]. All administrators of courts were instructed to act with civility in dealing with petitioners and those offering evidence. For cursing their punishment was a fine equal to three months' wages of the person insulted. The offender further was required to seek forgiveness from the offended, and whenever the offender employed force he was remanded to military courts.

Lest at this point someone seek to exculpate himself by claiming unfamiliarity with the laws of the state, the decree continued "When a decree is cited relating to some matter, and when someone neglects to act accordingly and subsequently pleads ignorance, punishment for the first offense shall be deprivation of rank and a fine equal to a year's salary. A second offense shall be punished by loss of a third of his property, and a third offense shall result in forfeiture of all property and dismissal from service."

THE ALEXIS NESTEROV AFFAIR

This utter disregard of the law and the state, so deeply ingrained in the mores of the Russian people, forced Peter to set a frightful example. He incarcerated and almost executed a man [Shafirov] who rendered him great service as senator and vice-chancellor. Coinciding with this affair which so burdened the Reformer another case arose concerning a man entrusted with uncovering and investigating abuses of power. Senior Inspector Nesterov was caught abusing his position. He had discovered an affair involving Savva Poptsov, a provincial inspector in Yaroslavl. As early as 1718 a citizen of Yaroslavl, the townsman[23] Ivan Sutiagin, sent a petition to the Senate against Poptsov, complaining of insults, ruin, beatings and mutilation. The petition was forwarded from the Senate to the College of Justice, whence it was dispatched to the Yaroslavl superior court,[24] and there it sat.

Sutiagin, whose character was expressed in his name,[25] refused to let matters rest. He sent another complaint to the Senate. When the Senate inquired why the matter was not investigated the Yaroslavl superior court answered that it must conduct an inquiry among the local residents who worked in the Chief Magistracy to determine why the sovereign's order had not been executed once the complaints were received from the College of Justice. The Yaroslavl superior court then returned the matter to the Senate.

These communications went back and forth for four years. Sutiagin still would not let the matter rest. In 1722 he submitted a plea to the sovereign himself, detailing his grievance against the inspector, who he alleged sheltered deserters, youths from the nobility and wanderers. Through his relative by marriage, Likharev, he illegally collected a grivna[26] from each of the peasant households in his district. He had not paid taxes or duties from the money collected from these peasant households and had not raised conscripts for many years. Instead he conscripted those whom he had seized and embezzled the treasury's money.

At this point the case began to move forward. "Regarding this rather important matter," wrote Makarov to Yaguzhinsky, "his imperial majesty has ordered that the petition and the specific accusations be sent to your excellency, that this matter be investigated by the Senate or, even better, by your office." Upon investigation it turned out that Poptsov, in violation of his instructions, had indeed taken part in those activities of which he was accused. He had his own court, he held people in the stocks, and he imposed fines on his own inspectors and on mayors, salt mine managers and people from other ranks.

Poptsov was sentenced to death. He spoke with Nesterov and in November 1722, following the decree from his imperial majesty, the lieutenant general and procurator general Pavel Ivanovich Yaguzhinsky, and Captain Yegor Ivanovich Pashkov of the Life Guards, procurator of the War College, pronounced the verdict. The finding on Senior Government Inspector Alexis Nesterov was based upon evidence provided against him by the former provincial inspector Savva Poptsov and upon his other criminal attempts to solicit bribes through threat of torture and then actually to order such torture. By order of his imperial majesty Nesterov was appointed to find and eradicate illegalities committed by others. Yet by neglecting this responsibility he allowed Poptsov to take advantage of his post to engage in extensive tax farming. Instead of suspending him and prosecuting his actions as circumstances required, Nesterov took bribes from him—a silver army watch worth a hundred twenty rubles, and a fox-hair quilt. He also agreed that Poptsov would advance him three hundred rubles in cash. In addition, Poptsov bribed him with rye, cattle, brocades and horses. Nesterov took a five-hundred-ruble bribe from Larion Vorontsov for installing him in Siberia as governor, and allowing him to farm taxes among the taverns, and other misdemeanors.

Not wishing to suffer further torture, Nesterov pleaded guilty to everything. Not everything came out during the torture because his statements were found to be inaccurate. The matter passed to the Superior Court where the generals, the middling nobility, staff and senior Guards officers presided. The esteemed senior inspector was sentenced to death, and the verdict was carried out.

Few grieved for Nesterov. In January 1722 on the occasion of the election to the presidency of the College of Justice Nesterov complained that not one of the dozens involved kept him informed [of what was taking place under his watch]. In this way the upper strata of society stubbornly persisted in its disgusted resistance to the inspectors. Nevertheless Peter did not eliminate this office. In the Senate protocols for January 1723 we read "Since a former senior government inspector now has been implicated in many crimes, his imperial majesty has instructed us to identify some good men among the general and senior inspectors. To that end we inform the colleges that whoever knows of suitable men for these posts shall inform the candidates and send their names to the general court."

EXPOSING MENSHIKOV'S ABUSES

Kurbatov died in custody. The Siberian governor Prince Gagarin and Senior Inspector Nesterov were executed. Senator and Vice-Chancellor Shafirov was sent from the block into exile, and the greatest man of the realm, the most illustrious Prince Menshikov, was exposed for his abuse of power and obliged to pay a huge penalty. Menshikov wished to take advantage of the Peace of Nystadt, Peter's pride and joy, by forwarding to him this plea on paper bearing a coat of arms. "I most humbly seek the indulgence of your imperial majesty for the joy of all the people about the eternal peace with the king of Sweden. In remembrance of the battle of Poltava and the capture of Baturin I request that I be granted as my property the town of Baturin with its outskirts, the district which belongs to it, as well as its homesteads and mills and lands with their inhabitants.

"I hesitated to trouble your imperial majesty with this request, considering that your imperial majesty saw fit to order the destruction of the city when it was taken and see to it that none of its inhabitants were left alive. Now people live there who formerly settled in the city's outskirts and in the surrounding district. Among them are people of every rank, in particular Chechel, who as hetman during Mazepa's treason was punished. He sought to skin me alive. Also there are his wife and children and others who participated in Mazepa's treason."[27]

The sovereign declined this request but Danilich [Menshikov] concocted other methods for expanding his domain in Little Russia by appropriating land and peasants near Pochep. The hetman complained and the notorious Pochep affair ended unprofitably for the most illustrious prince. At the beginning of 1723 he was compelled to seek Peter's forgiveness by writing "From my earliest years I was raised by your imperial majesty and I always felt, and do still feel, that your majesty has displayed his highest paternal mercy towards me. Through the wise and paternal welfare provided by your majesty I have been schooled and rewarded with ranks, villages and other income, as have others of my generation.

"Regarding the survey of the Pochep land, I recognize my culpability with respect to your majesty, and admit that I cannot justify my actions in this matter in any way. In all of this I tearfully and in utter humility beseech your majesty's merciful forgiveness and paternal understanding, for other than God and your highness I have no other hope for higher mercy. I submit myself in everything to the will and mercy of your majesty."

As was her habit, Catherine interceded forcefully on behalf of her old friend. Peter forgave him (although there continued to be repercussions from the Pochep affair), telling his wife "Menshikov was conceived in lawlessness, his mother gave birth to him in sin, and he will end his life in knavery. If he does not mend his ways he will end up shorter by a head."

At that time Danilich was very ill. Peter could not help writing him a letter expressing his concern. Menshikov revived and answered "I received with all my most humble respect and gladness your imperial majesty's all-merciful letter written in Grodno this past February 26. For this letter, and for your all-merciful expressions of concern over the illness which has befallen me, I most humbly express my obedient appreciation to your majesty, feeling no small measure of joy upon receiving this all-merciful letter. Freed from my illness thanks to the doctors' treatments, I most humbly give thanks that your majesty, in his exceeding paternal mercy towards me, has seen fit to let me keep my newly constructed house in Grodno and enough income to keep me in good health. I am telling your majesty the truth when I say that I built this house for your majesty's visit to the provinces so that your majesty need not worry about cockroaches."

The next year brought new failings to light and new pleas to the empress for her intervention. On April 4, 1724 Menshikov wrote to Catherine "I have requested most humbly the merciful forgiveness of his imperial majesty for my failings so that I can take part in tomorrow's festive celebration of Christ's resurrection, for which forgiveness I shall endeavor to send a copy of my request for your majesty's information. I most humbly request your most merciful maternal representation and intervention on my behalf, for other than God and your highnesses I have no hope for any higher paternal mercy."[28]

ELECTIONS

This is how it was with the most prominent gentlemen of the Senate. Still, in spite of these disappointments and the horrendous temptations of office, Peter believed in Russia's future, believed in the Russian people and in their perfectibility, steadfastly employing measures he thought could speed this process. He considered allowing people to participate in elections to be one of those measures. He himself loved the elections in the Senate and overseeing their correctness and impartiality.

At the beginning of 1722 the Senate was to cast ballots for president of the College of Justice. On January 19, leaving the Senate, the emperor and senators proceeded to the dining chamber, to which major generals, Guards majors and other officers, members of the colleges and a hundred men selected from the nobility were summoned. After taking an oath, they wrote down names of candidates, of which twelve were selected. The sovereign informed these candidates that neither they nor their relatives might take part in the balloting, or even be present in the chamber. Of the twelve individuals, three received the largest number of votes: Count Peter Matveevich Apraksin (seventy), Major General Ushakov (forty-one), and Stepan Kolychev (forty-one).

As happened commonly and everywhere the right to vote initially was regarded as a heavy burden. People attempted to avoid it, especially in areas having few nobles. Moreover, those on leave from their regiments wanted to stay home in peace. Consequently the nobles sent their stewards to vote in their place. In 1724 Peter instructed that the tax officials be selected from among the landlords themselves, making certain that their stewards were not selected. An order dispatched in December to all landlords, and in seaboard towns and other localities lacking nobles to the local subjects, to assemble at a regimental headquarters, and at the onset of the New Year to select trustworthy new provincial officials. If there were petitioners against a former official the landlords or subjects were to judge him. If guilty, they were to fine him and report the matter to the governors and commanders. Whoever deserved the death sentence or public punishment was to be remanded to the district court or, where there was none, to the military governors.

BUREAU OF THE SENATE IN MOSCOW

At the end of the reign St. Petersburg was established as the permanent site of the Senate. A Bureau of the Senate was set up in Moscow at which one senator always must be present. That senator, by virtue of his position, became the most senior authority in the old capital. In 1724 the representative of the Governing Senate in Moscow was Count Matveev, who characterized his activities in this way in a letter to Makarov. "Here everything is in good order. Although I am occupied with complicated matters and incessant problems, I am diligently clearing the local roads of thieves and bandits. In short time many have been caught and executed on the spot, without delay, on those very roads. Not so long ago the bandit chieftain known by the nickname Karpash was caught. This man, who for years carried out his banditry on the Mozhaika and Tatarka highways and on various other roads, was never subjected to torture. I have hopes of getting the upper hand over this numerous band."

One of the Senate's most onerous tasks was to organize the colleges, the district administration and the district courts. Its members wanted to appoint as few servitors as possible, owing to scarcity of servicemen and shortage of funds. This was extremely difficult because of the paucity of local educated people familiar with procedure, and capable of saving time, lessening the work, and expediting official business. The senators desired in particular to be rid of foreigners working in the colleges. These were brought in initially out of necessity, though not all of them proved to be capable and useful.

At the beginning of 1722 Peter, attending the Senate in Moscow, ordered "There shall be a review of the foreign college members in St. Petersburg and Moscow. We shall identify the presidents who are fit and necessary for their work. These we shall notify, and discharge the unfit." The colleges, which like the Senate moved permanently to St. Petersburg, were required to maintain offices in Moscow. Responsibility for identifying capable personnel for those positions, both in the colleges and in the provinces, fell particularly upon the procurator general. Yaguzhinsky wrote to Peter, who was away on campaign in August 1722, "We have not yet succeeded in appointing all the requisite personnel to the various ranks in the colleges and in the provincial administration. In truth, it has been difficult to find worthy men. Even now we cannot select a hundred such men. As the statute mandates, I have labored to equalize staffing levels as much as possible between the Admiralty and other colleges. It is just not possible in most instances to satisfy the others, especially the

Treasury College, given the small number of surplus servitors at the Admiralty."

REGIONAL ADMINISTRATION

The shortage of worthy men was felt most acutely in regional administration. Peter wanted to give a collegiate format to this administration by establishing district councillors, among which the governor would act "not as an administrator but as a president." In 1719 he substituted military governors. It is not known how these interacted with the civil governors. Neither is it known why Peter chose to abandon his earlier idea, although we might hazard the guess that his reasoning rested on the shortage of personnel.

We have a better understanding of affairs concerning appointments to the judicial court administration, which proved to be extraordinarily difficult, both because of the shortage of men and funds, and because men of high standing, the senators themselves, did not recognize the need for such a department. They did not miss an opportunity to apprise the tsar of the difficulty, harm and irreparable damage this matter was causing.

On January 10, 1722 General Admiral Count Apraksin suggested to Peter in the Senate that it was unseemly for civil officials to appoint judges in the governments, provinces and towns. In his opinion it would be better for the military governors to appoint these judges. Thus the Senate protocols included a clause regarding this recommendation. Not surprisingly, the suggestion was not presented in such an abbreviated form. Apraksin presented powerful evidence to support his opinion, from which it is apparent that Peter agreed with him since he ordered lower judges appointed by the military governors. Yet on February 12 we read in the protocols that the decree instituting the appointment of judges had been set aside. The deliberations of February 27 resolved that in towns without main courts the military governors must appoint court officers to hear minor matters. Around Moscow, provincial courts were established in three places, two in Galich and a superior court in Moscow itself.

On April 4 the sovereign ordered the governors, vice-governors and military governors in all governments and provinces to judge all felonies, except in towns having municipal courts. For important towns lacking municipal courts he ordered the appointment of two assessors, one assessor in provinces without an important town. For towns up to two hundred versts distant from provincial capitals, Peter ordered that a special court officer be appointed as judge to hear cases involving up to fifty rubles.

This officer served under the military governor. Peter further commanded that, to supervise the administration of governments and provinces and ensuring that justice prevailed, one senator from each college must visit them annually, on a rotating basis. At this time, when the Senate was involved in setting up the regional courts, it received a strange petition from the gypsy Masalsky requesting that he be put in charge of all gypsies in the Smolensk government. The Senate refused.

CENSUS REVISIONS AND TAXATION

"There are no people, there is no money!" was heard on all sides. The Senate had to remember the relevant point of the decree which created it. "Collect as much money as possible." The first census of 1722 counted 5,967,313 people from the tax-paying population,[29] among whom 172,385 were merchants. It also listed 340 towns in the empire. According to foreign data there were 273 towns, 49,447 households of urban lower classes,[30] and 761,526 peasant huts.[31] The Moscow government numbered 39 towns, 18,450 small townsmen's households, and 256,648 huts. Petersburg province contained 28 towns, 10,324 households, and 152,650 huts. The Kiev government listed fifty-six towns, 1,864 houses, and 25,816 huts. In the Archangel government there were twenty towns, 4,302 houses, and 92,298 huts. Listed in Siberia were thirty towns, 3,740 houses, 36,154 huts; in Kazan 54 towns, 2,545 houses and 20,571 huts. In Nizhny Novgorod 10 towns, 3,694 houses, 78,562 huts.

According to the count taken in 1710 state revenue reached 3,134,000 rubles. By 1725 it increased to 10,186,707 rubles according to Russian information. According to foreign sources, revenue reached 7,859,833 rubles by 1722. From peasants under crown and synodal authority, and from landlords' peasants and peasants of patrimony holders of every calling, a soul tax was collected at the rate of 74 copecks per soul. State peasants (black plow, Tatars, payers of fur tribute, etc.) owed forty copecks in addition to the other 74 in place of revenues free peasants paid the crown, synodal peasants paid the Synod, and proprietary peasants paid to landlords.

Once he paid these 74 or 114 copecks a peasant was free of all monetary and grain taxes and furnishing other provisions. Payment of soul taxes took place three times a year: January/February, March/April and October/November. From merchants and from craftsmen the state exacted a hundred and twenty copecks per soul.

Despite the increase in revenue and Peter's thrift state finances were unsatisfactory. Though the Swedish war had ended, the war with Persia continued, and for a long time there was threat of war with Turkey. A severe crop failure made matters worse. To maintain revenues it became necessary to resort to extraordinary measures, at the brink of which Peter usually stopped short.

In February 1723 the sovereign ordered "In light of the current need for money chancellery officials and those of comparable station shall receive as salary, in place of cash, goods from Siberia and other state domains, except for servicemen and master craftsmen." He then issued a new instruction that when money was needed to pay for something essential, means of collecting this sum must be devised. When this proved impossible, necessity required a ruble deducted from the salaries of all who held state rank, who received a salary from the state, clerical and lay, except foreign specialists in the sovereign's service, noncommissioned officers and those serving in the ranks and in the navy.

Lest anyone regard this as a personal affront, all must share this burden born of necessity, and no one could be offended by this exaction. Very soon, in April of that very year, more money was needed. Sources were found. "Let it be known that presently we have experienced a shortage of cash and grain, for throughout the whole realm little grain has grown. Moreover, we have learned that we are not safe from war with the Turks. Furthermore we are informed that the War College is owed a large sum for maintenance since 1720, and the Admiralty is owed for paying naval and admiralty servitors their wages." Instructions were issued to withhold a quarter of everyone's wages, to retain the tax in grain, to place the middling nobility and officers on half rations, to increase the tax on fortified wine by ten copecks a pail, to impose an excise tax on French wine, and to increase the price of stamped paper.[32]

THE ARMED FORCES

The huge deficits of the War College and Admiralty remained unpaid. These accrued because the largest expenditures were devoted to the recently founded army and navy, which gained Russia new prominence in Europe. On October 25, 1722 Menshikov addressed the Senate as president of the War College, accompanied by Major General Lefort[33] and three colonels. He announced that the War College received complaints from many places and regiments that pay was in arrears, and soldiers were deserting.

In addition to salary matters, this speech raised the important question of how to maintain the standing army. In 1724 the Senate found it impossible to billet soldiers in peasant households. The villages for billeting lacked sufficient space and faced huge burdens. Therefore it was resolved to construct settlements[34] housing one sergeant per hut, and other noncommissioned officers two per hut, those in the ranks three per hut, and at least as many for corporals, but no additional signal companies. For every signal company quarters were to be constructed for the commissioned officers, two huts for high ranking officers and one hut for others. Housing for the staff also was to be built for the regiment—eight huts and an infirmary. Where no troops were available the peasants, townsmen and men of various ranks subject to soul tax were to construct these quarters.

At the end of Peter's reign the number of regular army troops reached 210,500, among whom 2,616 were in the Guards, 41,547 in cavalry regiments of the army, 75,165 in the infantry, 6,392 in the Ukrainian landed militia regiments, and 5,579 in the artillery and engineering companies.[35] The irregular army consisted of ten Little Russian regiments totalling 60,000 men, five cossack regiments in Settlement Ukraine[36] totalling 16,000 men, 14,266 Don Cossacks on salary, 3,195 Yaik, 1,800 Terek, five hundred Greben and 214 Chuguev Cossacks. In the outskirts of Kazan there were 3,615 old-style military servicemen, in Siberia 9,495, in all 109,085 irregulars not counting foreigners. The navy consisted of 48 ships of the line, 787 galleys and other ships, with a crews of 27,939 aboard.

The number of serving men was augmented by nobles from the newly-conquered provinces, as the Baltic regions were called. In 1723 a decree assigned the nobility from Lifland and Estland to Russian military service on a different basis than that of Russian noble sons. Parity was based upon salary. Liflanders and Estlanders, as Russian subjects, received the same salaries as their Russian counterparts, but foreigners invited to serve in Russia received more. Still earlier, in 1722, the sovereign decreed that patriarchal nobles[37] henceforth were to be reduced to equality with other nobles. They were not to be inscribed as patriarchal, nor listed separately. Nobles who for one reason or another were freed from service had to pay for this privilege.

TRADE

We have in front of us a curious request dated from this time, specifically from 1723, from the noted Princess Nastasia Golitsyna. "I have been ordered by your majesty's decree to accept as payment from Miloslavsky, the son of Alexis, monies charged against him in lieu of service, total-ling three hundred rubles. This Miloslavsky gave me payment for 1719, but has not paid anything since. I request that you, sovereign, order Miloslavsky to make amends and give me those monies due to me from him."

Under the then especially unfavorable circumstances revenues were not sufficient to cover expenses, which increased at an extraordinary rate as a consequence of the Reformer's activities, in particular his establish-ing a standing army and navy. Income was growing at this time because Russia gained access to the Baltic coast. In the summer of 1722, 116 foreign ships arrived in Petersburg, 231 arrived at the port of Riga, and 235 left Riga loaded with goods. The tax on this trade amounted to 125,510 efimoks,[38] excluding the portion which went to the respective towns.

As early as 1724 twenty-four ships arrived in Petersburg, 115 in Narva, 303 in Riga, 62 in Reval (Tallin), and 28 in Vyborg. In Septem-ber 1723 price lists were ordered of foreign goods in the most prominent commercial cities of Europe "so that we know what is cheap and what is expensive." Russian ships appeared in foreign ports. Thus in May 1722 Bestuzhev wrote from Stockholm that a Russian ship belonging to Barsukov arrived from Petersburg. Bestuzhev further reported that at the very same time Russian merchants came from Reval and Åbo with coined money. They brought some linen, wooden spoons and roasted nuts, which they sold from their sleighs. Some cooked kasha[39] on the street by the bridge where the ships docked.

Hearing of this, Bestuzhev forbade them to sell nuts and spoons. So that henceforth merchants would not go to Stockholm with trinkets or cook kasha on the street, they were required to rent a house and conduct their business there. One of Prince Cherkassky's peasants visited Stockholm wearing a huge beard and brought with him some small wares. Bestuzhev wrote that the Swedes jeered at this peasant. "Russian mer-chants," wrote Bestuzhev in another report, "are unruly. They are con-tinuously drunk, swearing and acting vulgarly among themselves, from which considerable discredit is cast upon the Russian nation. Although I have informed them of your majesty's decree commanding them to live peaceably, comport themselves seemingly and dress neatly, they still go around in a slovenly manner. Some walk about in old Russian dress, without a cravat, and some appear in public with beards."

In the West Russian merchants were merely mocked but in the wild Crimea matters were worse. "It is not merely useful, but essential," Nepliuev wrote from Constantinople in 1724, "to introduce into the current treaty of alliance the possibility of having Russian consuls in Shemakha and in the Crimean towns of Khotin, Bendery and Perekop. Perhaps your majesty's court does not yet know how your subjects in the Crimea suffer even in peacetime, as I myself have witnessed. Many merchants are insulted, robbed and thrown in jail, and fines are taken from them all in violation of the treaty. Consuls could defend the merchants and all who come there."

Both the founder of Petersburg and the merchants, Russian and foreign, were preoccupied by the question of shifting the movement of goods to the Baltic and White seas. In 1721 it was resolved to deliver goods to Archangel by water from areas accessible to the [Northern] Dvina river system, and to route all hemp to Petersburg, and to ship goods for Riga on the Kaspel, Dvina and Torop rivers. The Pskov merchants were given sole rights to carry goods to Narva. Work on the Ladoga canal proceeded apace because the esteemed General Münnich,[40] recommended by Prince Dolgoruky from Warsaw, was in charge.

Peter was very pleased with Münnich, for he dreamed of sailing from Petersburg to shores of Moscow, at the Golovinsky Garden on the Yauza river. Not everyone involved with Münnich was satisfied with him, as his abrupt and hot-tempered nature gave them pause. Major Aliabiev, who had worked in the Ladoga Canal Chancellery, wrote in 1723 to Menshikov "I report with all humility to your illustriousness that when he was in the hamlet of Nazie, Lieutenant General Münnich twice jostled me at the gates, called me a daredevil[41] and a rascal in the presence of several witnesses, and reproved me in Russian."

Trade had to be strengthened now that the Russians had gained access to seacoasts, and the concerns of a government which well understood their significance had to be addressed. But the old ways of doing things, which no government was in a position to undo, raised some horrendous barriers to the hope of strengthening trade. Over several centuries the service estate had grown accustomed to living directly at the expense of the manufacturing population. In an agrarian state, urban manufacturers were unable to obtain sufficient standing to constitute an aristocracy of moveable property. A plutocracy, they were unable to achieve an independent prominence and activity, or to see to their interests.

MERCHANTRY AND URBAN ADMINISTRATION[42]

The self-administration of towns granted by Peter caught this group unawares, and the townsmen reacted in a very disoriented manner. Assuming the obligations of self-governance amounted to an extra burden. The rich ended up squeezing the poor, who felt they were better off under the military governors. Moreover, the old relations of *men* to *peasants*[43] led servicemen to have contempt for those in industry and allowed them to practice every kind of violence against them. These ancient relations produced the chronic feeling that the self-governance granted to the manufacturing estate strengthened the animosity of those who had lost to it. Let us offer a few examples.

The Chief Magistracy had drafted a long list of traders held prisoner by various governmental bodies and courts of law. Contrary to a formal memorandum from the Chief Magistracy, neither they nor their cases were remanded appropriately to the relevant magistracies, and several had died in harsh custody. The mayors and town council members[44] of the Moscow magistracy informed the Chief Magistracy that the town council members from the merchantry did not attend the sessions. Consequently [the council members] could not act on any cases. "In 1719, after a fire," the Kostroma town council members reported to the Chief Magistracy, "the town assembly hall was rebuilt with revenues from the merchant communities. The former military governor, Streshnev, took possession of the town hall entirely on his own initiative. Now the military governor Colonel Griboedov conducts his business there. A house near the town assembly was confiscated from a poor townsman in lieu of taxes, and given to Major Tatarinov in 1722 for his quarters. Now Assessor Radilov is residing there without permission and without being evicted. During this expropriation of the town assembly hall, records of cases have disappeared somewhere. In necessity the town assembly leased a very small and cramped cell in the monastery of the St. Nicholas hermitage at Baibaki. There were no other urban households nearby. Because of lack of space to store tax revenues in kind, tax collecting has collapsed."[45]

In one case the Kolomna magistracy was ordered to send a mayor to Zaraisk, then the Kolomna magistrate reported "There can be no mayor in Zaraisk because the Kolomna magistracy has only one mayor to whom it can assign business. The other mayor, Ushakov, was beaten to death by General Saltykov on his way from Kolomna to Nizhny Novgorod. Because of this time is needed in Zaraisk and in the Kolomna magistracy to accomplish anything."

Here is what actually happened to the first mayor. Commissioned Officer Volkov, assigned as ambassador to Persia, sent dragoons to the magistrate and together they brought Mayor Tikhon Bocharnikov to

Volkov and showered him with profanities. Volkov commanded the dragoon who had thrown the mayor to the ground to grab him by the hair and arms, and then Volkov proceeded to beat him with his staff. He ordered the dragoons to beat Bocharnikov with clubs, trample him and then whip him to death, from which beating Bocharnikov lay dying. On Volkov's orders the dragoons beat Alderman Diakov with clubs, and they also beat the town elder. Because of these beatings in Kolomna the townsmen could not settle any litigation as instructed.

Then in 1716 some soldiers killed Yevdokim Ivanov with a handgun, and clubbed the mayor [Ivanov] so badly while he was making collections that he died. In 1718 dragoons shot a leading merchant,[46] Grigory Longinov, in his own house. Further, long list of offenses against town residents also was sent by the Pskov magistrate to the Chief Magistracy.

What could be done for people in trade to spare them such assaults, such dishonor? In the old days they would have attached themselves to powerful men who would defend them from their brethren. In the seventeenth century strict measures were introduced against such forms of patronage. It grew difficult to form alliances with private individuals, consequently merchants began to seek the patronage of members of the tsar's household. We have seen that coachmen enriched themselves by bringing hay stokers to the quarters of Tsarevna Natalia Alekseevna.[47] A final decision emerged from the Senate in 1722. "The tax-exempt trading peasants[48] shall have their own shops, but merchants shall not own villages."[49]

The Chief Magistracy then issued regulations for executing this resolution, at which point the men serving at the court of the duchess of Mecklenburg, Catherine Ivanovna, made this request of her. "In past years we had free time for trading, and we traded without prohibitions, only paying a fee of 25 rubles per year to the Tax Assessment Office, from our businesses, to the Shipping Office two rubles. As townsmen we gave ten rubles apiece to the district for general assistance, and we also paid taxes. At the current time, in 1724, the Chief Magistracy issued instructions to all trading rows [rows of trading booths] commanding us to describe the functions of trading peasants, survey their shops and forbid them to trade, as if the tax-exempt settlers stood on an equal footing with the merchants. We could not carry out such an order in the district because their fathers once served at the sovereign's courts, and we now serve at the residence of your majesty.[50] We request that we be instructed to conduct our trade as we did previously."

The less well-to-do merchants valued their connections with servitors at court who had small houses in which they could trade with fewer insults and more profits. The wealthier strove to occupy more prominent sites in larger households to escape their insecure standing. In the beginning of 1722 the eminent man[51] and manufacturer Alexander Stroganov was informed by the Senate that he had been named baron. In 1724 Maria Stroganova and her children, Alexander and Nicholas, petitioned "that for the well-being of my younger son (Sergei) we now be appointed to the chambers of the sovereign tsarevna. I, your slave, am ignorant of how to arrange these matters between myself and others. Moreover, my sons do not hold any rank. By your majesty's decree various ranks and places have been assigned to all citizens based upon their standing that everyone might know his own true dignity in relation to others. We request that I be assigned such a place, and that my sons receive ranks in time for the coming nation-wide celebration of the empress's coronation."

The example of the Stroganovs was emulated by the merchant's son Alexis Guriev, who made a similar request to Empress Catherine. "My father came from the merchantry, from the Merchants' Hundred, and he worked as an inspector in St. Petersburg and died in 1714. I was left with no standing [on the Table of Ranks] and came under the protection of Tsaritsa Praskovia Fedorovna. Since she passed away I have had to endure numerous insults and misfortunes at the hands of many. Never previously was I obliged to conduct work or commerce among the merchantry, nor am I now. I request your majesty's great mercy that in light of the universal gladness (the coronation of Catherine) I be directed to reside at the court of your highness and live in Moscow, and that you grant me your sovereign order regarding this in recognition of my father's service and for the heartfelt gladness and benefit that accrued to your majesty when my relatives constructed with their own funds a town built of stone on the Yaik river and a storehouse for the fish that they caught. Even now it is known by our family name—the town of Guriev—and it has come to be worth 289,942 rubles. Income is collected from this town for your treasury totalling several thousand rubles."[52]

It was difficult to resist the allure of leaving the commercial estate after what happened to the merchant Bogomolov, based on the account of his son-in-law Ivan Voinov. "My father-in-law Alexis Vasiliev Bogomolov, a member of the Merchants' Hundred, was a prominent and wealthy man in Moscow. He had precious stones, items made of diamonds, pearls, gold and silver dishes and thalers, and he provided a great deal of money to the treasury. From the lofty gentlemen—the eminent man Stroganov, leading merchants and members of the Merchants' Hundred from the Chernaia free settlement, foreigners including Greeks—and merchants, all received various ranks in exchange for money. His house in Moscow stood in the White quarter at the foot of the Ascension convent of St. Barsonuphius. It was a many-chambered structure with a stone fence, and that house cost him five thousand rubles or more. My father-in-law dedicated that home to the blessed memory of Prince Boris Alekseevich Golitsyn, because the prince had purchased many expensive wares from him.

"Based upon this acquaintance, Prince Boris Alekseevich's son, Prince Sergei Borisovich, came to my father-in-law's house just to visit. Seeing that my father-in-law was aged and alone, without a wife, children or relatives except for me, he ordered his followers to evict everyone who lived with my father-in-law in that house. In their place he installed up to ten people in my father-in-law's house. To avoid public knowledge, he ordered his followers not to permit my father-in-law to leave the house, nor allow me or anyone into the house to see him.

"When my father-in-law tearfully requested that he be allowed to go to church, the prince's men followed him, not letting him go alone. It is well known to the priests, the sacristans,[53] the mother superior and the nuns of the St. Barsonuphius convent that we are their neighbors and are parishioners of that church. In 1713 Prince Sergei Borisovich threw out my father-in-law's belongings and other things, taking over the place for himself, lock, stock and barrel. He also seized the storehouses where the possessions of debtors, those who had mortgaged houses and shops, were kept, and he took possession of all my father-in-law's belongings, as well as those of mine which had remained with my father-in-law.

"This ruination brought me to a state of unrelieved poverty and obligations to others, and I wander with my wife and children from house to house. The prince and his followers have dispatched my father-in-law to the Epiphany monastery against his will. My father-in-law was constantly in tears there because the prince separated him from his home and belongings, and from his promised cemetery plot in the St. Barsonuphius convent, where my father-in-law left instructions that his body be buried because he had constructed a church at that convent, and now his burial plot is there. From this misery my father-in-law died a pauper in the Epiphany monastery where he is interred."

FACTORY DEVELOPMENT AND ITS OBSTACLES

Factory production intensified although not to the extent that Peter wished. Addressing this problem, Peter wrote in a decree of 1723 "Either those responsible fail to observe and execute the decrees with vigor, or there are few willing to engage in industry. In addition, factory owners are undercut by goods imported from abroad. For example, one peasant discovered a method for making paint for buoys. I ordered our painters to try it out. They said that it was inferior to that made in Venice, equal to the German, another was better, and it took a lot of work to prepare it. Thus no one buys ours because of the large quantity imported from abroad. Other manufacturers also complain. This matter requires us to oversee this practice with firmness and to communicate about it to the College of Commerce.

"If the college is unable to attend to this practice, this should be reported to the Senate and we should be informed, for other nations are deeply covetous of our manufacturers, striving with all their means to ruin them through bribes, as many have experienced. That there are few willing to venture manufacturing is true enough, for our people are like unschooled children, who never learn their ABCs unless compelled to do so by the schoolmaster, and at first find it irksome, yet once taught are grateful. All our current activities show this to be evident. Is not everything accomplished against their will? Already we hear expressions of gratitude for much that has been done, and our labors bear fruit. Thus, even in manufacturing, do not merely offer suggestions, as is done in those lands where people are already accustomed to it. Here men are covetous without first establishing themselves and abandon their work, as happened not long ago when a textile mill could not be completed for the lack of one machine. Instead impose requirements, and assist them with exhortations, machines and all possible measures, like good stewards, aided by a measure of coercion.

"Let us offer an example. Where fine rugs are made oblige the craftsmen to make hats as well, supplying them the necessary master craftsmen. Do not let them sell their rugs if they fail to produce their quota of hats. Where they make leather, have them use the hides for making chamois and other things for which hides are used. When they can manage their own affairs they may continue without our oversight. We shall delegate inspection specifically to the mayors of these towns, who will be given samples with the college's official stamp, which will remain with them. The mayors shall examine the wares to determine whether they can be sold at the trading rows. If the work has been poorly done the mayors can impose fines.

"Master craftsmen from other countries shall be examined expeditiously to see whether they really know their trade. If not, send them back without any recriminations. If they are capable, fulfill any needs that they may have. When a contract has expired, and our artisans have learned what they need but the master refuses to go, do not under any circumstances dismiss him. If he wishes to leave, notify the college and investigate whether or not he is leaving of his own accord or whether he is under compulsion, whether he is leaving on good terms. If he says he is content, let him depart. If he says that there is some problem or something displeasing, or if he does not say so but his demeanor shows discontent, make certain that the college looks into the matter aggressively, severely punishing anyone responsible, then endeavor to induce him to stay. If he simply does not wish to live here, let him go with complete satisfaction, that those who have come here have no complaints that we treat them badly. Thus we will stem the continued outflow of master craftsmen.

"When our own factories and manufacturers can manage their affairs it will be appropriate to impose a tax for all imported items, except broadcloth. Paints and other materials shipped to factories from foreign lands should be kept on hand in reasonable quantities by the college, and samples sent to the state, so that we do not have to search for such materials. Promise satisfactory compensation for the cost of shipping."

It stands to reason that unfavorable conditions existed for factories since the same was true for commerce. Factories owned by powerful magnates were better supplied than those belonging to merchants. The government at least did everything it could to encourage the establishment of light and heavy industry.[54] Anyone who established an industrial enterprise was freed from service, as were cofounders who entered into the firm no later than a year and a half after the enterprise was established. During this time, many manufacturers were mentioned: silk firms belonging to a company in Moscow and St. Petersburg owned by the Moscow stoker Miliutin; the coach builders Sukhanov and Company in Kazan and Astrakhan; the silk plant of the Armenian Safar Vasiliev located two days' journey from Terek; the Karchagin lace works in Moscow and St. Petersburg; the Tomilin needle factory in a district of Pereislavl-in-Riazan; Prince Menshikov's sail making shops in the Moscow region on the Kliazma, Filatov in Little Russia, Plavilshchikov in the Moscow region on the Kliazma, Khvastlivy and Company in the Orel and

Riazan districts; linen and starch factories belonging to the empress in Ekaterinhof; the linen factory of Thomas, or Thompson and Company in Moscow; the broadcloth factories Shchegolin and Company, Sobolnikov, Voronin, Aleksandrov, Pran, Fibik—all in Moscow; a state factory in Kazan and two in Voronezh; a state cloth factory in Petersburg, Volkov's in Moscow; a state wallpaper manufacturer in Petersburg, a wallpaper stamping firm also in Petersburg; the leather works Isaev in Petersburg, Istomin in Narva, Zhukov in the Moscow region; a chamois works, also in the Moscow region, a state chamois shop in the Voronezh government; state-owned wax works in Petersburg; a horse-hair factory belonging to Kobyliakov in Moscow; hat and stocking makers in the Voronezh government; the stocking factory of Mombrion in Moscow; a state paper mill in the Moscow region, Bagaret's paper and box mill in the Petersburg region; a sugar factory in Petersburg belonging to the foreigner Westhoff and Company.

Thanks to the duke of Holstein's visit to the Thomas, or Thompson, factory in Moscow we know about it in considerable detail preserved in the diary of the duke's bookkeeper Bergholz.[55] All those who worked at benches were Russians, and there were Russian master craftsmen with whom Thomas hoped soon to replace the foreign. The factory had a hundred and fifty looms and prepared varieties of linen, from crude to the most delicate, excellent tablecloths and napkins, narrow and broad ticking, delicate thread for camisoles, and colored handkerchiefs. The costs for operating the factory amounted to about four hundred rubles a month. Thanks to this same Bergholz we know some details about Baron Stroganov's famous gold thread establishment located at his home in Moscow. Here around a hundred young girls worked. Paper factories ran successfully enough that in 1723 all colleges and chancelleries were ordered to use Russian paper.

Among the state factories was a cloth works in Petersburg whose wares were not widely purchased because its prices were virtually the same as cloth imported from abroad, which was much better and wider than the Russian. Peter ordered the products made at the Russian factories to be sold more cheaply, in particular the linen and the woolen ribbon,[56] except for those used as compensation for master craftsmen who were instructed to accept linen at the Bureau of State Accounts in lieu of wages. The College of Manufactures reported, however, that although the price was reduced by five copecks per arshin,[57] there was no hope that people would buy it at that price. The appraisers sent by the magistracy priced the cloth very cheaply, from three to ten copecks, at a time when the factory cost per arshin was about fourteen and a half copecks. Since this cloth manufacturer now was left without any cash to continue to operate, the College of Manufacturing requested that the Cabinet direct these woolens be taken to the Bureau of State Accounts and paid out in lieu of wages or that they be sent to the War College for sailors' uniforms, for which it would transfer money to the College of Manufactures.

TATISHCHEV AND THE URALS

Factory production thrived in the Urals, where the town of Ekaterinburg was established in 1723 in honor of the empress. Gennin, who demonstrated his proficiency at the Olonets factories, was relocated there. In September 1723 he wrote to Peter "Although I have thrown myself into this work I cannot build and increase the production of iron and copper any sooner. In truth, I did not cause this delay, you must believe me, but there is delay nonetheless. I have several skilled people in mining and production, still I cannot be everywhere and see to everything for this sprawling enterprise. Moreover, the local carpenters are not as good as those in Olonets. In light of all of this I need the College of Mines to send me more mine foremen to prospect and excavate copper and other ore."

We cannot resist presenting still another curious letter [from Gennin], one dated April 4, 1724. "Ekaterinburg's factories and all its manufacturers are in operation. At the Ekaterinburg fortress and at Uktus output amounted to fifteen hundred puds[58] of pure copper which has been dispatched to the docks for shipping to Moscow. Moreover, one factory on the Polevaia river has received shipments of copper ore sufficient for an entire year, in a short period of time with minimal losses. I must thank God for the good fortune of having a site so richly endowed with ore. At the moment things are even better on the Polevaia. I hope that in a very few years the entire cost of setting up the Ekaterinburg factories will be recouped, and that abundant income will flow. Your other iron smelters have improved, both in Katerinburg (sic) and at the Uktus, Kamensk and Alapaevsk factories. They have been producing ore, coal and charcoal for a whole year. Where does the rich iron ore that exists at the Alapaevsk sites go? Half of it leaves there as iron, whereas at Olonets it is only a fifth, a great difference!

"Presently cannon for the artillery are forged at the Kamensk factories. Captain Tatishchev and Sergeant Ukraintsev constructed the mine at Pyskor on my instructions. Now they are occupied with shipping ore.

The Stroganovs now see that with God's help much ore is available. Before this they lived like Tantalus, everything in gold and encased by gold. Copper was not good enough for them, and they were avaricious. Now they want me to go into partnership with them and allow them to engage in shipping, to construct a factory at their cost, and assign them three ore sites on the Yava. I am more than happy to do this except I shall not hand over your sites, in light of the previous loss you incurred when the factories first were organized. Those losses must be recouped, and the College of Mines must make good the arrears in wages.

"For anyone who is willing there is sufficient ore, since in addition to your own rich site there are others which are satisfactory. For the time being I shall not bring the works at Pyskor into production. I shall await your order. As long as I have the authority I am glad to do this work. My friends can brag about my work in my absence. Without authority this would not be possible. Please hear me out and decide about the mining activity yourself, rather allow me to remain in charge.

"I wish for the best not for myself but on your behalf. I want all of the earlier losses that you have incurred in mining over the last twenty-five years to be returned to you. Do not yield the underground and surface mines[59] at Polevaia and on the Yava river where I get ore for you, which we obtain in great abundance and without much effort. Moreover, there are sufficient other such sites nearby where we managers of the company can obtain ore. I do not wish your interests to suffer. These sites I could appropriate for myself here, which I do not want to do, for I only wish you well. For the time being let the College of Mines look into this matter since truly no one there knows anything about it now, save for the official who actually works here. I have set mining affairs on the right road, please therefore give me assurances that when you grant an audience to others not far from me, you will choose not to halt this enterprise even while you might oblige them." Gennin also adds some comments about Captain Tatishchev as builder of the Pyskor factory.

The renowned Vasily Nikitich Tatishchev began his career as a mining official. More than anything he found himself at odds with the Demidovs. They complained to the sovereign, whereupon Peter ordered Gennin to investigate the matter. Gennin presented a report. "(1) Until Tatishchev took charge of the local factories and districts, and reported on outpost sites, goods passed freely by way of hidden roads in the forests, and foods by other means, arriving at the Demidov factories without levies or taxes, all of which currently are paid. When this practice was halted some local peasants were annoyed and complained to another member of the Demidov family, lying even more to avoid paying these heavy exactions. This peasant Demidov is stubborn. Once he saw others watching his lands. Without asking further, with peasant malice he complained. Heretofore no one was brave enough to reprimand Demidov, in fear, and he plundered here as he wished.

"(2) It would not be very advantageous for him if your majesty's factories flourished because now he can sell most of his iron at his own price, and the free workers labor at his factory rather than yours. When Tatishchev realized this shortly after his arrival he expanded your majesty's installations or rebuilt them. He wanted to secure the right of his mines to fell forest trees, and further wished to conduct an honest survey of the ore sites. All of this annoyed Demidov, who did not want anyone interfering with him on these matters.

"(3) Before Tatishchev arrived the officials at your majesty's factories did as they pleased. They were lazy, having little regard for the product of the factory. The incorrigible Gagarins drove the peasants to ruin yet could not withstand Demidov, who did as he wished. I expect he rejoiced that there was little activity at your majesty's factories and that the workers were deserting them.

"(4) Inasmuch as Tatischev acted still more boldly toward him, the old man did not appreciate having such a neighbor. Since he could not bribe him to shut your majesty's factories, he sought to drive Tatishchev away.

"(5) He was irritated by the fact that Tatishchev requested a tenth of his iron. Your majesty deigned to give me Sergeant Ukraintsev of the Guards to oversee the factories in my absence. Although he is a good man, he has no feel for this matter, and even ten Ukraintsevs would not cope.

"Hence I am informing your majesty from my grateful and loyal heart, as if to my own father, that in this matter it is better not to find against Captain Tatishchev. I hope your majesty will see fit to believe that I represent Tatishchev without prejudice, not out of affection or intrigue, or to further some request. Personally, I do not like his ugly Kalmyk face, but I see that he is completely in the right in this matter, and that he is sensible, judicious and diligent in constructing factories. In addition, although I have made representations to him about this, he pleads that he is in an impossible position.

"He believes, first, that your majesty harbors anger and suspicion toward him, causing him to fear that he cannot know how to act appropriately and that he will not be upheld in this matter. Moreover, without any sign of appreciation from you he thinks he has no hope of reward for his labor especially because at such a distance you cannot recognize his immense efforts unless word is conveyed by others. Third, when justice does not prevail against Demidov for his slander, and Tatishchev's losses are not compensated, their relations will be marked by enmity and distress, a circumstance which cannot fail to harm your majesty's interests. Therefore Tatishchev does not desire to remain here any longer. Please do not harbor anger against Tatishchev. Release him from his misery and instruct him to remain here either as chief director or as senior councillor."

SHEEP BREEDING

In the Northeast the Stroganovs saw the profits earned from mining ore, and requested the help of an expert to launch their own operation. In the South landholders were prevented forcibly from engaging in the improved system of tending sheep. In 1722 the Senate ordered that livestock in sheep pens be distributed to local sites to holders of several estates, proportional to the number of their villages, even if villagers refused to accept them. These sheep were to be tended at these sheepfolds, just as they were at the mills. The villagers were to keep the lambs and the wool was to be sold to cloth mills at a fair price.

In 1724 a decree was circulated to Little Russia. "We are informing all our loyal subjects, Little Russian residents of all rank and standing, that for the benefit of our entire state we have established cloth mills which require many fleeces. God has blessed Little Russia more than other regions of our realm with good air for the proliferation of sheep and high-quality wool, but the Little Russians, unfamiliar with the art of sheep herding, or making wool, conduct the wool trade unprofitably (even though they have a great deal of it), and sell the wool for next to nothing.

"We discussed this problem with Hetman Skoropadsky in Moscow in 1722, and instructed the College of Manufactures to inform the hetman and Notary General[60] Savich and Colonel Polubotok, that the lords in Little Russia maintain their sheep in the customary manner, and we have sent them rules about raising sheep. So far Little Russia has been completely unsuccessful in this endeavor, for Hetman Skoropadsky died shortly thereafter, and Polubotok and Savich, both of whom are ill-disposed to their fatherland and to us (in which they have been exposed), had no desire to see our order put into effect. They concealed it and apprised no one of the regulations sent to them. Moreover several Great Russian landlords, like those in the Settlement Ukraine regiments,[61] have begun to tend their sheep according to the regulations.

"This practice brings them a large income compared to what they earned previously. Now they sell wool for two rubles and two grivnas [a pud] or more, whereas wool of sheep raised in the former manner fetches only half a ruble and twenty altyns a pud. Once again we instruct the residents of Little Russia to tend their sheep according to regulations and sell the wool to our cloth mills. We have ordered that experienced sheep breeders be hired to instruct them how to maintain their flocks." Despite all the above barriers factories and manufacturers at the end of Peter's reign numbered two hundred and thirty-three.

HANDICRAFTS

In 1722, 1723 and 1724 Russian master craftsmen arrived from England, Holland and France where three cabinet makers for household furniture were apprenticed, four cabinet makers for official furnishings, two joiners for making beds, chairs, and tables, four coppersmiths, two foundry smiths, one engraver, and one maker of mathematical instruments. Peter ordered houses built for them and salaries for two years. Each received money for a workshop and assured of compensation for their work. He ordered them informed of this that they might acquire and train apprentices and expect no further salary until they did so.

Because this trade was organized into workshops in the West, it was deemed necessary to introduce this system in Russia as well. Peter ordered the Chief Magistracy to set up workshops and organize a model workshop in Petersburg. That work proceeded slowly, causing Peter on January 19, 1722 to issue this order to the senior president of the magistracy. "A decree and regulations have been in existence for some time about straightening out a matter placed in your hands, namely the initial organization of a proper magistracy and workshops in Petersburg, modeled on other towns, and then to establish them in Moscow and elsewhere. To date we have had little success in this matter. Therefore we have resolved that if these two matters, namely the magistracy and workshops, are not established in St. Petersburg within five or six months you and your colleague Isaev will be sent to forced labor."

In April 1722 the Senate issued an order to Dmitry Soloviev "to learn about workshops from foreign establishments and forward this information to the Senate." Soloviev promised to do this by the next morning.

Idle *talk* had it that such eminent brothers would not remain in disgrace for very long, at a time when knowledgeable and level-headed people were in such demand. The other brother, Osip, was already an assessor in the College of Commerce. Still, they produced instructions for organizing the magistrates only at the end of 1724, by means of which the Reformer wanted "all the Russian merchantry to gather its scattered temple."

MAGISTRACIES

Magistracies were to consist of a president, two mayors and four town councillors. Gathering this scattered temple was to be accomplished by charging the magistracy to list all merchants and artisans in all localities and register them in a town and for tax purposes. But these same merchants and artisans refused to be registered with the townsmen or pay taxes. They found ways to abandon their settlements and forged documents alleging they were transferred into another rank, into the peasantry or as pledgemen[62] for some obligation.

The new institution had to commence its existence by struggling with a problem which ancient Russia could not solve, fire fighting in the towns, especially assuring that a town had sufficient equipment for that purpose, and issuing instructions together with the supervisors of public property and other townsmen whom the magistracy designated for related matters. The magistracy maintained a census of all citizens, male and female, their children, brothers, brothers-in-law, nephews, grandchildren, adopted children, servants, employees, and the poor.[63] Their charge was to know when someone was born or had died (information obtained from the parish priests), and send annual reports to the Chief Magistracy of the numbers of births and deaths.

Town dwellers were divided into three categories, not including the leading merchants and the Merchants' Hundred. The first group, called the first guild, included the leading merchants, town doctors, pharmacists, physicians and shipowners. The second guild consisted of small traders, suppliers of eating establishments, and artisans. The remainder, in particular the lower classes[64] who hired themselves out for unskilled labor and so forth, although they too were in essence citizens and were counted among the citizenry, did not rank among notables and regular citizens.

Each guild selected from among the men of consequence a few to act as senior guild officials who, especially in the first guild, assisted the magistracy in all civil councils. Of these senior officers, one was named an elder[65] and one as his aid. They assisted in seeing to everything pertaining to civil affairs, offering appropriate suggestions to the magistracy. In important matters the magistracy was obliged to summon the elder and senior officers and consult with them. At the third stratum, among the lower classes, elders and tensmen[66] were selected, and they informed the magistracy of their needs. The elders and senior officials, with the consent of all the citizens, made equalizations in tax rates, ensured the circumstances of all citizens, provided them adequate means and access to non-familial relief lest the middling and poor folk, and people with families, be burdened.[67]

The magistracy was expected to work to avoid duplication in manufacturing and handicrafts, especially those which did not exist earlier. It was instructed to force the shiftless and idlers to work, and lead the children of the well-to-do and the poor to study reading, writing and arithmetic. Towards that end the magistracy was obliged to establish schools at churches or wherever appropriate. It was to settle the impoverished, especially the aged and ill, both male and female, in town almshouses, but not to admit outsiders. Wherever possible it was to establish fairs. It was expected to see that these fairs did not become scenes of idleness or noisy quarreling over prices with town citizens of various ranks by outsiders, visiting traders and craftsmen, or directed at visiting merchants and people attending from outlying districts.

All holders of urban ranks and the merchantry were to be encouraged to employ the lesser classes or impoverished citizens in appropriate work, allowing them to sustain themselves from their earnings and pay their taxes. When at the death of a citizen minor children were left unattended the magistracy was required to see to it that the executor of the will named by the parents took responsibility for the proper welfare and upbringing of the young orphans, keeping them in good health. If the parents had not named an executor, the magistracy was obliged to choose good people to be entrusted with the welfare of the children. "The magistracy," the instructions stated, "must conduct itself correctly, honestly and with decorum, thereby achieving the prominence and honor that magistrates have in other lands, and gain the respect of the citizens as their legitimate government and be worthy of the status bestowed upon its members by his imperial majesty."

The negligence and disorder reigning in the earlier town assemblies when choosing mayors obliged Peter to establish a separate college for urban administration having standing members respected by citizens as their legitimate authorities. Town residents through their elders and senior officers also were to participate regularly in the affairs of urban administration.

PEASANTS

The most populous class of primary producers, the ploughmen,[68] continued to file protests about their unenviable situation with respect to runaways. The government could not improve their lot by freeing them from their serfdom. It did reiterate the standing decrees requiring the return of runaways and peasants to their former landlords along with their wives and children and their belongings. It stated again the penalties awaiting elders and overseers for sheltering runaways, and the expropriation of villages from landowners who accepted runaways and provided them housing.

Landowners wanted an agreement with sharecroppers,[69] but the government restrained them. In 1723 the emperor instructed the census takers to reach an agreement with the landowners of the northern regions (the seaboard towns) regarding sharecroppers who moved from one land parcel to another. The census officials were to forward to the Senate the views of landowners about methods to prevent sharecroppers, when moving from place to place, from evading the soul tax. The census taker Brigadier Famendin offered the opinion that sharecroppers not move to other places, that they be forbidden by fiat to move. Colonel Solntsev made an identical suggestion, but Major General Chekin wrote that although landowners believed that the state must settle sharecroppers for them, as it did for holders of military service tenures,[70] in his view it did not make sense to treat sharecroppers the same as the regular peasantry.

In January 1725 the Senate agreed with Chekin, allowing sharecroppers free passage from private to crown land and the reverse, stipulating that an individual sharecropper might move only within his own district. Two methods were available to the government for lightening the peasants' load. One was to prevent the service tenure holders, who used the law for their own purposes, from imposing their personal rule over the peasants. The other, under especially dire circumstances, was to allow the village to lower the peasants' taxes. In relation to the first, the [Senate's] decree commented "Among both the upper and lower ranks of people it happens that moveable and immoveable property is left as inheritance to children who are such fools that they are unfit for any study or service.

Others, in consequence of their stupidity hand over their daughters and female relatives to marriage for riches. People such as this offer no hope of benefiting the state. Moreover, once they receive some property these idiots dissolutely squander it. They beat and torment our subjects, causing their deaths and wasting their immoveable property.

"Accordingly we command both the upper and lower ranks that when someone currently has such people in their family, or will have at any time in the future, he must convey that information to the Senate, before which he must testify. When on the basis of this testimony it is determined that there are individuals unfit either for study or service, who never will be fit, under no circumstances may they marry or remain as hereditary nobles, neither may they inherit villages. We command that such villages be managed by fiat [rather than by the village council], and that those villagers who cannot work profitably be fed and then handed over to their nearest relatives. If there is no immediate family, they must be entrusted to next closest relatives."

In the summer of 1723 the Senate received a report from Moscow and other provinces that, as a consequence of two successive years of crop failure, the peasants were in dire circumstances. They ate linseed and acorns mixed with chaff. They went days at a time without eating. Many were swollen and dying. Other hamlets and villages stood empty because the peasants scattered in search of food. Moreover taxes in kind excluding monetary collections in the Moscow government alone fell into arrears in the amount of 472,832 chetverts of grain. The Treasury College issued stern measures for recouping the arrears, commanding the population to sell their belongings and to sentencing defaulters to hard labor. As a consequence, poor peasants themselves volunteered for hard labor. The Senate resolved that such exigencies necessitated that they hold off collecting taxes in kind until September 1 of that year, and for the year 1723 collect taxes in kind in August, by which time the next harvest would ripen.

The census of peasant souls proceeded with difficulty. In the hamlet of Lopatki in the Voronezh district the priest Gerasim brought distress to the residents by leading them to the cross and gospels.[71] They concealed people and peasants to help them avoid having to testify about each other. The Kurkins, a family of single homesteaders,[72] with the consent of the priest, concealed peasants and even swore them to secrecy. The guilty were executed. In April 1723 male souls to the number of 70,492 were discovered in the Petersburg government, in its provinces and in the district of Olonets, in addition to those previously listed in the tax records.

PUBLIC SECURITY

Success in every branch of trade and industry depended upon the condition of roads and public security. These new requirements confronted major barriers, above all the natural conditions of the country, so large and so sparsely populated. In the autumn of 1722 it took the Dutch resident agent about five weeks to travel from Moscow to Petersburg because of the mud and dilapidated bridges. At one station he had to wait eight days for horses. Yet the long delays and inconveniences in travelling were minor discomforts in comparison with the absence of security on the roads, in the villages and on city streets. Senator Matveev, who remained in Moscow as the head of its upper administration, gave top priority in his report to the need for capturing and executing brigands.

The senators deliberated this matter in 1722. They notified the Moscow vice-governor Voeikov that numerous violent robberies occurred around Moscow, and inquired about the measures he adopted to eliminate them. Voeikov responded that he assigned special officers for this purpose to Mozhaisk and other places, and would send others to the remaining trouble spots. The dragoons were old and ill, and had no horses. According to the Dutch resident's account, twenty-four brigands were executed on a single day in 1722 in Petersburg. They were hanged, broken on the wheel or suspended from their ribs. These harsh executions did not end the violence. As before, local officials tried to reduce the number of vagrants.

In 1722 an order was issued in Moscow that all priests' children who appeared on the census as unattached be assigned either to a town or to someone at court as a means of eliminating vagrancy. Regulations against the indigent continued to appear, proof positive of their ineffectiveness. "The blind, ill, mutilated and aged who cannot work must not be arrested. They must be cared for by the community, which should not worry about to whom they belonged, but rather place them in an almshouse. Those underage who cannot remember to whom they previously belonged, who are ten years of age or older, shall be enlisted as sailors. The younger shall be placed with anyone willing to accept and raise them as their permanent wards. Those who accept them shall be so identified in the soul tax. Those whom no one accepts must be placed in an almshouse until reaching the age of ten. Then they too shall become sailors."

Everyone in Moscow, in both the Kremlin and the Kitay quarter, was ordered to build stone houses on the streets rather than in courtyards, and to lay down flagstones in front of every house to function as walkways (pavements). Inhabitants were ordered erect grating instead of fences to prevent easy entry by thieves. The trading rows were instructed to place candles in street lamps in front of the icons. Where there were no street lamps they were forbidden to place candles because they would pose a major fire hazard for the commercial district, which could ruin and impoverish many merchants. Checkpoints were placed at the ends of streets, through which people must pass at night. Armed guards were stationed there from among the residents of that street. Those without arms were told to carry large bludgeons, and all were required to have rattles.

Famine elicited the following measures in 1723. Where there was famine an inventory of extra grain was ordered compiled and its non-resident owners listed. An estimate was to be made of how much grain was required annually for each person for their own and their peasants' needs. Enough grain for a year or eighteen months was to be maintained for them. The remainder was to be distributed as a loan until the next growing season among peasants having no grain, as much as was required and its sources recorded. At the next harvest the amount shown on the lists was to be returned to those from whom it was seized. During the grain distribution particular vigilance was required to ensure that whoever hid their grain could not claim poverty and no grain, then take some. An inventory of grain held by merchants and manufacturers was ordered to prevent them reselling it at a high price, thereby causing great burdens to the populace. The Treasury College was directed to obtain weekly statements from the governments and provinces about the grain crop and posted prices.

RESILIENCE OF OLD WAYS

If the accounts of the barriers to improving material life suggested that they derived from the material conditions of the country and were rooted in the moral level of society, this explanation was far from satisfactory. The feud between Shafirov and Skorniakov-Pisarev in all its details, the behavior of magnates, inspectors, the mutual attraction of the powerful, the serving men and the manufacturers demonstrate this insufficiency. Peter's contemporaries recounted this incident. The emperor, attending a Senate hearing concerning an embezzler of state property, grew enraged and told Procurator General Yaguzhinsky "Compose a personal order that when someone steals enough to purchase a rope, he shall be hanged." "Sovereign," answered Yaguzhinsky, "do you really want to be left all alone as emperor without servitors or subjects? All of us steal, the sole distinction being that some are more conspicuous than others." Peter roared with laughter and said nothing more about it. We can offer a few more acute examples of a different character. A diplomat with whom we have long been familiar, Grigory Fedorovich Dolgoruky, had an unpleasant experience in 1722 which he described to the emperor. "On December 18 at your majesty's triumphal public entry (upon returning from the Persian campaign) I was in the company of your majesty at the Preobrazhensky offices. After your majesty's departure Prince Ivan Romodanovsky, who was crafting some particular harm against me on behalf of people who wished me ill, assaulted me [verbally] and barked out every imaginable kind of foul epithet, calling me a thief and traitor to the state. He insinuated that not only would your majesty punish me with the knout, you even intended to have my head cut off.

"Fearing your majesty's ire, I heeded him in everything and requested Gavrilo Ivanovich (Golovkin) and others to take my sword and place me under arrest as if I were a genuine thief, and I was held for several days. When I was freed on order of the most merciful sovereign empress I requested satisfaction from your highness for the mortal offense done to me. I now implore that you do me this kindness so that I do not have this insufferable profanity forever with me, that the public affront committed against the law of the land by the privy councillor and your majesty's cavalier [Romodanovsky] not be allowed to pass without being avenged. For pity's sake, sovereign, do not abandon me, now that I am advanced in years, to end my spotless service prematurely, in dishonor."

This is how others described the same incident. "On that day along with Prince Romodanovsky at the Preobrazhensky offices there were some festivities for the most eminent Russian magnates, which the emperor attended. Upon leaving the sovereign asked the host to let his guests continue their festivities, even though all of them were utterly drunk. Bad blood existed for some time between Prince Romodanovsky and Prince Dolgoruky. Because Dolgoruky refused to respond in kind to the toast that Romodanovsky offered him, both of these old men swore at each other fiercely and then grabbed each other by the hair. For at least a half hour they pummeled one another with their fists. No one present could separate them.

"Prince Romodanovsky, by then frightfully drunk, appeared, as they say, to be coming off second best. After the brawl he commanded his guards to arrest Dolgoruky who, upon being released, refused to go home while under arrest, saying that he would request satisfaction from the emperor. This feud probably will not reach such a decisive end because this sort of fist fight happens here fairly often when people are inebriated, and they are left behind without any repercussions."

The new order of affairs is expressed here in that Dolgoruky protested in the name of the law of the land against a public affront perpetrated [in a separate incident] upon the privy councillor (Cavalier Andreevsky). Stepanov, a member of the College of Foreign Affairs, when complaining against Vice-Chancellor Shafirov, wrote "I am not speaking of my person, only that the dignity of a chancellery councillor does not permit me to tolerate the beatings and swearing." This man did not feel himself safeguarded. Thus, individuals safeguarded their ranks by citing the nation's laws.

We ought to welcome this new way of doing things for by this path, by powerful individuals turning more and more attention to the laws of the land, a society gradually comes to respect the inviolability of a person as a person, not only as a chancellery councillor.

Gradually, for the customs of the nation do not change by fiat. When a privy councillor and a cavalier were not safeguarded against public affront, what did people who were not chancellery councillors have to endure? We spoke earlier about the situation which manufacturers confronted. If dignitaries and princes in their personal or family feuds engaged in public defamation and assaulted one another without understanding the harm they brought themselves, it is hardly surprising that those engaged in commerce undermined their own positions even more through such internecine quarrels.

Here is one example. The Viatka merchant Alexander Shein had about a hundred thousand rubles in capital and paid the treasury three thousand rubles in tax from his business. He quarrelled with his wife and got it into his head that, according to an old custom, he would have her tonsured. Shein's father-in-law Filatiev learned of this and asked Secretary Nesterov of the dreaded Preobrazhensky Chancellery for help. The secretary did help. He and his mates seized Shein, brought him back to the Preobrazhensky headquarters and declared that Shein was guilty of intrigue for slandering his father-in-law. By this act he condemned himself to ruin and was sentenced to death. Thanks to the amnesty following the Nystadt peace Shein kept his head. He was knouted and exiled to Siberia forever, with confiscation of all of his property.

When in 1723 Peter began to recognize the grave misdeeds perpetrated at the Preobrazhensky he directed that the names of those who suffered at the hands of the officials of that chancellery be made public so that all would know. As a consequence Nesterov was found guilty of multiple transgressions. The emperor ordered his moveable property be given to the elders of the Moscow meat market in compensation for meat taken from them without payment by the Preobrazhensky.

The governor of Astrakhan, Volynsky, continued to distinguish himself by the lack of ceremony he accorded those close to him. This habit drew Peter's ire but his ways did not change. As a consequence of the Persian war he was ensnared in some difficulties with two generals in his government, Kropotov and Matiushkin, with whom he was feuding. One letter, in the course of complaining about them, recounted the following to Peter. "In this matter I am reporting on my own behalf to your majesty. Midshipman Yegor Meshchersky spends his time at the Astrakhan port. He is a genuine fool and drunk. He does not deserve to be a midshipman, and he is unfit to serve even as quartermaster. We are unable to order him to do anything, that is the honest truth. Those naval officers know him and they can testify to this on their conscience and honor, that he is just as I report. Now we can confirm that several pranks have been played on him. He was taken for their private amusement to the home of Lieutenant General Matiushkin, who openly ridiculed him, threw water on him, poured wine over the heads of his comrades, set fire to him, covered him in sooty grease and humiliated him with some other stupidities. Then, having endured all of this, he abused and lashed out at many of them, which they all put up with and then left.

"During the merrymaking at Matiushkin's house Meshchersky insulted me, my wife and daughter with such foul offenses that no one could ever tolerate what we heard. Matiushkin not only made no effort to prevent it. In fact he kept laughing at the fact that I was so offended. I told Matiushkin that this abuse caused me harm which I did not deserve. Although it might anger Matiushkin, I would not tolerate such profanity from his idiot. He told me that he would not get angry on the idiot's behalf, and I could do whatever I wanted with Meshchersky. Once I realized that I would receive no satisfaction from Matiushkin I managed to draw Meshchersky's attention to me, because he had amused the others at my expense, sat him down on a wooden horse and let him know that I would tolerate no more of this defamation."

When it came to insolence, the women yielded no ground to the men. In 1722 a palace courtier, Derevinin, was being held in the Privy Chancellery. One night Tsaritsa Praskovia Fedorovna appeared there, took Derevinin away in front of the guards and beat him while her servitors scorched him with candles, poured strong vodka over his head and face, and set him on fire. The unfortunate Derevinin would have burned to death had the guards not extinguished the flames.

THE YOUNG CANTEMIR

The Russian people understood that knowledge of the laws of the land must serve as a counterweight to all such arrogance and the sole means of living like other, educated nations. This circumstance obligated them to seek education. Peter understood this better than most, not wanting his daughters to behave like Tsaritsa Praskovia Fedorovna. Thus, beginning in 1715, Tsarevnas Anna and Elizabeth were given daily French lessons by Rambour.

A young man, a recent arrival, who became an adopted son of Russia and was destined to be one of the first figures in our young literature, Antioch Cantemir, turned to Peter in 1724 with the easiest request for the Reformer to grant. "I have the greatest desire to study, and I recognize an inclination within me to win merit through the Latin language, in particular through knowledge of ancient and modern history, geography, jurisprudence and whatever is appropriate for political service. I am more than willing to study mathematics, and also paint miniatures in my spare moments. These sciences are pursued more zealously, and are studied more easily in the vaunted academies of neighboring realms, a fact demanding that I be sent abroad for a number of years and that I have some means of support. My orphanhood has left me with a complete lack of funds, the circumstances of which has been conveyed to your imperial majesty, and in light of which I request an allowance, however small, for my maintenance abroad."

TATISHCHEV

At the end of his reign Peter sent someone else abroad, a man who subsequently distinguished himself as an eminent toiler in the service of Russian scholarship. We first met Tatishchev at the Ekaterinburg factories, where Gennin had come to recognize his talents. In the end Peter did not grant Gennin's wish that Tatishchev remain as head of the factories, instead sending him to Petersburg. Tatishchev himself related that Demidov accused him of graft. To Peter's question whether the accusation was just, Tatishchev answered "I bear witness that in this matter I have sinned neither before God nor before your majesty," and went on to explain that a judge is not guilty when he resolves a matter properly and is thanked for it. To protest such gratitude is harmful because judges would lose their incentive to devote time to affairs over and above what is prescribed. This would inspire delays, thus burdening those involved in court cases.

"That's true," replied Peter, "but we cannot permit this practice because judges who have no conscience will, under the guise of accepting well-meaning gifts, stoop to extort them forcibly." Other contemporaries gave this response to Peter. "You have forgotten that for a good judge service is a sacred obligation. For such a man temporary profit will not enter into his thinking. What another may do out of bribery, he does out of virtue."

Tatishchev understandably must have made the same impression on Peter as he had on Gennin. They might not have liked him, but at the same time they could not deny his immense talents. Peter did not return Tatishchev to the factories, where he could have offered his theory of gratitude to the judges, he sent him to Sweden to recruit needed specialists for mining and minerals. At Tatishchev's departure Peter instructed him to examine notable structures, works, mining enterprises, factories, monetary affairs, offices, libraries and especially the Obig canal, and obtain blueprints and descriptions of everything wherever possible. He was to take several young Russian students to Sweden to study mining, to observe and report about the political situation, Sweden's public activities and its secret intentions.

Tatishchev returned to Russia by the time of Peter's death. He presented his report about useful institutions in Sweden and the harmful conditions there. He was not permitted to hire specialists in Sweden. He brought only one master craftsman into Russian service, a man skilled in cutting and polishing hard stones, though he did succeed in placing sixteen Russian apprentices in various Swedish factories.

STUDENTS ABROAD

In 1723 the young men sent to study philosophy in Paris returned in Petersburg. These were Ivan Gorletsky, Taras Posnikov and Ivan Kargopolsky.

Peter ordered the Synod to examine them in their subjects and to assign them appropriate work. It is not known to what manner of behavior the decree of 1723 on Russian students in England referred. "It has come to our attention that some of you, fearing punishment for your disorderly life in England, fear to return to the fatherland as we have ordered. For this we command with all our mercy and without any risk of our will being contradicted, that when Mr. Golden, the English merchant, comes to send you back to Russia in accordance with our orders, you can return to the fatherland without fear. We forgive all of you everything, even though some of you may have misbehaved. We assure you that you will suffer no punishment, but will be accepted mercifully. Some of you already have returned home to pursue your own affairs, to apply what you have been studying, and to reap rewards granted by us in the form of wages and living quarters."

COMMISSIONING THE NATIONAL HISTORY

Peter had never abandoned his idea of commissioning a history of Russia. If Polikarpov's experience[73] showed him that it was still too early to consider writing one, at least he wanted to prepare materials for this great enterprise. In February 1722 he ordered all dioceses and monasteries to send all their manuscripts to the Synod in Moscow, including chronicles, books of degrees, chronographs,[74] and so forth. He ordered them copied, the copies deposited in the [Synodal] Library, and the originals returned. Peter then ordered Feofan Prokopovich to compose a history of his own time.[75]

During the Persian war he contemplated editing and augmenting this history, sending his notations back to Prokopovich. "In the decree sent by your majesty concerning the memorable history of your majesty's glorious activities," Prokopovich answered him, "you have ordered me to correct and augment the manuscript, and I shall sincerely endeavor to do so. Compiling this history has been no easy matter. Still, I hope to do so without excluding other glorious and noteworthy deeds, the substance of which is currently missing either through ignorance or through the negligence of the people who keep records. On this matter the idea recently came to me that your majesty's current campaign should be described thoroughly, so that when something noteworthy and deserving of inclusion in the history takes place, it will not be lost. Everything would be noted in appropriate detail. A convenient way of accomplishing this, it seems to me, would be to direct adjutants, or someone else given this responsibility, to observe all events and happenings, after which they should describe it or appoint designated record keepers. During some lull in the campaign these descriptions can be conveyed to Lavrenty, archimandrite of the Resurrection cathedral, who accompanies your majesty. He would preserve these notes and later write an account in a simple style without any adornment, from which we may eventually compose such a history with adornments."

SCHOOLS AND THE ACADEMY OF SCIENCES

Special schools continued to appear in response to awareness of specific needs. In the new government and judicial institutions it was impossible to proceed without people who knew legal procedures. Foreigners were utterly inappropriate, the number of Russian youths sent abroad was entirely inadequate. In November 1721 Peter issued a decree "to establish a school where clerks are to be taught the necessary skills, in particular arithmetic and book-keeping, appropriate to each occupation. Whoever does not learn these skills shall not be employed. Specific subjects shall be assigned, in particular arithmetic, book-keeping, mathematical tables, writing style and other learning appropriate for a good clerk, at schools to which chancellery officials[76] shall send their children, as would others wanting their children to become clerks. The Senate also is assigned the task of designating young nobles to study at colleges."

The sentence concerning young men at colleges is used in the same sense as in the instruction to the master of heraldry, where it was said "For the present, the academies shall be improved so that they can devise a brief course of instruction where representatives from all the notable and middle noble families can study economics and civics."

"For the present, the academies shall be improved." That is, for the present the academies must generate educated young people for the civil service. What did the reference to academies actually mean? A decree published on January 28, 1724, exactly one year before the death of the Reformer, said the following. "To found an academy in which languages are to be studied, as well as other subjects and noteworthy arts, and books are to be translated. To maintain these endeavors we designate the revenue collected from the tariffs and licenses in the towns of Narva, Dorpat, Pernau and Arensburg, in the amount of 24,912 rubles. For the purpose of organizing the arts and sciences two models usually are employed. The first model is called a university, the second an academy, or a society of arts and sciences.

"Currently in Russia an establishment for the revival of arts and sciences must be founded, but we cannot follow the models adopted by other states. It is appropriate at present, when we survey the current state of the realm, to identify students and teachers, and found an institution through which the state earns widespread glory for its success in practicing science here. Through study and the deployment of these sciences, their usefulness to the nation will progress. In organizing a simple academy of sciences we cannot employ both models. An academy enables the arts and sciences to develop in their own setting and then to be disseminated, but they do not quickly bear fruit for the nation.

"Establishing a university promises even less. There are no proper schools, secondary schools and seminaries in which young people can learn basic subjects and then explore the higher sciences, which then could be welcomed. Therefore under current circumstances a university cannot have value. It would be more useful to found here an institution comprising the very best scholars dedicated (1) to producing and perfecting scientific works, but in such a way (2) to teach sciences to young people publicly, and (3) to lead a few of their students to be among the first young people to study the fundamental principles of all sciences. In this manner one structure suffices, at little cost but with great utility, whereas other states require the three different assemblages (an academy, a university, and a secondary school)."

"We cannot follow the models of other states here." This impossibility derived from Russia's lack of development. In a small locale where demands on citizens are very limited, industry and trade are not widespread, everything necessary being sold in one shop. In other words, luxuries are for the rich, the most basic commodities are for the very poor. This little locale then begins to grow, its population starts to increase, its needs grow, and this one simple shop where everything was sold in one place now consists of several shops where only the best-known wares are sold. This is how development is started, then it progresses extensively in the cities. This law of development is general in a nation's life, bringing good to those realms which do not violate it, know how to manage development correctly and fear to push it along too quickly. The undeveloped Russia of the first quarter of the eighteenth century could be satisfied with an institution combining an academy of sciences, university, pedagogical institute and secondary school all in one. Its destiny was to become the seed from which all these institutions ultimately would spring.

The lack of schools at this time is evidenced also in that the academy founded in Moscow before Peter's reign had a mixed church-civil character, owing to the level of social development of the times. It retains this stature even now despite the law establishing an academy with a purely civil character. That the Moscow academy preserved its prior character derived primarily from the fact that the Petersburg institution was too small for huge Russia.[77]

According to Peter's decree the new academy was charged with translating books. Until the academy was organized the newly-established Synod was obliged to do this. Translation of needed books was never very far from Peter's thoughts, no matter where he was or what he was doing. From Astrakhan during the Persian campaign in July 1722 Peter wrote to the Synod "The book which Sava Raguzinsky translated from Italian about the Slavic people (*Orbini il regno degli slavi*),[78] and another, which Prince Cantemir translated, about Islamic law,[79] when published, must be sent here without delay. If they are not yet ready, see that they are published quickly and sent here." In October 1724 Peter wrote to the Synod "I am sending along with this a book by Pufendorf containing two treatises: the first about the responsibilities of man and citizen, the other about the Christian faith.[80] The first must be translated immediately. I do not see that there is any need for the other."

There is another curious note from this time directed to the Synod written in Peter's own hand, which vividly reflects the sort of man he was. "An order to those laboring at translating books on economics. Foreigners commonly fill their books with many worthless narratives simply to enhance them. It is inappropriate to translate these except for relevant material and the brief commentaries that precede each subject. Even commentaries should not be added for the sake of frivolous adornment, only for edification and instruction in something honorable. Therefore edit even a treatise on agriculture (excising what is not worthwhile). As an example I am sending you books without these unnecessary narratives, which merely waste time and try the patience of worthy people."

In the latter years of his life Peter also turned his attention toward the priceless Patriarchal Library, now renamed the Synodal Library. At the beginning of 1723 the Synod received instructions to publish at once the catalog of manuscripts of this library compiled by Skiada, and to present it to the emperor. In the spring of 1724 Peter desired that the library be housed in the sacristy "and that nothing be sold from it, as happened earlier." The arts also were not forgotten. In 1723 the director of construction was ordered to employ two architectural apprentices who had been in Rome, Usov and Yeropkin, bring them to Petersburg and in their place send two other good lads to Italy.

The Academy of Sciences, which at that time functioned both as a university and as a secondary school, had urgent need of teachers. Russia was concerned also about the education of other Slavic nations. The Serbian archbishop Moisey Petrovich visited Russia to congratulate Peter on the peace at Nystadt, bringing with him a request from his nation. The Serbs hailed Peter as the new Ptolemy. The written request and the archbishop in person implored him to provide two teachers, in Latin and Slavonic, as well as church books. "Be a second apostle to us, enlighten us as you have your own people, and our enemies will not say 'Where is now their God?'"[81] In response Peter ordered some books—four hundred primers and a hundred grammars—be sent to twenty churches.[82] The Synod was to find and send two teachers to Serbia at salaries of three hundred rubles each.

IV

THE ORTHODOX CHURCH AND POPULAR RELIGION

THE SYNOD'S FIRST YEARS

The Synod survived this difficult period, the time of its initial activity, in the midst of such a remarkable era! In September 1723 a charter from the patriarchs of Antioch and Constantinople recognizing the Synod was made public. Yet when Feodosy, archbishop of Novgorod, presented the charter to his imperial majesty he reported (1) about the Synod's impotence. The decrees which it directed to the Senate and dispatched to the colleges and chancelleries appeared to have no effect. From the very founding of the Synod in 1721, among communications sent to the Senate, which numbered more than a hundred, and those to the colleges and chancelleries, many decrees were ignored and for a long time went unanswered. (2) According to information sent to the Senate, the master of petitions Pavlov,[1] suspected of being a schismatic, was not ordered to appear before the Synod. (3) Members of the top four ranks responsible for revenue collection did not permit the Synod's servitors to collect what was due for that year [1721], causing the Synod's activity to halt.

Once the emperor heard this report he ordered that a personal decree be read in the Senate stipulating that the Synod receive satisfaction on all these points. The master of petitions was dispatched immediately to the Synod. After the death of Stefan Yavorsky[2] the Synod remained without a president. This title was established at the outset on the basis of the Synod's status as a religious college but the Synod very soon distinguished itself from other colleges to stand at the level of the Senate, which did not have a president. The title of metropolitan was eliminated because it suggested the subordination of other church hierarchs to it, which in fact was not the case.[3]

The question of salaries to be paid to Synod members posed a serious problem during these first years. The scale for their salaries were by the standards of the day significant. The vice-president received 2,500 rubles, a councillor a thousand, and an assessor six hundred. Where was the money supposed to come from? The revenues associated with the Table of Ranks were set. Accordingly in 1721 and 1722 members of the Synod and chancellery servitors drew their salaries from money the Synod collected from schismatics and from those who had not taken confession, from fines and from infirmary funds.[4]

In January 1723 the Synod received a threatening decree. "Word has reached us," it read, "that the Monasterial Chancellery, now absorbed into the Synod, has failed to distribute a substantial sum to the proper places. Because of this failure the field army has stopped paying its poor soldiers, who have not received wages for nearly a year, and others have been waiting for more than a year. Therefore, so long as the undistributed sum has not been paid out by you to the designated places, you are prohibited from giving cash salaries to yourselves and to your subordinates, and to monastic servitors (even for construction), except for grain and other essentials appropriate for survival."

"Regarding your majesty's decree," responded the Synod, "on collecting and paying the undistributed sum (caused not so much by the Synod's negligence, as by unsatisfactory accounting at the Treasury College and the Senate's failure to assign the officers and palace guards[5] needed for these collections), the Synod has and does observe this charge assiduously, now reasserted through these decrees and stern warnings. Regarding payment of salaries and construction we offer the following report.

"Currently a medical hospital is being built in Moscow in accordance with your majesty's personal order, for which several payments have been made. Still more money is required and cannot be refused. Moreover the Synod's own members and servitors of civil rank have no sources of income other than the salaries designated for them. It is now said that they need their salaries to move to St. Petersburg, and it is utterly impossible for them to do this without their salaries." "Give salaries for half a year," wrote Peter, "to those moving to Petersburg who have no patrimonial lands and rely upon their salaries for subsistence."

Feofan Prokopovich, archbishop of Pskov, then turned to the emperor with a plea. "Constrained by my poverty, and hoping for your majesty's paternal mercy, may I be so bold as to trouble my all-merciful sovereign with this request. The diocese placed in my care is quite poor. In the past year I received a message from the archepiscopal chancellery that, after distributing funds to church and household servitors, all that remained was one ruble, thirty altyns and four dengas. I found the archbishop's residence utterly dilapidated and badly in need of repair. We hoped for one good crop of grain, but it turned out to be poor. Three hundred households are said to survive only with great difficulty, and much work is done in a sea of devastation.

"For several years preceding my arrival, and during my entire stay here, there have been major crop failures. I could endure this poverty most easily in Pskov. Yet I have been ordered to reside in St. Petersburg (which for me is very enjoyable and pleasant) and even the cost of maintenance would not be covered by current revenues. We can purchase beer, firewood and sometimes even hay, but there is no place to keep cattle, nowhere to run the horses. The villages around Moscow (which the all-merciful sovereign granted to me) do not yet provide me income (other than hay for the horses) because of the many years their fields lay fallow. I need to buy horses and other livestock for manure and other purposes, and hurtful circumstances continue.

"Everything of benefit still depends upon hope and patience. Had your imperial majesty not granted me several thousand rubles at first, in truth our need would be dire and we must begin all over again. Now all hopes rest with the salaries from the Synod. I have still other uses for this money. I am teaching, feeding and clothing up to twenty young men, and also assembling a proper library. I have bought already sixteen hundred rubles' worth of books, and if I could I would never stop buying, for in indulging this fancy of mine it seems I also serve the general welfare. I cannot think of selling the library to anyone (even though we are in dire need), and if I am responsible it will go where the sovereign pleases. Yet now not even my salary has been authorized. I am reduced to the most extreme level of need.

"Upon your majesty's well-known mercy immense hope rests. Last year I used 3,200 rubles from the synodal treasury, hoping to pay it back from my salary over a four-year period. I bought a house even though it required much additional construction. Now, at the recommendation of the senior procurator of the Synod, it will assist me in paying this debt only when I have nothing left and my salary stopped."

In January 1724 a personal order conveyed the following. "When members of the Synod receive from their dioceses, monasteries and churches a sum after expenses equal to their salary, let them retain it. In that circumstance they shall not demand a salary. If these same monies do not provide enough to equal the rate of pay, or if in general no money comes in at all, they shall request and receive their salary from state funds."

APPOINTING THE CHIEF PROCURATOR

Feofan Prokopovich mentions here the chief procurator of the Synod. On May 11, 1722 the sovereign ordered the Senate "to select a good man for the Synod from among the officers, courageous and capable of administering synodal affairs, to serve as its chief procurator. Provide him with instructions similar to the those of the [Senate's] procurator general." The man chosen was Colonel Boltin. Subordinated to the Synod were the chancellery (1) for the religious courts in Moscow administered by a synodal councillor and an archbishop on a rotating basis, with three archimandrites as assessors; (2) the Monasterial Chancellery administered by a judge, assisted by a councillor and two assessors, all lay officials; (3) the Chancellery of Church Affairs where an archimandrite served as judge and an abbot assisted him; (4) the Chancellery for Uncovering Schismatics. A representative of the Synod also attended the Senate.

The members of the Synod often were summoned to the Senate for joint consultations, both secret and open. Sometimes the sovereign himself attended these sessions. Thus it was on April 22, 1722 when these issues were discussed and resolved. "When a betrothal is agreed the fathers and mothers of the groom and bride shall swear that the marriage was arranged with the consent of their children. Among the lower ranks priests and civil judges shall administer this oath. Notables must swear before members of the Synod and bishops. Private chapels shall not be maintained in houses of the leading notables. Monasteries shall have one convent church, a second for visitors, and a third for the sick, to limit long services, and other churches must be left open for annual holidays.

Concerning this last matter the bishop of Novgorod, Feodosy, suggested that there was no need for more than three churches because iconostases, church vestments and roofing cost much money. "We should be ministering to infirm soldiers sent to monasteries instead of to the elderly, who are already lost, and care for the soldiers at the monasteries. Whoever does not want to live in the monasteries shall not be provided sustenance." Menshikov remarked that this could not be done because many of the invalids had wives.

This same session decided to acknowledge the energetic measures undertaken for supporting Orthodoxy in the Polish areas. Feodosy of Novgorod offered one particular suggestion for protecting the Orthodox in Mogilev. Peter responded that a commissioner would be assigned there as an observer. If persecution continued, he would deal directly with those responsible and instruct them how to behave properly. Each locality with an Orthodox population shall receive a cleric with instructions to purchase a house and construct a church for the Orthodox. It further was resolved to place gravestones in the ground at monasteries and churches and engrave the name of the deceased on them. Other stones must be set aside for paving and repair of churches. It was decided to build hospitals on the grounds of convents, which must be relocated to buildings having stone enclosures. The Synod recommended that schismatics wear special clothing, as did those with beards, old-fashioned in style except for its red color inasmuch as schismatics wore red identifying cards[6] on their clothing. The sovereign agreed to this suggestion.

The moment it was established the Synod was obliged to consider a notorious event, the divorce of the Saltykovs, a new and difficult matter. Feodosy of Novgorod wrote about this matter to Empress Catherine. "I most humbly report to your majesty concerning the matter of Saltykov and his wife, each of whom wants this matter settled according to the respective wishes of the parties, and neither wants to be held responsible. They both strenuously defend their own honor, neither making any concessions to the other. When she submitted a petition to the Synod against her husband he was not in St. Petersburg. When he arrived she already had left town. He refused to respond to her petition in her absence, a circumstance which has caused the Synod considerable difficulty.

"If they continue to behave in this manner we cannot begin proceedings. Your majesty, will you not allow us to speak to the tsarevna, the duchess of Courland, about Saltykova's beatings at the hands of her husband in Mitau, from her majesty's own doctor, to determine whether he gave her treatment after these beatings? Your majesty's secretary could take a deposition from the doctor's own hand, which would assist us considerably in resolving this matter, because no one other than a doctor can assess more precisely whether these beatings were life-threatening. Having written this, if there is something improper in it, I most humbly ask for your forgiveness."

This curious letter reveals causes for the delays so characteristic of our system of jurisprudence. Saltykova's father, Prince Grigory Fedorovich Dolgoruky, in a letter to the empress points out some additional causes for delays. "Merciful mother, this is an offense to all! Your majesty knows the intolerable offenses and deathly beatings my daughter suffered at the hands of her husband, and how she was completely cheated of her dowry. Now she is forced mercilessly to await a judgment. To this very day this matter has seen no proper resolution. Even worse, my petition for an inquiry into this notorious matter has been ignored. Many people in power are disreputable. They request and insist that people work on their behalf, they refuse to take any action on my truthful petition, nor do they permit me to act on my own behalf. As all this was going on my son-in-law went off to Moscow, and forever tours his villages. To this day he frolics about, cavorts and insults me, while I linger with my family in tears, barely living, because nothing is being resolved either at the college or through my own litigation. Justice is absent, nobody wants to find him guilty, and everyone shamelessly delays until such time as I leave here empty handed."

The main responsibilities of the newly-established Synod, according to the thinking of its founder, consisted of overseeing the clergy, especially the monastic clergy, opposing the Old Belief, investigating superstition and disseminating religious and moral enlightenment among the people.

Old Russia had passed on to the new a monastic clergy in a most unsatisfactory condition, attested by both church and civil authorities. Measures which the Reformer undertook to alleviate this harmful state of affairs proved unsuccessful, simply exacerbating the problem, evoking powerful hostility against the Reformer, who understandably responded in kind.

THE TEN COMMANDMENTS ACCORDING TO PETER

A note written in 1722 in Peter's own hand has survived in which he offers his own commentary on the commandments. The commandments were written on one side, and the sins which violated them were listed on the other. Next to the first commandment was written "Idolaters and atheists," next to the second "Whoever does not have a fear of God and regards everything lightly, others in ignorance of the teachings." Next to the third was repeated the comment listed next to the second, adding the debased and the lazy. Next to the fourth he repeated that written for the second and third. For the fifth he cited bandits and others like them. The sixth listed those who lacked fear of God either out of need or from uncontrolled greed. The seventh—thieves. The eighth—the heartless. The ninth—deceivers. The tenth—the same.

After listing the sins next to the relevant commandments [Peter remarked] "I find only the sin of hypocrisy or bigotry unlisted, and why? The fact is that, in essence, the commandments are different, and the crimes against each are different, so that everything listed above implies these sins in one way or another. Next to the first is atheism, which is predicated upon bigotry, for its first act is speaking about the visions commanded by God and the miracles as if they are fictitious. When they imagine all of this they are asserting that God did not do this, but that men did. What kind of faith do they have? If they have none, they are at heart true atheists."

Alongside the second commandment absence of the fear of God is listed, but when people prevaricate against God, what fear of God can reside in them? Next to the third: This is equivalent to the second, and in addition God suggested that they *worship him*, that is, pray. How can God receive prayer from people who are biased against him, a prayer offered by false miracles and in the places of the Pharisees, by an atheistic conscience? Next to the fourth: How is it that some people honor their natural fathers (though this for their good fortune for being born) but do not respect the pastors designated by God to be, in essence, second to their natural fathers? When the authority of the fathers [pastors] is based actually upon deception, and deals with hard times by striving ever more to subordinate pastors by slandering them to their superiors. The superiors in turn spread abusive words about the pastors among the people, thus provoking them to riot, as the heads of many in neck chains bear witness.[7]

Next to the fifth: In this world a bandit causes people only ruin, as when he is the ringleader of a riot. Yet these bandits couch everything they do as if it had some sacred purpose, in the guise of a lamb and cloaked in its skin. Against the sixth: As when someone dupes a man to take a wife unknown to him, especially when he is a cheerful and good man. It is hypocritical to take someone under his wing, lead him to church to be married [to someone he does not know] and after bringing him back home, to kiss his hands and bow down in supposed respect for his great virtue (the fact that he accepted such a son of hell to be his brother-in-law). Against the seventh: They all steal not just with one hand, but in spirit with both. Against the eighth: In this their mastery consists in what is written above.

Next to the ninth and tenth commandments Peter wrote "All of this demands no commentary, since how can they sustain themselves this way? It is said that an icon appeared either in the forest or elsewhere and there a vision appeared, saying to build a monastery on that very spot else it would become wasteland, because a monastery cannot exist without villages. Something of the sort happened not long ago in Preobrazhenskoe when two peasants came and spoke of such a vision commanding them to build a monastery at a certain place and to hand over the master's village located there. So one sin may include all of the others, while other sins do not. For example, let us say that a bandit started to blaspheme. Who would accept him into a workshop? If someone entered a tavern in a righteous manner and did not drink and carouse while all those around him were disorderly (drunken), would not all of them not shun him? If a young Orion came to a Venus in disguise to seek the young maiden's company, would he not be seeking friendship? If a thief behaved like Orion, he would find no comrades because they would expect him to lead them into temptation. In the end, Christ the Savior commanded his apostles to be fearless, although he most assuredly bade them to beware of the leaven of the Pharisees in their speech, lest it lead to hypocrisy."

REFORMING THE MONASTIC CLERGY

Peter ordered precise data gathered about the current number of monks and nuns, contemplating possible measures for limiting their numbers and involving those released of their vows in worthwhile pursuits. As it turned out, there were in all the dioceses 14,534 monks and 10,673 nuns, for a total of 25,207. In November 1722 a joint conference convened of senators and members of the Synod over maintaining retired officers and soldiers in monasteries. The archbishop of Novgorod said that the Synod had no resources available to support them. The senators raised the possibility of supporting them from salaries freed up by departing monks and fines collected from schismatics. The members of the Synod responded that these funds already were designated to pay salaries to chancellery employees. They then decided to draft a report to the sovereign, at which point Feodosy of Novgorod raised the question of whether it were appropriate now to profess novices into the monastic life.

These various points of view were conveyed to the sovereign, and in January 1723 he issued a decree. "Henceforth under no circumstances shall anyone be professed [into the monastic clergy]. In this way the large number of those who are monks and nuns will decrease. The Synod shall present monthly reports on this, and it shall assign retired soldiers to occupy the places left vacant."

Upon his return from the Persian campaign Peter devoted himself diligently to the issue of the monastic clergy. His basic thinking on the subject already was conveyed in January 1723 in a decree concerning the Moscow Miracles monastery,[8] "to keep in residence only those monks needed for a church administration. Those who are just occupying space shall be dispatched to other monasteries where the monks support themselves by their own labors." After several redrafts of the initial note Peter set out his views on the monastic clergy and their origins. "The monastic clergy appeared, at first, from among people wishing solitude and who acted out of conscience without passion or thought that their salvation was otherwise not possible in this world, rather basing this choice on their natural inclinations. Others became monks as a way of sheltering themselves from tormentors and persecutors, and still others against their will, even though this would save their souls.

"The monasteries located in those very wastelands had a special set of rules for the hermits, who lived there without requiring labor from others for subsistence. At one time certain Greek emperors abdicated and then began to act blasphemously even with their wives.[9] Then some swindlers approached them and sought permission to build monasteries in towns, for which they demanded financial assistance. Even more brazen was their desire not to labor but to satisfy their needs through the labors of others, towards which the emperors appeared to be completely inclined. This practice brought a large measure of ruin upon themselves and their nation, when along the channel of over thirty versts from the Black Sea to Constantinople there were three hundred monasteries. Just as in their lack of foresight in other matters, so too here they brought an added element of poverty upon themselves. When the Turks made their assault on Constantinople less than six thousand men could be assembled. This gangrene also began to spread here in the church under the protection of the [Greek] tyrants. Yet still the Lord God did not deprive the former masters (that is, the Russian sovereigns) who held them in check, of their paradise, as he had the Greeks.

"Might not our monks carry out their calling through their work? The northern climate of our country does not permit it, and they are utterly unable to subsist without their own labors and those of others. Our monastic clergy has developed in three wrongful ways. (1) As a way of directly satisfying the conscience of those who wish to be monks. (2) Bishops did not permit us to live without monks even though previously, in the three hundred years after Christ, there were no monks and many miracles took place at gatherings. (3) Those who wish to follow the apostle Paul who, in spite of denouncing circumcision at every opportunity, nevertheless for the sake of the Jews circumcised his own pupil Timothy."[10]

In January 1724 a personal order was forwarded to the Synod. "Although the Ecclesiastical Statute[11] has directed how the monastic clergy shall be supported, we shall restate the rules briefly because even at that time there was need for clarification. At one point the monastic clergy was enlarged by the bishops who following the example of the Roman Pope endeavored to distribute them to several locations contrary to God's commandments. In this matter, those who sought truth have borne the major burden of correcting this practice. With God's help we have made a determination, corrected it and issued decrees.

"Now that we have some free time after issuing formal decrees relating to affairs of state, and having informed people in detail about their ranks, once again we issue these regulations and resolutions to serve the eternal and immediate benefit of our people as well as the well-being of society. It is fitting that we seek a different path useful in the eyes of God and neither shameful nor deceitful before the people because the monks' way of life in its current form is based on the laws of others. Considerable harm results since most monks are essentially parasites. The seed of this woe produces idleness, numerous superstitions, schisms and scandals, as everyone already has learned [by previous decrees and the Ecclesiastical Regulations].

"We have respect for all who have settled among us, in that they have remained here. It is apparent that they have not renounced the good and satisfying life that they have here, rather have embraced it, for there are three constituent elements of the economy, namely one's own home, a state and a landlord. With the monks, all of this is now prepared. Where they do their own labor they must become free settlers because now they do only a third of the work that settlers do. Are they diligent in their understanding of God's word and teachings? In every way no. They say that when they pray, everyone prays with them, but St. Basil rejects this reasoning. What value does our society derive? There is an old proverb that truly explains the situation. [Monastic prayer] is neither for God nor for mankind's benefit because numerous [monks] flee from taxes and in laziness, as if bread were free. There is another way of life that is a form of idleness but which is useful to God and not dishonorable, serving the poor, aged and young."

The result of this thinking was to identify two functions for the monastic clergy: (1) to serve the suffering, and (2) identify candidates for service in the church hierarchy. Retired soldiers and other poor folk were dispersed among the monasteries, and the monks were expected to tend them. The monks and nuns also must care for the aged and the sick of their own sex, and rear orphans. Certain monasteries were assigned these responsibilities, the rest required to engage in handicrafts, and the monks to tend the land. For the training of educated monks two seminaries were to be established, one in Petersburg and another in Moscow.

FOUNDLING HOMES AND HOSPITALS

In 1715 Peter ordered hospitals constructed to care for abandoned children, of brick in Moscow and of wood elsewhere. The number of children under care increased year by year. In 1724 a single chancellery of the Moscow government had 865 children, 396 males and 469 females of various ages from under six months to eight years. A total of 4,731 rubles was spent on them, five rubles, fifteen altyns and five dengas allotted per year for each.[12] Wages were paid for 218 wet nurses, each of whom received an annual allotment of three rubles in cash and three chetverts of grain.[13] The chancellery reported that the wet nurses and children lived in a variety of locations because the hospitals were not yet built. Among the illegitimate children there might be some who in fact were legitimate, which was currently impossible to know because there was no way to tell. An audit of accounts revealed two youngsters kidnapped by wet nurses and subsequently identified by their father and mother, along with several other children in the custody of their natural mothers for the prescribed nursing. Two monasteries were named for temporary upbringing of abandoned children in Moscow.

In May 1724 Guards Captain Baskakov received an order. After collecting revenues from the monasteries he must distribute them (1) to monastic servitors, (2) for church expenses, (3) and the remainder in three parts, two thirds for the sick and one third to the monks who ministered to them. (4) Of the funds designated to aid the sick some must be used for bedding and other necessities as defined by the Regulation on Hospitals [1715]. (5) Monasteries with orphans must meet the first and second requirements, just as other monasteries. (6) For nuns so employed, the same rules applied as to monks. (7) The daily life of infants, toddlers and children up to the age of seven shall be organized as [the monasteries] require and done as if in a home. Clean bedding was strictly required. (9) When orphans reached the age of five they were to be taught literacy by the nuns. (10) Instruction in arithmetic and geometry must be conducted at designated monasteries. (11) In Moscow the monasteries assigned to care for the sick, aged and crippled were the Ascension and the Miracles; for orphans the New convent. The Synod was to determine which monasteries must house schools.

With regard to the orphans at the New convent, Baskakov issued this regulation. The convent was to house thirty-six six-month-olds, each of which was allotted two rubles annually. Eighteen wet nurses were assigned, each to receive three rubles and five chetverts of grain per year. For the thirty-six yearlings were allotted two rubles and one and a half chetverts of grain each. Eighteen nuns also were assigned to them, each paid six rubles and five chetverts. Two-year-olds received the same level of maintenance. Three- and four-year-olds received three rubles and two chetverts each, and one nun was assigned for every three children, each of whom received six rubles and five chetverts. The five-year-olds received the same maintenance allowance, but they were assigned only one nun for every four children. The six-year-olds received three rubles fifty copecks and two-and-one-eighth chetverts of grain each. Six nuns were assigned to them for literacy instruction.

In May 1724 the Synod received a decree. "Holy Synod! The money collected in fines from the schismatics shall not be disbursed for anything without our order. These funds are needed for construction in the monasteries and teaching orphans, at a time when your entire economy is coming to an end."[14] Since not all convents were to have foundling homes, it was resolved that the other nuns must learn spinning. In 1722 fifty trained spinsters and their tools were attached to the Synodal Chancellery[15] from the spinning workshop at the Intercession monastery and distributed among the convents to instruct the nuns in their art. In this instance the Senate suggested that the Synod need not subordinate all nuns to the elderly women and girls sent from the spinning workshop. Some nuns were mature women, and some very aged as well, who knew how to spin.

PARISH CLERGY

Matters were more difficult with the secular clergy since they did not flee the troubled world nor did they require a more tranquil and freer existence. For them the primary concern was how to improve their material existence, where to find the means for this under the financial conditions then prevailing. To improve the life of priests the authorities previously attempted to limit their number at churches and to free priests from having to purchase houses from personal funds. Now an additional regulation dealt with deacons and sacristans who were required, like priests, to live in houses purchased and supported by funds which the church collected. The means for supporting them were meager, and at the combined conference of senators and Synod members held in November 1722 more active measures were sought, but in vain. It was decided, as was usually resolved in those days in difficult circumstances, to learn how this was handled in other countries. The protocol of the meeting stated "Concerning the appointment of priests and sacristans at churches, a discussion was held over supper. We recommend assembling information on the relevant laws among other Christian peoples, which we will hold for future joint consideration."

For the time being church governance continued in the old manner. Construction of new churches was prohibited without an order from the Synod "because it is known to every clear-headed person the kind of negligence of the glory of God that transpires when there are excess churches and too many priests." The revenues of parish priests were diminished by the fact that wealthy people had their own priests in their household chapels. In regard to these private chaplains, a measure was proposed. "Concerning chaplains, limitations shall be established as to who may have them because there are far too many and they are impossible to control. When a head of household is permitted to have a chaplain he must provide support to his own parish priest, equal to that of the chaplain for a year, and he must answer for any neglect of the parish priest.

"If no one is permitted (to have private chaplains) priests who are induced to become private chaplains must be fined and compelled to perform forced labor for a long time. Others then would have fear and not follow in their footsteps without permission of their bishops. Orders must be posted at the city gates that priests and monks, even though just beginning their ministry, who have not been summoned and certified by their bishops, shall not be permitted to enter St. Petersburg. The same shall hold true for lower clergy who have absconded from their posts because they too can cause considerable harm."

Necessity compelled even prominent people to engage in the above-cited practices, the illegality of which they clearly recognized. In 1722, while the Synod was in Moscow, a priest at the church of the Nine Martyrs, Mikhail Timofeev, delivered a written complaint [to the Synod] that in 1719, while working in the consistory, he labored tirelessly for two years without any compensation. Lacking income from the church for celebrating rites, he fell into dire poverty. Merely to feed himself and his household he was obliged to accept voluntary contributions of money, food and drink from those who petitioned the courts.

Now he was employed in investigation matters, and because he wished to absolve himself of all suspicion he presented a list of all gifts he had accepted, and on the occasion of the peace treaty with Sweden pleaded that he be forgiven all his misdeeds. The Synod apparently was troubled by this confession and delayed the case until the middle of 1725. It determined that torture would be inappropriate, and instead suspended him from the investigator's office and gave him no new responsibilities. Instead he was sent back to the church of the Nine Martyrs and ordered not to defame anyone about bribes, which he could not seek to repay (totalling 97 rubles and three thalers, and food worth 196 rubles, 93 copecks), so that no one would petition about [recovering] them.

Peter earlier issued a regulation calling for the formal education of children of the secular clergy prior to ordination, *when they so wished it*, to encourage them to become useful priests. He came to recognize the necessity of not limiting schooling just to those who desired it and in 1723 he published a decree. "All sons of priests, deacons, and sacristans," it read, "who are capable of studying shall be selected to attend school. Those who do not wish to study shall remain in school against their will and receive instruction in hopes that they will join the clergy."

Peter was of the opinion that military chaplains should be capable of doing more than just administering the rites. In 1723 he wrote to the Synod to instruct it to assign to the regiments priests who had studied in schools. With respect to village priests and peasants, the Senate in its combined session with the Synod ruled that on holidays the parishioners attend church in sequence so that their homes would not be left empty. When a peasant disobeyed a priest in some manner the priest, prior to writing to the bishop, must notify his parishioners and peasant elders so that the peasant was not detained in a town on the basis of a letter from a single cleric.

The Senate then turned its attention to widowed priests and deacons, forbidden from remarrying without first leaving the clergy. In April 1724 Peter ordered that widowed priests and deacons who studied at schools and who could serve by preaching the word of God be reassured that if they entered into a second marriage they could be teachers when so requested by the bishop, and work at church councils and administrative offices.

Previously Peter demanded that churchgoers observe proper decorum in the churches and stand without chattering during religious services. He turned to them again in 1723 and ordered several measures through a personal decree sent by the Synod to all bishops and other church authorities. They must announce that under no circumstances could petitions be presented during the reading and singing of the word of God in the sacred churches, nor might chancellery clerks interrupt with reports save important state documents and those that simply could not wait. Moreover the church authorities were instructed not to allow petitioners to approach them during services. They must think of God and concentrate on their prayers, thereby giving the praying parishioners a model of proper decorum in the churches.

Charitable contributions offered in church during the liturgy were ordered separated into two purses, one for church needs, the other for hospitals.

PROTO-INQUISITOR, SCHISMATICS AND HERETICS

Just as the organization of government inspectors was linked to the establishment of the Senate, so too the establishment of the Synod created the position of proto-inquisitor, or chief inspector, in matters relating to churchmen. The proto-inquisitor in turn selected provincial inquisitors. Their responsibilities consisted mainly in certifying that every rank carried out its obligations, and in reporting transgressions.

Above all else, the inspectors were charged to look for schismatics. The first order of business for the newly-established Synod was publication of a pastoral admonition to the Old Believers. At that time the Synod invited all teachers among the schismatics freely and without fear to attend debate at the Synod, observing only responsible civility in the debates. No one would be detained even when they disagreed with the Synod. Whoever failed to appear within the designated time was liable to civil judgment and punishment. In January 1725, in an admonition to the Orthodox against preachers of the Old Belief, the Synod complained that none of the schismatic teachers appeared for debate in response to the invitation. "When previously they were brought to court involuntarily and punished for abusing God's church and for corrupting the simple folk, they circulated elaborate calumnies among the people, saying 'We suffer unjustly on behalf of ancient pieties, we suffer persecution and submit to execution because they who refuse to listen to our justifications and arguments, these imams of divine scripture, sentence us to exile, to chains, to dungeons and to death.' Yet now when they are summoned freely to a friendly, safe and honest discussion, they do not show their faces. What can be the reason? None other than the fallacy of their arguments."

Besides inviting schismatic teachers to debates the Synod announced "Anyone having doubts about something in books we have published previously, and in books still to be published after discussion and resolution by the Synod, shall come forward to the Holy Synod to present their doubts without risk of suspicion and danger. The doubt that he raises shall be resolved by holy scripture."

Further on in this notice the Synod spoke of the schismatics. "Anything presented to them as the truth, although it be utterly false and indecent, they will accept as their belief." Alongside this passage Peter wrote in his own hand "In this they remain even unto death, submitting to torment, of which we offer one example here. In 1701 the thief Talitskoy, as a way of stirring people up, wrote letters suggesting that the Antichrist had appeared, and that a certain saddlemaker Ivan Savin followed his teachings. He expressed astonishment at the torture that he endured for not observing the church's precepts, and for his evil doings he was sentenced to death. All of this he accepted with gladness.

"At the time of Talitskoy's execution by fire he broke and repented. As he descended from the pyre, the other heretic, Savin, saw him and asked the guards why he was reprieved, who provided the [new] information, and to what had he confessed? Savin then asked about his own fate, since they also reprieved him, and he wished to see Talitskoy. When this was allowed, he asked whether he had really repented. If so, to what? Talitskoy related everything to him in detail, and said that everything that he had taught him was false. This caused Savin such sadness that he tearfully repented, and reproached Talitskov [sic] for the harm he had done him, that he was glad to suffer, but not for this, only for the truth."

The Old Believer teachers did not attend the Synod for debates on faith, neither did they desist from spreading their teachings. The Synod demanded firm measures. In 1722, at the joint conference of the Synod and Senate in Moscow, Archbishop Feodosy of Novgorod said that many schismatics did not pay wages according to the fixed rate. At Butyrki, he alleged, there were few residents, and not all the Old Believers gave the money for wages to the workers' agents, threatening to beat them even though officers would be sent there if they did. Responding to these points in their report to the sovereign the Synod said "To capture the Old Believer teachers who while furtively staying at home maintain a regular residence elsewhere, spread their Old Believer charms and turn the simple folk away from the church, it appears very useful to have an order stating that agents sent by the church authorities to capture these teachers shall be obeyed without restraint, nor may the civil authorities demand a written order from their superiors in such matters.

"If in pursuit of these false teachers (this is appropriate for cleansing their souls) the Synod is not granted such freedom of action it will grow more difficult identify and eradicate them. Even worse, such lack of authority will allow the teachers sanctuary and protection, enabling them to expand their numbers without fear and to beguile many others through their blandishments. This would be very harmful to the holy church, for the news from Moscow suggests that Old Believers have grown more numerous. In some parishes there is no one else and all identify themselves as schismatics by a special notation under the double taxation scale.[16] The civil authorities fail to assist officials in pursuing false teachers, and even place obstacles in their way. An appeals judge, Oprianin from the Viaznikovo settlement,[17] sent a scribe and some bailiffs who forcibly seized from behind a grate in a courtyard the scribe Liutov, who was involved in the Old Belief. They held him under guard for his religious activities but contrary to the order of the Chancellery of Church Affairs, Oprianin made no report.

"Take those whom the Synod designates [as Old Believers]," responded Peter to the report, "wherever they are supposed to be sent, and the civil authorities shall do the same without imposing obstacles. Rather, they shall offer their assistance. Whoever disobeys this ruling shall be fined as a violator of the law. When church bailiffs search for someone merely in malice and without just cause, after seizing him, the bailiff is responsible for bringing the culprit to the civil authority. There he shall be remanded or, by mutual consent if at a remote place, sent to the district authorities. At that point the chief civil official must question him. If a schismatic, see that he is remanded to the church bailiff. If it is determined that he is not a schismatic also hand him over [to the civil official], and tell him that he [the bailiff] must write to the Synod and the Senate about the matter, and when he is handed over, write immediately. When the report is received the Synod, in the company of two members of the Senate, shall investigate and decide whether he is innocent."

Bishop Pitirim of Nizhny Novgorod continued his activities against the Old Believers. In July 1722 he apprised Peter that two Old Believer teachers, the elders Nikon and Pakhomy, were reconciled to the holy church. With the aim of returning still others, he had assigned them [to join] with officials to oversee their community at Kerzhenets. He and his acquaintance Rzhevsky wrote to Peter that, on the basis of a decree, he placed the schismatics at hard labor while they were being reconverted. Once they returned to Orthodoxy they would be delivered to the Synod for a determination of their faith. At first he did not allow them sent to Siberia, but when a captain from Petersburg appeared in Nizhny Novgorod with forced laborers in stocks, Pitirim ordered them to be sent to Siberia.

"We were informed," wrote Pitirim, "that the schismatics sent with the captain included Vasily Vlasov, a factory owner who propagates the schism's harmfulness, were not reconciled to Orthodoxy. He [Vlasov] should not simply be sent into exile. In our opinion he is not fit to remain on this earth. Moreover many schismatics, both dangerous and harmless, flee and settle in the Siberian towns. If schismatics at hard labor are permitted to live in these towns, and freedom is granted them, once they join the runaway schismatics they can do much mischief to stir up the people." Peter responded with a decree to the Senate. "Henceforth under no circumstances shall you order schismatics delivered to Siberia, for even without exiles there are already many schismatics there. Order them sent instead to Rogervik."

The Old Believers persisted in awaiting the Antichrist. In March 1722, at a bazaar in Penza, a monk climbed onto the roof of a shop, raised his hood on a stick and shouted that Peter was the Antichrist, that he would place a mark on everybody, that only those with marks would receive bread. After hearing this half-crazed monk Varlaam the local captain of dragoons, Vasily Levin, fell into a severe illness. Levin slandered several people to the Secret Chancellery, including Metropolitan Stefan Yavorsky, whom he blamed for his illness, and repeated what he said earlier. He was executed in Moscow.

In 1723 Old Believers went about the villages and taught "Two years have passed (since the Treaty of Nystadt) was celebrated for two weeks, when bells rang in all the churches for an entire day from morning to evening. Since that time the Antichrist has sat on the throne. Red Gates have been erected in Moscow, through which only our Old Believers refused to pass. Seven more years shall pass and the Antichrist will appear and inspire seventy visions."

In connection with their wait for Antichrist, one of the most curious episodes in the history of the schism occurred in the life of the monk Samuel. "Once there was piety, now it is no more, as in Rome. Tsar Peter is the Antichrist because he rules by himself, there being no patriarch. Then there is his mark, that beards be shaved, and thunders echo from the dragoons." Thus spoke the monk Sava in Tambov to the scribe Stepan, who was frightened and stopped going to church. He turned to his confessor, who slowly and carefully recounted "When we were in Voronezh in the choir we sang before the sovereign. He cursed some traitors in our presence and the discussion moved on to Talitskoy, and the sovereign said 'What a brigand that Talitsky is! So now I am the Antichrist! O, Lord! Now I am the Antichrist in your eyes!' We heard this and thought 'Why is he saying this, God knows.'"

These words from his confessor moved the scribe Stepan to even stronger doubts, becoming convinced that the Tsar Peter was indeed the Antichrist. Moreover in a Cyrillic book published in the old orthography it was written that Peter arranged to have a proud prince to enter the world as Simon, the Antichrist. Stepan then resolved to be tonsured. He spoke with a woman who said that her relatives were in Suzdal, where the tsaritsa was being held,[18] and the tsaritsa told the people "Keep the Christian faith. This is not my tsar, there is another on high." Stepan was tonsured by his own wife in the Tambov Treguliaevsk monastery, and renamed Samuel. He was told that his first suffering would take place at the monastery. "There is no need," he responded, "I shall go out into the hills."

At the Treguliaevsk monastery Samuel met another monk, Filaret, who told him "The one who rules us now is not our sovereign, Tsar Peter Alekseevich, but the son of Lefort.[19] Tsar Alexis Mikhailovich told his own wife 'If you do not produce a son I will stop loving you.' She gave birth to a daughter, and at the same time Lefort's wife gave birth to a son. In fear the tsaritsa switched the infants. Samuel's uncle, the monk Nikodim, inquisitor of the Migulinsk Trinity monastery, then visited the Treguliaevsk monastery. His nephew told him of his doubts regarding the Antichrist. 'No, it is not the Antichrist,' answered the uncle, 'not even his precursor.'"

Elsewhere rumor was spreading that the Nizhny Novgorod schismatics called the local bishop Pitirim the Antichrist for his persecution of the Old Belief. Shortly thereafter the monks of the Treguliaevsk monastery gathered in Voronezh for some occasion. While there Samuel wrote a letter claiming that Peter was the Antichrist and threw it at the stoop of an unknown house. The monks were given permission to leave. On the road from Voronezh, in the village of Izberdeo, Samuel met the junior boyar[20] Kezhnev, who said "A rumor is about that our sovereign went to Stockholm and there he was incarcerated, and this man is not our sovereign." Samuel then thought "The Antichrist! An order arrived commanding us not to read the Book of Ephraim and the Sobornik, and then the Ecclesiastical Statute arrived.[21] It is obvious that the Antichrist reigns. We must forsake the monastic clergy and flee into the wilderness!"

Samuel fled but was captured and returned to the Treguliaevsk monastery, where he was put in chains. While in confinement he was grief-stricken that the Antichrist reigned, and refused to bow to the abbot. "How can I bow down to him? He is a servant of the Antichrist." At last Samuel escaped from his chains. He fled to the cossacks, where he found a bargeman, a simple soul, whom he told that the Antichrist reigned. He came upon a priest who went on at length insisting that instead of "the emperor" it was "the crusher" and explained "It is 'the crusher' because he grinds down the people."[22]

Then a change took place within Samuel, thanks to his impressionable nature. Books fell into his possession distributed by the government against the schism, and they dispelled his doubts. Returning to his monastery he preached the Orthodox faith, then new temptations came his way. He was delivered from the Treguliaevsk monastery to the Epiphany monastery in Moscow, where he was required to attend school. Samuel was not averse to reading books and thought about what he read but for one such as he, no longer in his childhood, studying grammar proved difficult. He did not appear for his lessons, and lashes from the prefect awaited him. Once again he chafed at the new order and its perpetrator, even though he no longer considered him the Antichrist. Here arose an even greater seduction. Word had come that his wife had married some-one else. That she had fornicated was his fault according to the Acts of the Apostles. Where was the guilt in this situation? It was with Peter himself, because his wife had wanted to have him tonsured, but was for-bidden. Still, there was jealousy. Samuel could not remain unconcerned at the thought that his wife belonged to another. His companion, the monk Peter, inveighed mightily against the Ecclesiastical Statute, and his swear-ing inflamed Samuel. Finally he could tolerate it no longer, and composed profanities against the emperor on scraps of paper. The authorities found one of these notes and hauled Samuel off to the Secret Chancellery. He justified his writings by stating they were not meant to be spread among the people, but were for his own conscience. They did not believe him, and he was executed.

Instances of self-immolation continued. The authorities learned that there were Old Believers in Ishimskaia district, and Colonel Parfeniev visited there to warn and appeal to them that if they did not return to Orthodoxy they must pay a double tax. In response the Old Believers trekked into two wastelands and immolated themselves. The members of the Vyg[23] community continued to live peaceably. A curious incident oc-curred among them. The scribe Sablin forged an order granting him full authority to withdraw money from the Vyg community. Some experi-enced members recognized that the order was a forgery, and Sablin was assigned to hard labor in the Petrovsk factories.

Such things were found among the Old Believers who, in their own words, held to the old faith, that is, the old books. We have observed other such manifestations and heresies. The notorious heretic doctor, Dmitry Tveritinov, repented while in confinement and in 1722 asked to see a confessor, yet the inclination toward heresy did not ebb. In 1724 a certain Alexis Popov wandered the land and preached that worshippers who prayed to the heavens would be received by God in spirit and in truth, but it was unworthy for them to worship icons, fashioned by hu-man hands.

In Moscow there appeared a man of advanced age. Was this not John the Evangelist? At a later time he appeared variously as John the Evan-gelist, Elias and Enoch.[24] Once, when the emperor was waging one of his campaigns, it was said that a man of great age appeared in the regiments, and they called him a hero-adventurer.[25] Was this not Enoch? The next year [1725] the heretic Artemy Ivanov was prosecuted for saying that the son of God was not crucified, that the prophet Eusephius[26] took his place. Ivanov said that icons were idols, and those who worshiped them idolaters. The church was a den of thieves who had obliterated the mysteries of the church.

The schism, a defection from the church, had the very same consequences in Russia as in other countries. Once they broke free from the authority of the church the schismatics splintered into multifarious sects. This splintering, intensifying over time, knew no limits. The Protestant influence is undeniable. It is obvious, for example, in Tveritinov. Even without the Protestant influence splintering expanded by way of the well-known downhill road. Troubled times, a multiplicity of interpretations, the impossibility of reaching the truth through human reason, reinforced the schismatics' determination to trust themselves to Holy Scripture alone.

Even Scripture was subject to various interpretations. To escape these interpretations schismatics strove for an unmediated bond with the spiritual world, with the deity. They came to see themselves as awaiting the appearance of individuals appointed as heralds of a mighty upheaval which would obliterate troubled times and bring back the kingdom of truth. Along with the appearance of the Antichrist they anticipated the appearance of John the Evangelist, Enoch and Elias. In the end, they came to act in an agitated and unnatural manner, believing that in this state they renounced this earth and received inspiration from above, the gift of prophecy.

Among those most adept in these beliefs people began to see Christs, and among the women mothers of God. This was the last step. The historical Christ now had disappeared. Each of the adepts, by means of exercises which elevated them to a state of rapture, could become a Christ. The means of achieving a state of rapture for religious purposes is the same at all times and among all peoples. This is true whether with shamans and dervishes, Finnish wizards about whom the ancient Russian chronicle speaks, the shaking peasants and old women mentioned in the Hundred Chapters,[27] and in Western European sects. To suggest that the radical Russian sects of the eighteenth century, and those which exist today which developed from the religious movement of the seventeenth century which we call the schism, were produced by the ancient Bogomils[28] is as mistaken as it would be to derive them from the Quakers. It would be just as much a stretch of the imagination as it would be to derive the western Albigensians from the Bogomils. We shall return to this subject when we describe the discovery of the existence of these sects by the government and society.

RELATIONS WITH PROTESTANTS AND CATHOLICS

During its struggle against the schism the Synod never lost sight of the Protestants and Catholics. Thus it sent official notification to the Senate of a report from Joachim, bishop of Astrakhan, that a Father Anthony of the Roman faith reached Astrakhan through Persia in 1718, and in 1721 built a Catholic church with a cupola and a cross near the Orthodox church. When questioned by the bishop, Anthony responded that he built the church on the order of Governor Volynsky. In 1720 the Lutheran pastor Johann Sikilis built his own church [also in Astrakhan] near the Orthodox church. He placed a four-pointed cross upon it, and in 1721 he wed to a dragoon of the Lutheran faith a married Orthodox woman.

This affair generated an investigation of the pastor which proved fruitless for fear of Governor Volynsky, who forbade the ecclesiastical chancellery from passing judgments without his direct order. The Synod's report expressed its wish that henceforth Volynsky not interfere in religious affairs. The Senate sent Volynsky an order to this effect, demanding a response to these charges. At the end of 1723 a curious decree was published stating that Catholics who resided in Petersburg were permitted parish priests only from France. This preference for the Gallic church, which was more independent of the Pope, is understandable. Moreover, it might serve as an avenue for friendly relations with France.

COMBATING POPULAR RELIGION

Along with eradicating the schism the Synod was obligated by the Ecclesiastical Statute to expunge superstition. As was true everywhere, here also the Reformer preferred to act through persuasion and instruction. A silver ark was taken to the Synod from the home of the secretary of the Monasterial Chancellery, Makar Beliaev, which included a depiction of the martyr Christopher. The ark contained relics which, according to testimony, had the appearance of an elephant's bone. The emperor ordered the contents of the ark emptied into a reliquary, that the elephant bone be placed in the Synod's Chamber of Artifacts, and a book written explaining that in an earlier time, when there were no church examinations, these and similar superstitions evolved from Greeks who came to Russia. Under the Synod's watchful eye superstitions have been overcome.

In 1723 the Holy Synod decided to issue an admonition announcing that piety did not require the faithful to save the annual Lenten bread and water of the Epiphany. The holy bread might be received at every service, and water was often consecrated. Crafting golden and silver frames for icons, or candlestick holders and icon lamps, especially for the glory of God, did not enhance piety. In places which housed artifacts which were not consecrated, but which monastic and church authorities decided on their own to fashion, great care must be taken in overseeing the edifices built by pilgrims and others engaged in unsanctioned religious practices.[29] The synodal ruling further specified that unconsecrated icons worn round people's necks be delivered to a church office for disposal as the church saw fit. Chapels were demolished and processionals of the cross abolished. This excess of zeal aroused grumbling among some people, including those who were not superstitious yet feared that this endeavor to purge society of superstition transcended the boundaries of responsible conduct.

In the sovereign's absence, the Senate considered itself obliged to intervene in this matter. In July 1722 the lords of the Senate summoned the Synod's senior secretary and told him that the demolition of chapels caused crosses and cupolas to be thrown away. These lay untended and scattered, which gave rise to great temptation. The Senate further protested that it was inappropriate for the Synod to abolish processionals of the cross. When synodal people could not accompany them, someone from the free population might replace them.

The reasons for restraining holy fools[30] are fully revealed in the following episode. In 1723 a report from the Kolomna inquisitor to the Synod depicted Vasily Bosoy as a holy fool. Once it heard the details of the investigation the Synod decided to dispatch Bosoy to the College of Justice because the holy fool testified that he simply pretended to be a holy fool. He killed a priest in the town of Belev because the priest refused to hear his confession. In Orel he pushed a young boy from a bridge because the boy teased him. On the Romodanovsky estate, in the hamlet of Prosviriakovo, he used magic to drive a peasant from his wife.

While going around villages he used his magic to entrance young maidens, and seduced twenty of them. While in Kaluga he taught his magic to ten people. To avoid the cold while walking in winter with just a shirt and barefoot he uprooted a small nettle plant [the previous] spring, put it in a pan without water, squeezed out some juice and rubbed it into his skin. He gave instructions in making a two-fingered cross.[31] He employed demons in his service. He gave the water demons all the cattle they demanded. When the water demons drove the cattle to go drink he dropped them into the water, and the air demons obeyed him without question or qualms. As with the water demons, they did nothing without a little bribe, and Mikh the Satan headed all the demons. The holy fool also could travel from Kaluga to Kiev in seven hours by his demonic power.

PROKOPOVICH AND CHURCH PRIMERS

Episodes such as these might be reduced through the spread of religious and moral enlightenment among the people. The Ecclesiastical Statute called upon the Synod to prepare three books the statute deemed essential to the nation. Feofan Prokopovich composed a primer published under the title of *A Student's First Lesson* [See Note 21]. In the introduction he says "Because many of us who have been accorded rank by the fatherland nevertheless have little knowledge of the laws of God, there is a general need to issue a small book with commentary on the ten commandments handed down by God.

"Such booklets have been used very little in Russia because those in existence were written in a high Slavonic dialect and not in simple speech. For that reason pupils hitherto were deprived of a proper upbringing. Seeing the nation's lack of pride, the all-Russian monarch, our emperor and most merciful sovereign Peter the Great, father of the fatherland, was pained in his heart by the unhappiness of his subjects and began a careful deliberation about establishing a functional and necessary regimen in Russia for the upbringing of children. In answer to his wish God inspired him with wise counsel to command that a short book be written containing clear explanations of the laws of God, the symbols of faith, prayers to the Lord, and nine blessings.[32] This he instructed published with a primer so that young children learning to read the letters and syllables can study these commentaries rather than the psalms and prayers, and learn to read texts by using these commentaries.

"In doing this we have learned that the precepts of our faith and the laws of God show us that teaching psalms and prayers can be useful. Thus by the order of his imperial majesty a little book was published with which children who are studying can know God's will and learn to fear the Lord from their early years."

A brief note written in Peter's own hand has been preserved which states "Also make some sort of small book for peasants that they read for understanding in church." In February 1723 the Synod ordered "in the place of the previous books of readings, Ephraim the Syrian, the *Sobornik* and others,[33] the primer with the explanations of God's commandments shall be read during Lent in the churches. They shall be distributed in reasonable quantity so that those who come to church and prepare for confession and the holy mystery of the Eucharist, having heard God's commandments and the commentary about them, and examining their own conscience, may better prepare themselves for true repentance."

In April 1724 Peter sent a decree to the Synod. "Holy Synod! Because I have long expressed my conviction, which I now put into writing, that we compose these brief teachings for people (because we have dangerously few educated preachers), we also must issue a book to explain God's indispensable law and advice, the traditions of the fatherland and various incidental practices used only for ceremony and ritual. This is to be done without fail, and with time and experience the current state of affairs will change and people will learn the high regard this booklet holds.

"Regarding the first point, it seems to me that we must write the book simply in such a way that even a villager can understand. Or perhaps we could prepare two: a simple version for the villagers, and for the towns a more elegant one selected for the sweetness of its sound. Whichever approach is demonstrated to us as the more appropriate for presenting precepts conveying the existence of a direct path to salvation, specifically through faith, hope, and love (for regarding the first and last they know perilously little, and nothing directly or even indirectly) shall be chosen. Hence all their hopes rely on church singing, fasting, ritual and similar things, including building of churches, candles and frankincense. Regarding Christ's suffering, these activities explain only original sin and receiving salvation through one's deeds, as is written above." Still earlier Peter ordered that Catholic, Lutheran, and Calvinist catechisms and other books of church activities be assembled. Once translated into Slavonic they were to be published as sources of knowledge and information.

V

THE UKRAINE

THE UKRAINIAN COLLEGE
From the movement for reform in Great Russia let us now turn to similar movements in Little Russia and its circumstances prior to the end of
the Northern War. Once it accepted the rule of the tsar's government
Little Russia was compelled to devote its energies to the security of
Russia as a whole. The Peace of Nystadt permitted Russia to act more
decisively. At the beginning of 1722, while the new emperor was in
Moscow celebrating the treaty, Hetman Skoropadsky[1] arrived to convey
his congratulations. He was received honorably, but matters did not end
there. "To bring to an end the disorder," announced a decree of April 29,
"that has arisen in the Little Russian courts and army, Brigadier Veliaminov and six staff officers from the Ukrainian garrisons are ordered to remain with the hetman on the basis of treaties concluded with previous
hetmen."

By this order the one official assigned to the hetman was recalled. In
response to Skoropadsky's complaint that this arrangement undermined
the terms to which Khmelnitsky agreed,[2] Peter drafted an answer in his
own hand. "In place of what was agreed to with Khmelnitsky, that supreme authority rest in the hands of Great Russian military governors, this
(namely the college) has been established. Thus you are not to imagine
any breach in the terms to which Khmelnitsky agreed. Rather, the college
will assume responsibility for executing them."

A manifesto was promulgated in May [1722] establishing a Ukrainian
College under the chairmanship of Brigadier Veliaminov. The responsibilities of the new college were delineated in the following way. (1) To
conduct official business expeditiously and impartially in all localities,
and ensure that offenses received lawful satisfaction. (2) To account accurately for monetary, grain and other collections, and receive them from
Little Russian village officials and town elders. (3) To pay infantry officers and their soldiers from the income of the hetman's council, to
maintain account books and present them to the procurator annually in
the Senate. (4) To prevent the general overseers and colonels, by means

the hetman's council, from impoverishing the cossacks and lower classes. (5) To arrange quarters for the dragoons without exceptions, whether on the hetman's personal service lands and dwelling, or at the households of officials, priests and sacristans. (6) Together with the regimental commanders to review all complaints from the lower ranks and Little Russians. (7) To require that the decrees of the sovereign and Senate sent to the hetman are registered in the general chancellery, and make their reports available. The college was instructed to prohibit the hetman's scribes from signing universals[3] in his place. These must be distributed directly by the college.

ADMINISTERING THE UKRAINE

With this present in hand Skoropadsky returned home. In July [1722], while the sovereign was still absent, the Senate grew alarmed at news that the hetman had died on the third. It quickly resolved that until a new hetman was chosen Little Russia would be administered by Colonel Polubotok of Chernigov, and the local officials.[4] They were instructed to consult Brigadier Veliaminov in all matters and in all councils, and in issuing orders, regarding which the Senate promised a formal charter. It was determined to tell Brigadier Veliaminov by express courier to go to Glukhov as quickly as possible by postal coach. Once arrived, he was to ensure that while the hetmanate remained vacant there would be no civil violations either in local or other jurisdictions, and that the populace would not become agitated. He was instructed that no orders or letters concerning official matters be circulated without his approval about which [Veliaminov] was secretly apprised.

General Prince Trubetskoy, governor of Kiev, also was ordered to Glukhov immediately by postal coach. He was to observe the situation and through discreet inquiries block secret correspondence and activities of factions abroad or at home arising during the confusion. He was instructed in particular to make sure that the Zaporozhians, Orlik or other traitors, as well as the Crimea, engage in no subversion. The existing town gates were to be properly maintained and new ones added. In this matter it was decided also to send an order to the commander of the army, General Weissbach.

A commotion arose in the Senate over whether to rely on Polubotok. "Please allow us," wrote Senior Procurator Skorniakov-Pisarev to Makarov, "to append these steps to his majesty's orders sending someone to Little Russia to govern the hetmanate through the notables. I have no confidence that Polubotok will administer the hetmanate appropriately, for he is uncooperative." In addition, two high-ranking deputy commanders were dispatched to Peter in Astrakhan to request that he permit a new hetman to be chosen. The senators informed Count Peter Andreevich Tolstoy, who was accompanying the emperor, that it was after widespread consultations that they sent the Little Russian envoys to Astrakhan. If this were not done doubts might arise in Little Russia whether the request would be honored.

The governor received written instructions [from Tolstoy] to detain them in Astrakhan. Should the sovereign order them returned they were to be told that selection of a new hetman must be delayed until his return from campaign. "Thus," wrote the senators, "they will harbor no doubts, and we can await his imperial majesty's will. We have ordered that this matter not be assigned to Brigadier Veliaminov and the local officials, thereby assuring at the very outset that they are not troubled. Meanwhile we request a specific decree."

Peter agreed with the senators' opinion. He answered that the Little Russians' request should be granted once he returned from campaign. Yet before his return the two figures of authority working side by side in Little Russia revived their feud. In October Polubotok and his confederates complained directly to the Senate, to the Little Russian College, bypassing local officials, who were neither consulted nor advised. They ordered the colonels to inform them how much land there was in each regiment, how many mills, and other useful information. In addition, ten officers were named to the regiments from the Glukhov garrisons, for reasons unknown.

The college demanded that the Little Russian military chancellery send all notes, local orders, searches, deeds of purchase and other documents if they related to petitioners who submitted complaints to the college. The military chancellery was unable to comply because it never maintained such records, nor did it employ many chancellery officials. The college demanded special tax collectors, yet nowhere in the monarchy did instructions exist for such a position. The college sent decrees about these petty matters to local officials in the name of his imperial majesty, demanding responses and appropriate action none of which, in light of the chronic difficulties arising in the administration of Little Russian affairs, could be carried out .

For his part Veliaminov complained that local officials executed imperial decrees poorly, and that they did not answer to the Little Russian

College. The Little Russian officials then addressed a complaint to the emperor. "Your majesty ordered that there be a college in Little Russia for appealing high matters, yet the Little Russian College accepts hearings into its own court which bypass our regimental and civil courts. It sends a common soldier to gather complaints lodged against notable people and local officials, and then decides these affairs at its own discretion. Consequently our own courts soon will be left without any cases. We are commanded to withdraw from the College of Foreign Affairs and to subordinate ourselves to the Senate. Yet the Little Russian College sends your majesty's orders to us every day, instructing us to comply with them and pressing submission of reports on us, forcing us to submit to its authority."

Reviewing these complaints, the Senate resolved that in private matters Veliaminov must not demand official documents or copies from the chancellery. When local officials convened over important matters Veliaminov was to participate and to assemble relevant regulations and copies of local orders without interference from the college. The college could be involved only in appeals, and in these hearings was instructed not to send directives to local officials. Rather it was charged with reviewing case files with in a civil and correct manner, and under no circumstances was it to make threats. When the college encountered resistance, it must write to the Senate. When it needed information about estates, mills, and other local matters the college was not to involve the regimental commanders in any way, unless advised to do so by local officials.

After expressing their gratitude to the Senate for resolving these relationships in their favor, the local officials reported that they now knew why the college dispatched officers to the regiments. They were sent with orders to notify the entire nation [that is, all of Little Russia] that everyone who held a grievance should present his complaints directly to the college in Glukhov without fear of local officials, and the matter would be resolved quickly. But the populace [which heard this pronouncement] would grow restless. Now people stopped heeding local officials and their own landlords, and even revived old conflicts both with landlords and officials, and among themselves, all of which were resolved long ago.

One after another, the colonels got up and marched straight away to the college. These same officers made an extensive inventory of mills, baths, apiaries and other places, and this census raised questions among various people. Veliaminov charged that the local authorities established their own court in Glukhov in place of the general court, without notifying him. This new court was supposed to choose judges from the regimental officials, three men from each regiment, to reside in Glukhov on a rotating basis for a month, then be replaced. Veliaminov wrote that the Little Russian College only accepted petitions submitted to local officials in the name of the judge, scribe and captain of the cossacks, who were not permitted to petition the general court and were close at hand.

In response to this communication the Senate ruled in February 1723 that when the general court met on important matters without Veliaminov being informed the brigadier was to inquire privately into any intrigues or bribery. Once fully aware of a situation he was instructed to pass judgment against a relevant local official, report to the Senate, and see that no harm came to the Little Russian people. When someone petitioned against a judge, the petition must be heard by a judge other than the one accused. When someone appealed a decision of the entire court as unjust the matter was to be referred to the Little Russian College.

Since Little Russia just heard of the emperor's return to Moscow the local officials forwarded a request to Menshikov requesting permission to submit a petition for a decree about selection of a hetman. Once the local officials learned in January 1723 that Peter was in Moscow, they appealed directly to the emperor that he fulfill a promise given during the campaign to allow a new hetman to be selected. Receiving no response, they sent a new request to Petersburg in May [1723]. "Please send your decree to Little Russia that in recognition of the rights granted to us and the custom of the Little Russian army the hetman may be chosen by free elections without delay. Governing without a hetman incurs great hardships and difficulties."

To this request were appended still others, among them selection of colonels from Little Russians at places long since not represented in Starodub, Pereiaslavl and Poltava districts, easing regulations for Little Russians on return of runaways, army posts, and sending cossack detachments for work on the Ladoga canal[5] and the fortress of the Holy Cross.[6] In 1722 the Starodub regiment petitioned the sovereign to grant it a colonel "from among the Great Russians, in particular the Guards colonel Fedor Protasiev or someone who fears God and will protect our freedoms," because the regiment experienced horrible oppression at the hands of its previous colonel, Zhurakovsky.

In response Peter commanded that Great Russians be assigned to Little Russian towns. Initially they were to be called simply commanders so as to prepare the populace for the change. In the beginning of 1723 Peter decreed the following to the Senate. "Notify the cossacks and other service populations of Little Russia that, as they wished, Russian colonels have been assigned to the Little Russian regiments. Notify them as well that if these Russian colonels offend them in some manner they may circumvent them and report the offense directly to his majesty. Let them know that the colonels are ordered that their instructions [to the cossacks] must not offend anyone as stipulated in the Articles of War,[7] which threaten execution for such offenses."

The instructions given to Colonel Kokoshkin, who was appointed to the Starodub regiment, stated "The residents in the district of the Little Russian Starodub regiment have suffered unbearable offenses and ruin from Colonel Zhuravka [Zhurakovsky], because of which they petitioned for a Great Russian colonel. Therefore Kokoshkin shall keep in mind this instruction which states why he was sent. In particular he must understand that the Little Russian people must be free of the burdens with which their own officials oppressed them. The previous colonels and local officials plundered their own subjects, took their lands, their forests and mills, burdened them by seizing food and drink. They forced them to work on constructing their houses, and made the cossacks who had left service obey them. Now they were instructed to obey Kokoshkin.

"We must be as fearful of this kind of conduct as we are of fire, and gather provisions only from regimental lands. The previous colonels dragged out matters in the courts, but Kokoshkin must act correctly, sincerely and efficiently as a judge. He must dissociate himself from the usual arrogance and severity of previous governors. He must behave in a kindly and generous manner with the regiments.[8] Should he nevertheless fail to practice his instructions and governs like the previous Cherkassian colonels, he will be summarily executed even for a small infraction, as a violator of his order, a violator of the law and subverter of the state."

In addition to appointing Great Russian colonels the Senate determined during its session of October 22, 1722 to write a special and secret communication to Veliaminov, instructing that as circumstances permitted he encourage the Little Russians to petition that a court be established for them according to the Law Code and the laws of his majesty.

CLASHES OVER CHOOSING A NEW HETMAN

Thus Skoropadsky's demise led to a clash in Little Russia between two policies. First, the attempt by the imperial government to exploit the discord

between the local officials and the rest of the population, and thereby to
govern Little Russia as it did Great Russia, and second, the attempt by
local authorities to preserve the old order and the hetmanate. Among
those seeking the latter were two colonels, one of them from Mirgorod,
Danila Apostol, who understood where power resided and who wanted
to receive the hetmanate for himself from the emperor. In March 1723 he
wrote to Peter "Your imperial majesty is aware that I serve you as a colonel, and that I have served unfailingly for more than forty years. In the
course of my faithful service, when I have been received by your imperial majesty, your most exalted and merciful word has comforted me on
several occasions. Because a hetman currently has not been chosen for
Little Russia, and because there is no one more senior than I in the Little
Russian regiments, may your supreme authority[9] command that I, your
most humble slave, be appointed for my faithful service as Little Russian
hetman in place of the deceased Hetman Skoropadsky, for which most
exalted bounty of your imperial majesty I am forever prepared to shed my
blood in your service." At the very same time Apostol sent a letter to
Menshikov bidding him to solicit the emperor about this issue. Menshikov and Apostol were in a long-standing correspondence in which the
colonel showered the most illustrious prince with flattery.

In this particular letter Apostol delineated his prior service. But the
Chernigov colonel, Pavel Polubotok, whose vigor in defending the independence of Little Russia stood in marked contrast to Skoropadsky's
chronic weakness, was more eminent. Apostol wanted the emperor to
appoint him as hetman. Polubotok, who administered Little Russia in the
absence, and now after the death, of Skoropadsky, attracted a party of
notables, whose interests he was prepared to advance in whatever way he
could, to the detriment of the lower classes. At the end of 1722 Polubotok
and the council of local officials suggested that Veliaminov distribute a
circular throughout Little Russia that the common people, in their abuse
by thoughtless individuals displayed willful determination not to offer
dependable and obedient service to their masters. Should resistance appear anywhere the guilty parties must be imprisoned and, after confirmation of their guilt, be punished publicly without mercy.

Veliaminov responded that he did not agree with such a circular because those in positions of authority would use it as a pretext to oppress
the lower classes without cause, as they did previously. Veliaminov suggested that when peasants displayed resistance to their masters the matter first should be investigated, following which punishment could be

imposed. There was no need to arouse fears by issuing a formal warning without cause.

POLUBOTOK AND HIS CONFEDERATES

Polubotok and his allies paid no heed. They circulated orders as they wished at a time when this was forbidden by decree without Veliaminov's consent. Peter had no patience for disobedience to his decrees. The time had come to demonstrate that an order from the emperor or from the Governing Senate had the same force in Little Russia as in Great Russia. Moreover under the circumstances of that time it was important to remove the most obstinate and unreliable people from Little Russia. Polubotok, together with the scribe of the general court, Savich, and the chief judge, Chernysh, were summoned to Petersburg to explain themselves.

Simultaneously a decree emanated from the Little Russian College ordering that revenues be collected for the treasury, in cash and grain, by the village police and town officials of the Little Russian people. These collections must be paid to the college by officials designated for this task. These revenues were to pay salaries according to the terms agreed by Bogdan Khmelnitsky. To guarantee that the collectors behaved honestly, taking nothing for themselves from the receipts, the agreement with Khmelnitsky called for the War College to appoint one overseer to every regiment from the good men among retired noncommissioned officers. The collections paid earlier in Little Russia for the hetman, colonels, hundredmen[10] and other local officials of the poor cossacks and common people, but which the local authorities, cossack notables, army officials, monasteries and churches now had not met, must be paid by all equally, from the highest to the lowest ranks, with no exceptions.

Some common people petitioned for entry into cossack service at places where they served previously. Their grandfathers and fathers, and even some of the petitioners themselves earlier served among the cossacks for many years. The local officials and other authorities had seized them, some against their will, and subjugated them to their own authority, thus depriving them of their cossack status. To inquire into these petitions the decree of the Little Russian College stated "We shall review the former and present cossack registries of the military chancellery. If this inquiry reveals that grandfathers and fathers of the petitioners indeed were among the cossacks, they too shall be inscribed. When registers from long ago cannot be found, testimony shall be taken from the Little Russian residents, and on this basis whether to inscribe them shall be decided."

The more decisively Peter acted on behalf of the common people, the more entrenched grew the notables' desire for a hetman, from whom they hoped to find support against the hated college and its president. They pressed their requests more aggressively, manufacturing burdens and intrigues to achieve their goals. In May 1723 the local officials once again submitted a petition to allow them to choose a hetman. They turned also to Empress Catherine to beg her patronage in convincing the sovereign to order a hetman chosen by the free elections of the Little Russians.

Peter responded to this effort with a decree in June 1723. "Everyone is aware that from the time of the first hetman, Bogdan Khmelnitsky, and even until Skoropadsky, the hetmen behaved as traitors, from which our realm has suffered great harm, especially Little Russia, where the memory of Mazepa is still fresh. It is fitting, then, for us to seek a hetman completely faithful and reputable. We have striven unceasingly to bring this about. Until this hoped-for eventuality takes place the government has chosen to appoint individuals to act as your government, ordered to act in accordance with the instructions they have been given. This is to ensure that, until a hetman is chosen, there will be no disruption of official business. Consequently it is not appropriate for us to intervene in this matter." This decree is remarkable because, in the context of informing them of his efforts to seek a worthy man as hetman, the sovereign announced that the hetman would be appointed, not elected.

Once Polubotok, Savich and Chernysh arrived in Petersburg they petitioned the emperor to maintain Little Russia under its previous laws. There were two sides in Little Russia, and soon the cossacks Sukhota and Lamaka appeared in Petersburg, dispatched from the Starodub regiment, along with the priest of Liubech. They too presented a petition to the sovereign wherein they complained about the offenses of the local officials. They asked that their colonels, as well as the officers of their judicial court, be Great Russians. Polubotok and his confederates then alleged that Sukhota, Lamaka and the priest were dispatched by the Little Russian College. Receiving this petition, Peter sent a trustworthy man, Rumiantsev, to Little Russia to examine the towns. Rumiantsev was ordered to use this assignment as a pretext for gathering information: (1) whether all Little Russians desired Great Russian colleges and courts; (2) whether they wanted Great Russian colonels; (3) regarding the petition submitted in the name of the local officials, whether the local officials and cossacks actually knew about it; (4) whether people were fleeing because of the posting of dragoons or because of the oppressive behavior of landlords and local officials; (5) the offenses local officials committed against the cossacks in the process of seizing their lands and mills.

Polubotok, Savich and Chernysh were not caught napping. They bribed the Senate clerks to inform them about Rumiantsev's instructions. They then sent an instruction to Little Russia, to the Little Russian administrators, about how to react, in particular to urge the [Little Russian] nation to respond unanimously to Rumiantsev concerning the hetmanate by demanding that the previous order be preserved. No one approved the spirit of the petition brought by Sukhota and Lamaka.

To accomplish this the colonels suggested that the local regimental chiefs, the hundredmen, offer compensation to whomsoever they offended and forewarn them of any complaints to Rumiantsev. The chiefs would say "Whoever was offended has received compensation. Henceforth anyone so offended can receive satisfaction in court." Polubotok, Savich and Chernysh further instructed that the colonels' letters to the general chancellery, reporting that people were moving away because of the posting of dragoons be presented to Rumiantsev. Further, the local officials needed to tell Rumiantsev that Lamaka, Sukhota and the Liubech priest did not come alone to Petersburg, nor did they compose the petition. Rather, it was written in the Little Russian College and then transcribed into Little Russian script. The clerks and others commandeered to work in the college for crimes they previously had committed signed it. Brigadier Veliaminov sent off Lamaka, Sukhota and the priest with this petition on postal coaches provided them for travel and transporting money.

Armed with this instruction, Polubotok's man Lagovich was sent to Little Russia with further instructions to convey a verbal order to Polubotok's son Andrei in his father's name to summon the Liubech hundredman and assure him that the elder Polubotok, upon his return from Petersburg, would give him full satisfaction if he would restrain his own people, the hundredmen, from petitioning, and would not himself petition against Polubotok.

Not satisfied with struggling just against the Little Russian College in the Ukraine, Polubotok and his companions wrote two petitions and dispatched the chancellery clerk Ivan Romanovich to go to Petersburg with them. On November 10, 1723, as Peter was leaving the church of the Holy Trinity, Romanovich presented him with the petitions. The sovereign went to the parlor (in a hostelry named the Four Frigates) and there unsealed these papers. Polubotok, Savich and Chernysh, along with many other Little Russians, were standing near the house waiting to hear what

Peter would say to them as he came out. They were not expecting that, finding in the papers "baseless and offensive petitions," the sovereign ordered Romanovich arrested, along with the senior officer and the Little Russians then in Petersburg. He ordered their papers confiscated, those with them in Petersburg and those in their homes in Little Russia, to allow Rumiantsev to investigate. Among these papers was found a draft of a circular to be sent to an envoy in Little Russia conveying what Rumiantsev had learned through his investigation.

On December 15 an inquiry convened among the local officials. "From whom," they were asked, "did you learn of Rumiantsev's message to Little Russia and about the contents of his commission? In your circular it is written 'Suggest to the gentlemen administrators that if they suffered and are suffering abuses and reproaches from Brigadier Veliaminov they write a complaint to the Senate. So counseled high-ranked personages.' Who are these people?"

"The circular," replied the senior officers, "was composed after general consultation with and consent by the senior chancellery clerk Nikolay Khanenko. They learned from Rumiantsev's bandore player that Rumiantsev was sent to inquire about the college, whether they wanted it and Russian colonels. Upon their arrival in August Peter Andreevich Tolstoy notified them that officials were being dispatched to Little Russia to ask about the offenses and confiscations. The chancellery clerk personally mentioned the advice of the high officials, although not on their orders."

At this point the senior officers announced that they knew about Rumiantsev's travel not from the bandore player, rather from clerks whom they bribed, as a consequence of which Peter issued an order to the gentlemen of the Senate in January 1724. "It has come to my attention," it read, "that scribes have been leaking secret matters to the Cherkassians. It is surprising that these include both commonplace and secret senatorial activities relating to rural districts. In light of this revelation you shall follow the example of the College of Foreign Affairs in seeing to it that secret matters be entrusted to especially trustworthy people and never again will you be afflicted with such transgressions."

In addition, Rumiantsev sent word from Little Russia that local officials from the general chancellery distributed impressive letters to the towns expressing their agreement with the instructions from St. Petersburg. He apprised the Senate that the secret negotiations in Petersburg were well known in Little Russia, that the confiscated papers revealed little about what they had been up to. "Those men from the chancellery," replied Peter, "wrote these opinions to the towns irrespective of whether they were knowledgeable in these matters. Whoever among them appears to be important shall come here forthwith, as must the scribe Valkevich. Select good people to take their places who are not bound by their current responsibilities and wish to be at the college.

"They must stay abreast of everything taking place in secret, and let them beware that such matters are being investigated here in the following manner. People are arrested once copies of the letters about which they spoke are found, that is, those the Senate scribes gave them. At this point three have been discovered, and they have confessed. Write a letter stating that little has been learned so far, which of course means that it has been kept hidden. Among the drafts of their letters it was discovered that they wrote home to have their houses purged of all incriminating evidence. In light of this discovery, you may question their household servants. In addition, it is appropriate for you to publicize the names of those who must account for their belongings, or at least to explain a satisfactory portion of them. Valkevich has reported to Polubotok and the others about the searches made here among the drafts of their letters. You shall carry out your other responsibilities in accordance with my decrees, and we have been satisfied with what you have done in this matter so far. Leave a specific place in your report for Danilo Zabela's testimony. Previously he submitted a report against the local authority, which at that time was not believed but which now has been recognized, and now he shall go to the Ukraine to complete the search for evidence."

Within a few days there was another letter. "In the past year the bishop of Chernigov wrote to the bishop of Pskov, who resides here, that Borkovsky spoke in the presence of witnesses in his own house concerning the correspondence between Polubotok and Orlik. On the basis of the bishop's letter the Secret Chancellery ordered the governor of Kiev to investigate. The governor sent to Chernigov investigators, whose work has no end in sight. Perhaps the only real news in this matter is that fear of Polubotok prevents people from telling the truth. Since Polubotok and others are now involved in serious crimes in Chernigov, we have appended a list with their names. We shall round up those implicated in the investigation and assure them that they may come forward and expose Polubotok without fear, and we shall send them here. Even though they are not under arrest an officer must escort them here."

The affair of Polubotok and his confederates was remanded to the Superior Court. They were asked above all why, without Veliaminov's consent, they circulated these intimidating orders among the simple folk. They responded that they heard no ban from Veliaminov himself. Independently they complained to the brigadier that he sent officers with a notice to all regiments that all who heeded the landlords and local authorities had nothing to fear. They felt they could proceed to petition against them [the colonels] to the college. In their view it was the brigadier's orders that caused the ensuing difficulties between the common people, the landlords and local authorities. Local peasants assaulted the landlord Zabela and pulled out his hair, and then beat the village elder of Pogrebki to death.

There was a second accusation. Polubotok and others were required to inform Veliaminov when they planned to attend conferences when important matters were discussed. Veliaminov was supposed to be present at all such meetings, yet [Polubotok and his confederates] had not in fact notified him. In response to this charge came the evasive answer that important matters often did not involve them. The third accusation was that in place of the general court in Glukhov they established their own without notifying Veliaminov. To this they responded that they did notify him, and he said "Good!"

Then came an accusation that the petition submitted by Polubotok, Savich and Chernysh on behalf of the entire Little Russian people appeared to be unknown to them. Polubotok and his confederates obliged a certain local official, formerly in Glukhov, to sign his name on a blank sheet on which a petition subsequently was written calling for an end to the Little Russian College and its replacement by a general court made up of seven individuals.

Polubotok and his associates explained this matter in the following way. They drafted the first petition in Glukhov in Little Russian script, to which the signatures were then affixed. Then they obliged the signatories to sign blank sheets so that the petition could be rewritten in Great Russian writing, which was done by Polubotok and his companions upon their arrival in Petersburg. Only then did they realize that they included the point about the general court of seven individuals in the petition without apprising those who had affixed their signatures. Officials from all the regiments, the hundredmen, the disobedient confederates and hundreds of cossacks from every regiment responded unanimously to Rumiantsev and protested about their signatures, insisting that they were unaware of this petition. Instead they thought they had signed petitions about reducing the revenues to be collected.

Polubotok, Savich and Chernysh, in their confrontation with Lagovich, acknowledged that they gave the instruction mentioned above. The residents of Starosenzharovsk gave testimony against their own hundredman Vybly. He had talked them into demanding with one voice the abolition of the Little Russian College [tax] and its collections. It was learned that when Polubotok's household servants heard about his arrest the housekeeper Maria burned his letters. It was further discovered that the retired executioner Ignatov and the widow Natalia Krivkaia were telling fortunes stating that Polubotok would be hetman, and that on Polubotok's order the milkmaid Maria Matveikha was killed.

The executioner Ignatov explained that Polubotok ordered him to kill the police[11] cossack Zagorovsky and others, lest they make a report against him. The Starodub townsmen presented a complaint alleging that Polubotok stole money from them. Even Apostol's name came up. Colonel Shemet was punished for not giving salaries to the cossacks who were in the Persian campaign and abandoned in the town of Terek because of illness. These monies were used instead to purchase a camel and five horses for Apostol. Peter also learned that Polubotok and his associates sent a letter to Zaporozhia. This was an especially important matter for him, as is apparent from his letter to Rumiantsev of March 14, 1724. "You should consider sending someone to Zaporozhia (better if it were someone who suffered severe harm at the hands of the local officials) to get hold of this letter which the local official [Polubotok] wrote to them. For that purpose you can use up to five thousand dengas (coins) from what was taken from the local officials, and I expect for that amount of money you can obtain it."

Peter's attendance was required at the Upper Court because Chernysh cajoled the chamberlain Chevkin to intercede with the empress on behalf of him and his companions. Chevkin advised them to bring Catherine a gift of five hundred thalers, either wrapped in paper or concealed in a glass. Polubotok, meanwhile, died in the fortress, and his comrades' fate was determined only in the next reign.[12]

COSSACK RESTIVENESS

Nepliuev, the Russian envoy in Constantinople, reported "The French consul has arrived from the Crimea. He told me in secret that at various times over the past year certain cossack commanders whom the Tatars call *barabashi* arrived from the Ukraine. These people turned to the chief Tatar, Murza (Prince) Zhantemir-Bey, with complaints that all their former privileges were abolished, about which they petitioned to Petersburg without success. Therefore, they maintain, the Ukrainian population seeks Turkish protection but cannot succeed without Turkish assistance because of the large Russian military presence in the Ukraine. "The murza advised Khan Saidet-Girey to look into these cossack affairs. The khan refused, first of all, because the Porte gave him strict instructions to maintain friendship with Russia and, secondly, especially because he is a peace-loving man."

In the other cossack territory, on the Don, the old forms of life yielded peacefully to new relations with the crown, whose overwhelming power was acknowledged after the failure of the Bulavin revolt.[13] In 1716 ataman Maxim Frolov wrote to Prince Menshikov "May it please my sovereign and dear father[14] the most illustrious prince Alexander Danilovich to assist me and plead with the great sovereign about the extreme need in which I presently find myself, that his sovereign majesty might give me a letter of appointment as military cossack chieftain for the army of the Don in recognition of all my years of service and in respect for custom, just as was the previous field ataman Peter Yemelianov. I have been selected as the field ataman by the general consent of the army."

In 1722 the ataman Vasily Frolov, Maxim's brother, sent his son and nephew to Moscow "to attend school to study books in Latin and German, as well as other political subjects." Vasily Frolov died the next year and Ivan Matveev replaced him, but the commission appointed to examine Turkish allegations of cossack brigandage sentenced him to pay compensation for the Turkish wagons[15] they plundered. An imperial decree arrived at the Don stating that, in light of this verdict, Matveev was unsuitable as ataman. Pursuant to a petition of the local authorities, it named Andrei Ivanov Lopatin to serve in that capacity. The cossacks responded that Lopatin "was an agreeable choice respected by the military atamanate."

UNREST IN THE SOUTHEASTERN BORDERLANDS

In the East the non-Russian population[16] continued to be uneasy. In 1720 the Senate dispatched a colonel, Count Golovkin, to allay the concerns of the Bashkirs and to separate the prisoners from them.[17] He returned in the spring of 1722 and brought a map of the Bashkir lands. He notified the Senate that from June 7, 1720 to March 1, 1722 he returned a total of

4,965 families of [Russian] runaways, a total of 19,815 persons of both sexes. Flight to Bashkir lands renewed in 1724 among men fleeing the military levies. A newly baptized person[18] was sent secretly, in the guise of a runaway, to collect information about developments among the Bashkirs. The Bashkirs received him and said "Why are you living in Kazan? Soon there will be a war with the Russians. This war will be like no other [because] the Siberian and Yaik Cossacks will be with us."

Word came that the newly baptized [Bashkirs] were cleaning spears and sharpening arrows, that the Yasy Tatars refused to pay the soul tax and provide conscripts. The Bashkirs gathered in the Ufa district on Lake Berseven. The warlord Aldako attended with seven hundred men, as did the son of the traitor Sentek, who fled in 1707 to the Kirghiz. With him came five hundred men. Bashkirs and Tatars assembled from many directions at this lake. They wanted to lay siege to Ufa because of its three judges. They demanded that Ufa have only one judge and that the other two be handed over to them. They did not need these bribe-takers.

EXPLORING THE FAR EAST

Even as disorders erupted on the Asiatic steppe Peter continued to devote some attention to his most remote Asian borders on the shores of the Pacific Ocean. These were territories he needed to satisfy the calls of science, as stated by Leibniz,[19] to determine whether Asia was joined to America. On January 2, 1719 the geodesists among the explorers, Ivan Yevreinov and Fedor Luzhin, received this. "Travel to Tobolsk. Once you have assembled provisions proceed from Tobolsk to Kamchatka and to further points you have been instructed to visit. Describe these places and learn whether America is separated from Asia. Do this with care."

Yevreinov and Luzhin were unable to determine whether America and Asia were joined. Instead they merely brought Peter a map of the Kurile Islands in 1722. Not surprisingly Peter was dissatisfied. In 1725 he wrote an instruction to Captain Bering.[20] "(1) It would be worthwhile to construct a ship or two with decks in Kamchatka or some other place there. (2) Sail on these vessels to the land towards the north, and based upon current expectations (because nobody knows where it ends) see if it appears that this land is a part of America. (3) You are to search for the site where Asia and America split apart. When you arrive at a town in European hands, go ashore and take first-hand observations. Once you have charted the site on a map, come back."

VI

PETER'S FINAL DAYS AND THE SUCCESSION

PETER'S STATUTE ON THE SUCCESSION

So it was in this new and strange empire, in the west abutting the Baltic Sea, on its eastern borders resolving the question of whether Asia was connected to America. Many both in Russia and abroad were preoccupied with their own thoughts about the future of this empire, about who would succeed the great man who had conferred new prominence on his nation. His eldest son [Alexis] was a victim of this new prominence. The younger tsarevich, Peter, upon whom his father's hopes were concentrated, died soon thereafter.[1] A grandson remained, Alexis's son Peter, but it was impossible to draw any satisfactory conclusion regarding the character of this six-year-old child, and so it would remain. To proclaim the young Peter heir to the throne would arouse the hopes of those who bemoaned his father [Alexis] who personified the old order, endangering the opponents of Alexis, the very men on whom the emperor relied most heavily to support his policies.

At the beginning of 1722, during the celebration of the Treaty of Nystadt in the old capital, Peter published a statute on the inheritance to the throne. "The Absalom-like malice which emerged from our son Alexis's arrogance is well known.[2] His intentions were halted not by his repentance, but through God's mercy towards our entire fatherland. This situation arose for no other reason than because of an old custom that the elder son received the inheritance. He was also the single male [heir] in our family at that time. For that reason I did not want to countenance any fatherly punishment. I do not know why this ill-advised custom became so entrenched, for such traditions of inheritance in fact were voided by some people based upon the deliberations of wise parents. Moreover, even the Holy Scriptures provides instances of its being voided. We even see such events among our own ancestors (the example of Ivan III).[3]

"When this matter was considered previously, in 1714, we felt mercy for our subjects and wanted to prevent their homes from falling into ruin at the hands of unworthy heirs. We issued the statute stating that immoveable property is to be given to one son. Nevertheless at that time we granted parents discretion to decide which son would be considered the most worthy. We recognized that a younger son might then pass over an elder, but we believed that this was the most appropriate way of guaranteeing that the inheritance would not be chiselled away. We must maintain our guardianship over the integrity of the entire state, which with God's help now has expanded, as is apparent to everyone. Thus we must compose this statute so that inheritance of the throne is always at the discretion of the ruling sovereign, that is, whom he so wishes he shall designate as heir. Once I have designated an heir, having seen the meanness that has transpired, I shall abolish this obscene practice. Lest his children and future descendants fall into such malice as described above, I have placed this curb upon myself." Not satisfied by the considerations expressed in this manifesto, Peter ordered Feofan Prokopovich to draft a detailed approval of these measures. Feofan's work appeared under the title of *The Right of the Monarch's Will*.[4]

POPULAR RESISTANCE TO THE STATUTE

Peter wanted his subjects to take an oath recognizing his will but resistance arose in some quarters. The Old Believers interpreted matters this way. "He took the Swedish woman[5] for himself since the tsaritsa bore him children and ordered all of us to kiss the cross to the future sovereign, and everyone kissed the cross to the Swede, the upshot of which will see a Swede come to rule." "You see," said the monks, "the sovereign selects a foreigner known to the tsarevna to take her place. He has banished his grandson. No one has any information about him, so now they close ranks around whomever the sovereign deigns to choose."

The residents of Tara did not take the oath because their fury was aroused by Colonel Ivan Nemchinov, the cossack Ivan Podusha, Peter Bogachov, Dmitry Vikhorev and Vasily Isetsky. Colonel Batasov came to Tara from Tobolsk to investigate, with instructions that he not treat resisters harshly, nor force them to flee. As a consequence of this order Batasov freed Podusha from incarceration once he paid his bail, but moderation did not help. Bogachov, the leading instigator of the trouble, fled the town, and Nemchinov barricaded himself in his mansion along with sixty hostages. He allowed forty-nine to leave, then tried unsuccessfully to blow up the remainder with gunpowder. All of them were rescued, though Nemchinov and four others who suffered the most from the explosion died. The rest recovered.

IMPERIAL TITLES AND TERMS OF INHERITANCE

The manifesto naming Grand Duke Peter Alekseevich as successor granted him this right only upon the approval of his grandfather, contingent upon his favoring the heir. If he happened not to like him, would Peter choose someone totally unknown? In the churches the tsar's family was commemorated in this formula. "Our most pious sovereign Peter the Great, the all-Russian emperor and autocrat, our most pious sovereign Empress Catherine Alekseevna, the sovereign ladies the tsarevnas, the lady Tsaritsa and Grand Duchess Praskovia Feodorovna, and the lord and master Grand Duke Peter Alekseevich, and the ladies tsarevnas the grand princesses."[6] Grand Duke Peter stood lower than his aunts the tsarevnas. People therefore naturally turned their attention to Peter's daughters, all the more so because they knew the influence Empress Catherine wielded over her husband. Thus the issue of the marriages of the tsesarevnas became a question of the utmost importance.

Not only Russians worried about this. The Viennese too considered it in their interest and their obligation to support the rights of Grand Duke Peter [Alekseevich], the blood nephew of the empress of the Holy Roman empire on his mother's side.[7] The Austrian ambassador arrived at the court of St. Petersburg with a remonstrance alleging that Grand Duke Peter did not receive a proper upbringing, that he lived in a palace surrounded by women. Consequently he could not acquire the necessary training. It concluded from this circumstance that his imperial majesty did not want to name him as the heir to the throne. Could any good come of this, the note inquired, in addition to the fact that it would lead to a rupture in the alliance between the two empires? The ambassador further informed the court that he heard that Tsarevna Anna Petrovna would marry Alexander Naryshkin,[8] whom the emperor then would name as his successor, and that Tsarevna Elizabeth would marry the duke of Holstein.[9]

The rumor about Tsarevna Anna's marriage to Alexander Naryshkin, which also appeared in the foreign press, turned out to be false. Peter went to great efforts to marry off the younger tsarevna to the king of France, long delaying his consent for the elder tsarevna to wed the duke of Holstein. Though the duke remained in Russia after the Peace of Nystadt, Peter kept silent about a wedding. The emperor was otherwise occupied with the distant Persian campaign and Catherine, who was well disposed toward the duke, accompanied him. The duke consequently was not announced as the fiancé.

DUKE OF HOLSTEIN'S BETROTHAL TO GRAND DUCHESS ANNA

Bassewitz [the Holstein privy councillor] addressed a letter to Peter. "Your imperial majesty, please consider most mercifully how contented and profoundly glad I was when his royal highness [the duke of Holstein] ordered me to arrange these affairs, and your majesty gave me his assurances in Vienna through General Yaguzhinsky. Now with particular sadness I see how his royal highness earnestly grieves that your majesty hesitates to permit him to wed one of the sovereign tsarevnas. What can be holding your imperial majesty back from concluding this union? His family is one of the most distinguished among the ruling houses. Thank God he is reasonably intelligent, exhibits no duplicity, and his fear of God and humility promise the tsarevna a very desirable life. His rights to the crown and principality are manifest, for the Holy Roman emperor will never sway from his guarantee regarding Holstein.[10]

"There is no doubt that the emperor would rather see the Swedish crown resting on the head of his royal highness than that of the prince of Hesse.[11] If your imperial majesty might arrange a peace with the English king, England would support the compromise of Bremen and Verden,[12] and assist his royal highness in every possible way in the Schleswig and Swedish matters. The Prussian court will observe the duke's will since he has given his consent on the matter of Pomerania. Holland wishes to assist the duke, as does the Polish king. Cardinal Dubois has promised the duke's envoy that France is prepared to assist the duke the moment your majesty conveys the decree to his ambassadors. The Swedish nation's love for his royal majesty is rather well known in France. Were they to learn that the duke has become your majesty's son-in-law, they would offer even stronger help in hopes of future friendship. In these circumstances a large proportion of states, as well as the notable people in Sweden who otherwise might not be inclined toward the duke, would approve of him.

"Your imperial majesty can conclude this important and glorious matter without war. Your majesty, as a wise monarch, knows that all states envy your increasing power, which upon the death of your majesty they will attempt to undercut. If on the other hand your majesty or your heir enters into an alliance with Sweden the enmity of the whole world would be in vain. This alliance can be effected best through the duke, for many there are on his side. Many others greatly fear lest your majesty abandon his son-in-law at this dangerous time. History suggests that a small army is sufficient to undermine opponents in a country where many people of goodwill are found.[13] In the Polish Sejm a hundred thousand rubles can accomplish much. We are ready and willing to give this amount.

"The residents of Lifland and Estland are permanently obliged to act according to your majesty's will. If your imperial majesty will grant one tsarevna to his royal majesty, the duke's supporters in Sweden may display their loyalty more freely. Should your majesty deem it unprofitable to yield the elder tsarevna, the duke shall be content with the younger. As far as I could observe, the duke admires the qualities of both sovereign tsarevnas sincerely, but it would be more suitable and better, because of his age, for him to marry the elder tsarevna.

"Since hitherto, in spite of numerous attempts, I have not had the happiness of receiving your fatherly consent to a marriage union with her highness the tsarevna, once again most submissively I express to you the painful distress that grows within me. I hope for a most merciful and expeditious hearing because this continued silence compels me to fear that I have suffered irretrievable loss. I cannot remain in the dark any longer."

"Most illustrious duke," Peter responded, "dear loving nephew! I have received your two letters, the one from you directly, the other from your ambassador Bassewitz. These discuss two matters. The first describes our house's relationship to you, and the other requests that I assist you in your affairs. Many powerful individuals have expressed their eagerness for us to act on your behalf. On the second issue let me answer that I, too, along with these potentates, am prepared to offer my entire willingness and to labor in all possible ways in that matter. As regards the betrothal, I am not ill-disposed. I want to be accommodating because I know your good character rather well, and I love you with all my heart. Yet I cannot commit myself until your affairs are brought into a genuinely better state because were I to arrange a betrothal now I might at some time be compelled to do something contrary to the will and well-being of my fatherland, which is the basis of my life."

Only in 1724 when, by means of an alliance between Russia and Sweden, the duke's affairs improved, did Peter give his consent to the duke's marriage to his elder daughter [Anna]. In July, during a conference between Peter and his ambassadors, a report was read about the duke of Holstein, about the doubts which Sweden still harbored regarding his betrothal to one of the tsarevnas, and about the intrigues in Sweden against the duke. Sweden wished to know how to act in the matter of the duke of Holstein so as to satisfy the treaty of alliance just concluded. After lengthy deliberations Peter informed Stockholm that he very much wished for one of his daughters to enter into a marriage with the duke of Holstein. In the interests of the duke it would be better to hold discussions at the Russian court and ensure that this matter resided first and foremost in the hands of the Russian sovereign. He concluded that he wished to deliberate further on this subject.

On November 24, the empress's nameday,[14] the betrothal of Tsarevna Anna and the duke was announced. On the basis of the new law which reserved the right to appoint a successor to the throne to the reigning sovereign, the tsarevna had to reject as part of the marriage contract all claims for herself and her descendants to the Russian throne.[15] The duke supported this renunciation and the pact was cemented by an oath of the bride and groom. The duke undertook to maintain his bride in the Greek confession, and to build and maintain a church in their future dwellings "according to the Greek custom." The princes born from this marriage were to be raised in the Lutheran faith, the princesses in the faith and confession of the Greek church.

The father of the bride promised to supply his "dear, sweet daughter" clothing, gems,[16] dresses and, beyond that, to give a dowry[17] of three hundred thousand rubles. The duke was obligated to make available to his "dear, loving spouse" an additional three hundred thousand rubles and to give her five percent of it annually. He also was required to give a "morning gift"[18] of fifty thousand efimoks, paid annually in installments of five percent until that sum was reached. Finally, he was to pay his spouse six thousand rubles annually for her coffers and expenses. Thus the future duchess received in all twenty-three thousand rubles per year and, as security for this income, the duke gave her mortgages for a specified number of plots of land. The duke also was to maintain his bride's servants at court. In the event of the duke's death the widowed duchess received the lands of Trittau and Rheinbeck together with properties in its environs sufficient to provide fifty thousand efimoks of clear income. If the duke gained the Swedish throne, upon his accession he was obliged to present his spouse everything appropriate for the consort of a king of Sweden.

EMPRESS CATHERINE

Peter also wanted to strengthen the rights of his own wife. Catherine, as always exercised great influence over her husband and, as before, everyone who fell into disfavor turned to her, as did those with some need or requests to intercede with the sovereign. As was her custom she willingly heeded these requests, willingly lent them the sense of her enduring and beneficial influence. This influence also extended to one line of the ruling house, that of Tsar Ivan Alekseevich. Ivan's widow, Tsaritsa Praskovia Fedorovna, was distinguished in all matters by her gentle nature, as witnessed by her treatment of the palace guard in the Secret Chancellery.[19]

Peter had granted her the island of Petrovsky, which previously belonged to Tsarevich Alexis's children, but insisted that the garden, which had belonged to Alexis's wife and which was separated from the island by a channel, was to remain with his grandchildren. Tsaritsa Praskovia held onto the garden in violation of this decree. Menshikov and Peter Apraksin made representations to her about the illegality of this action, to no avail. She refused to listen to anyone, making it necessary to write to Catherine about this matter. Previously Catherine had to mollify Tsaritsa Praskovia's anger at Peter Bestuzhev, who was then in the employ of Tsarevna Anna Ivanovna, the duchess of Courland. Perhaps on account of Bestuzhev, Tsaritsa Praskovia was also furious at her own daughter Anna Ivanovna.

Empress Catherine II recounted that in her assessment Tsaritsa Praskovia was so angry at her daughters, Catherine and Anna, that on her deathbed she damned them and their descendants. This legend has some foundation, though the affair was exaggerated by the misfortunes subsequently befalling Tsarevna Catherine Ivanovna's descendants.[20] In addition, perhaps they exaggerated with the hope that they might thereby drive a wedge between the glorious successors of Peter the Great.

We have no knowledge about Tsaritsa Praskovia's rage against her daughter Catherine, or her anger against Anna. This matter ended when the mother offered her forgiveness after the intercession of Empress Catherine. Tsaritsa Praskovia's deathbed letter to her daughter Anna has come down to us. "My most loving Tsarevna Anna Ivanovna! Because now the disease spreads within me by the hour, and with it the suffering, I have already despaired of life. I shall remember in this letter how you prayed for me to the Lord God. If my maker wills that I depart this earth and be separated from you, do not forget me in your reflections. I also have heard from my dearest sister-in-law, the sovereign Empress Catherine Alekseevna, that you find yourself in great doubt, supposedly over a ban or some spoken damnation from me. In this matter you now need have no doubt that I absolve you of everything for the sake of her majesty, my dearest sovereign sister-in-law, forgiving you in everything even though you may have sinned against me."

When Peter took the title of emperor a question arose concerning the titles which his spouse and children would receive. On December 23, 1721 the Synod and Senate, while in Moscow, conferred in the Synod's Sacristy Chapel. Since his majesty held the title of emperor and autocrat of all Russia it was consistent to confer a title on the sovereign tsaritsa and his majesty's children. They deliberated over this for a long time then agreed to call her majesty "empress" or "tsesareva," and the children "tsesarevna." They now resolved to exclude the formulation used in Catherine's title over the past several years "most serene, elect and esteemed." In places where the titles of the grand duke (Peter Alekseevich) and tsarevnas employed "nobility"[21] it was now acknowledged more accurate to use the expression "lord and master."[22] Otherwise it was demeaning to apply the title "nobility" to their highnesses according to current usage since "nobility" also was granted to the service gentry.

Peter concurred with this resolution, only instead of tsesareva he ordered that Catherine be termed "the empress her majesty the tsesarevna." In 1723 Peter reasserted his intention to have Catherine crowned and on November 15 a manifesto was signed. "Because everyone knows that all Christian states without exception observe the custom in which potentates crown their spouses, there being no question that even in the antiquity of the Orthodox Greek emperors this practice was observed many times (examples followed); and, because it is known that the past twenty-one years of war have witnessed so many trials and the most deathly fears about the well-being of our own person, we suggest that with God's help these tribulations for our fatherland have indeed come to an end, that Russia never before has experienced such a true and profitable peace, and that in all matters it has never known such glory.

"In these aforementioned labors of ours, our most loving spouse, the sovereign Empress Catherine, has been an eminent helpmeet. This is without question. Even during many military activities, notwithstanding her feminine delicacy, she was there with us by sheer force of will, assisting as much as she could. During the Pruth campaign against the Turks she conducted herself with the dignity of a man even in times of despair, not behaving like a woman. The whole army knows of this and through it undoubtedly the entire realm does as well. In light of this fact the title of autocrat[23] which God has granted us shall be granted to our spouse for these and other labors."

THE MONS AFFAIR

The coronation of Catherine culminated in Moscow with great fanfare on May 7, 1724. Then within half a year Catherine experienced a very unpleasant situation when her lover and the administrator of her chancellery of landed estates, Chamberlain Mons, brother of the well-known Anna Mons,[24] was apprehended and executed. On November 14, 1724 the Superior Court sentenced Mons to death for several crimes. (1) He seized the hamlet of Orsha and some villages from Tsarevna Praskovia Ivanovna in the name of the office overseeing the empress's patrimonial lands, taking the quitrent for himself. (2) He dispatched the former procurator of the Voronezh superior[25] court, Kutuzov, to seize that village, also sending him to the empress's patrimonial lands in Nizhny Novgorod for an investigation without prior permission from the Senate. (3) He took four hundred rubles from the peasant Solenikov of the village of Toninskoe because Solenikov had a grooming stable in a village belonging to his majesty.

This Solenikov turned out not to be a peasant, but a townsman. Mons's sister Matryona Balk was accused alongside Mons. She was beaten with a knout and exiled to Tobolsk. Also accused was Mons's secretary Stoletov, who after the knout was exiled to ten years' hard labor in Rogervik, and the noted fool, the gentleman of the bedchamber Ivan Balakirev, who was beaten with sticks and exiled to Rogervik for three years. The following explanation of the verdict was read to Balakirev. "Because after disappearing from service and from engineering classes you caused all this folly, and then through William Mons you were placed at the court of his imperial majesty where you served William Mons and Yegor Stoletov in accepting bribes."

PETER'S FAILING HEALTH AND DEATH

Added to these disagreeable experiences with Mons were unpleasant activities involving the incorrigible Menshikov, whom Peter was obliged to remove from the presidency of the War College and replace with Prince Repnin. Makarov and members of the upper court also were accused of taking bribes. All of this worked against Peter's health, and he had lived only fifty-three years. In spite of frequent illness and his long-established practice of referring to himself as an old man, the emperor hoped to live still longer and to arrange his monumental bequest in the interests of the Russian state. Yet his days already were running out. No one's constitution long could withstand the pace of such intense activity.

When Peter came to Petersburg in March 1723 after returning from Persia he appeared much healthier than prior to the campaign. In the summer of 1724 he grew seriously ill, although in the second half of September he appeared to recuperate, taking walks at times in his gardens and swimming in the Neva. On November 22 he suffered a serious attack. It was said that he emerged from it in such a temper that he pounded nails into the medical attendants, and verbally abused them, calling them asses. Then he recovered again. On September 29 he was present at the launching of a frigate, where he told the Dutch envoy Wilde that he felt somewhat weaker. Even so, at the beginning of October he travelled to inspect the Ladoga canal against the advice of his doctor Blümentrost. Then he visited the Olonetsk iron factories, where he forged with his own hands an iron band weighing three puds.

From there Peter headed to Staraia Rusa to oversee the salt works, then early in November he travelled by water to Petersburg. At the little town of Lakhta, seeing a boat carrying soldiers from Kronstadt run aground, he could not restrain himself. He personally helped pull the boat off of the shoal and save the people, which meant he stood waist-deep in the water. His seizures quickly returned. Peter arrived in Petersburg ill. This time he could not recover.

The Mons affair could not expect to attract much of his attention in the midst of this convalescence. Peter now was doing very little work, although he appeared in public as he normally would. On January 17, 1725 the illness intensified. Peter ordered a makeshift altar placed near his bed. On January 22 he made his confession and took the sacrament from his confessor. The life force began to leave the sick emperor, who no longer screamed from the severe pain as previously, but merely moaned.

On the twenty-sixth he took a turn for the worse. All convicts were freed from hard labor, pardoned except for those convicted under the first two articles [of the military statute] and of murder. That same day the last rites over the ailing tsar were pronounced. The next day, the twenty-seventh, all sentenced to death or to hard labor according to the Articles of

War were pardoned, save those convicted according to the first two points, murderers, and those guilty of repeated theft. Also pardoned were nobles who had not reported for duty according to the designated terms of service. On that very day, at the end of the second hour, Peter demanded some paper. He began to write, then the pen fell from his hands. From what he had written they could make out only the words "give out everything... ." He then ordered his daughter Anna Petrovna be summoned to write down what he dictated, but when she approached he could not utter a word.

The next day, January 28, shortly after five in the morning, Peter the Great was no more. Catherine remained with him almost continuously. She closed his eyes for him.

VII

EPILOGUE

In the throes of these frightful physical sufferings, with full recognition of his human frailty, and yearning for the solace of peace with God, this greatest of historical figures passed away. We have pointed out earlier that the entire previous history [of Russia] paved the way for Peter's activity, that his endeavors eclipsed Russia's prior history, how the nation demanded them even at the cost of traversing this perilous path of upheaval by expending extraordinary effort to abandon despair for a new road, a new life. This in no way diminishes the greatness of the man, who by completing such a difficult feat lent a strong hand to a great nation. By the uncommon force of his will, which drained his every ounce of strength, he gave direction to this movement.

History tells of no other nation which underwent such a monumental and complicated reorganization, accompanied by such enormous consequences, for its domestic life and for the community of nations. Western nations and Western historians, with their ingrained prejudices regarding the exclusive supremacy in modern history of the Germanic tribe, with their very understandable fear of losing their monopoly of historical interpretation, have difficulty with dealing with the complexity, indeed the impossibility, of studying Russia dispassionately and impartially, its present and past. They cannot, do not want to deem worthy of world-historical significance the events transpiring in Eastern Europe during the first quarter of the eighteenth century.

Nevertheless they have been obliged to turn their attention to the outcome of these events, to the decisive influence of Russia on the fate of Europe and consequently of the entire world. Moreover they have had to recognize Russia as representative of the Slavic tribe, by which the monopoly of the German tribe was destroyed. This is the source of all the anger and the effort to minimize the significance of the Slavic tribe and the Russian nation, to insinuate fear of a new actor's ambition, to instill the idea of threat to the civilized West gathering from the East. These unfriendly attitudes towards Russia expressed in the West and by representatives of its scholarship suggest all the more how significant Russia is, how significant Peter's actions were, in joining both halves of Europe together in common activity.

RUSSIAN ASSESSMENTS OF PETER

Let us leave the foreigners and turn to our own. In the consciousness of the Russian nation the Petrine upheaval, it stands to reason, represents a very important turn of events and has stimulated much scholarly excitement. The reverential and quasi-religious adoration of the Reformer's activity, which prevailed for a long time after his death, elicited a reaction late in the eighteenth century. This opposition was articulated as a progressive movement reflecting the moral and cultural development of the Russian nation. Amidst conditions grown familiar, new demands and outlooks were arising, a process whereby the historical life of a nation is nourished.[1] Adulation of Peter the Great's activity, the sanctification with which the fruits of his activity were regarded, naturally inhibited the progressive movement by rejecting every challenge as improper.[2]

Usually it is considered necessary to deny the propriety of the old in order to defend the claim of the new. In this way [reformers] strive to strip away the old, to demean its significance. Confronted by the opposition of the worshipers of the old, their opponents endeavor to chide them so as to smash the idol, desanctify the martyr and demolish the temple. They then erect another temple in its place, and install another idol. In this case Russia's progressives were not content with this outcome in relating Peter's activities to the new activities of their own time. For them it was not enough to say "Peter the Great created the body, Catherine the

Great gave it a soul." They set about reproaching Peter by maintaining that even for his own time he behaved improperly and illegally, transforming a better antiquity into a worse modernity.

The extreme quality of this critique did not resonate widely although the eighteenth century did bequeath to the nineteenth a multi-volume panegyric to the activity of the father of the fatherland. Golikov's book then gave way to Boltin's,[3] which concluded with sharp jibes against the Reformer's activities. The underlying tendency of Golikov's work, his attempts to endow everything his hero did with eternal approval, suggests that in the second half of the eighteenth century Russian thought was trying to come to terms with an epitome of greatness, and contrary views collided.

In the nineteenth century once again new circumstances of national life evoked opposing views of Peter's activities. The radical nature of the French revolution, the shock to the powers of Europe, the violence practiced against the nations which the French empire brought forth in the wake of the revolution and fear of revived revolutionary movements,[4] compelled Russian thinkers in general to treat all rapid assaults on the old with hostility. Furthermore the legacy of the French revolution reinforced the conservative inclinations which characterize especially the author of *A History of the Russian State* [Karamzin], who preferred Ivan III to Peter the Great.[5] Other arguments soon appeared which evinced an outlook in literature hostile to the deeds of the Reformer.

Above all, eighteenth-century thinkers had the man in mind, abstractly considered, along with his abstract laws. The nineteenth century opposed this tendency, which it thought one-sided. The anger the French empire stirred among the nations inspired nationalist sentiment, the nations throwing themselves into the study of their own pasts with the aim of clarifying and reinforcing their own national consciousness.

This practice even led to the supremacy of the principle of nationalism, in the name of which important events occurred and still occur in our own time. This tendency, in its essence high-minded and beneficent, gave rise in extreme forms to Germanophilism in the West and to Slavophilism in Russia.[6] The Petrine upheaval proclaimed the inadequacy of the ways of Old Russia, of the purely national way of life, and demanded that the nation adopt the institutions and customs of other nations. Such an upheaval could not arouse much sympathy from people who served with great enthusiasm and were inspired by the principles of rulership of their own time. This [Slavophile] outlook combined the view, taken to extremes, of the significance of the popular masses, without defining specific roles in terms of their relationship to historical representatives. Peter loomed as a frightful despot who, managing affairs by his arbitrary will and according to his personal outlook, violently compelled part of his nation, the upper strata of society, to exchange their ancient ancestral life for new and alien customs and ways. At the same time the lower strata, having rendered great and sacred service to the fatherland, remained true to the old ways. Thus a split developed between the upper and lower strata of the population which, in this [Slavophile] view, constituted the main harm Peter's reign brought to the Russian land.

THE JUDGMENT OF SCHOLARSHIP

Scholarship cannot accept this second protest against Peter's activities, this nineteenth-century protest. We have a complete right to be sympathetic towards the radical transformation of the nation's life. Storms do clear the air, though the devastation they leave behind shows that cleansing is bought at a heavy price. Severe illnesses call for strong medicine. We know that pre-Petrine Russia suffered many illnesses, and particular contours of the reform era reflect this fact even more. The body politic recovered, gaining the means to extend its life, which proved rich in powerful endeavors. Nevertheless the historian falls into indefensible one-sidedness were he not to acknowledge that these strong means usually leave behind unwelcome consequences for the organism. The Petrine epoch of reform is no exception.

It is not the historian's business to celebrate unconditionally all features of this epoch, or to approve unequivocally all means employed by the Reformer for treating Russia's chronic ailments. In presenting flesh-and-blood activity and obliged to include its darker side the historian also has the right to portray Peter's activity as that of a great man who served more than others his nation and humanity.

A time of upheavals is troubling for a nation. Such was the case for the era of reform. Complaints against great burdens resounded from all sides, not without reason. A Russian had no respite from mobilization, from heavy and continuous military service in the infantry and the new navy, from forcing workers into new and burdensome forms of labor in remote and unfamiliar places, from forced schooling and assignment abroad to study. For the army and navy, for work, schools and hospitals, for maintaining diplomats and diplomatic bribes money was essential, but poverty-stricken Russia had no money. Burdensome taxes in cash and in kind weighed down everyone. When necessary the state deducted taxes from wages. Many were ruined by having to build homes in Petersburg.

Having taken all that could be taken, the government farmed out the rest. In this poor nation oak caskets became an object of luxury. These the government appropriated and sold at a high price. The Old Believers paid double taxation. Those with beards paid fines for them. Peter had a prescription for everything: look for ore, look for paint, supply *monsters*,[7] tend your sheep not like before, dress the skins, establish new kinds of courts, weave no more narrow linen, take your goods to the West not the North. Drowning in these new government offices and new courts people did not know where to turn. The people in these offices and courts knew nothing about dealing with the new terms of business and circulated papers from one office to another, producing horrendous bureaucratic delays. New forms of poverty cropped up as the standing armed forces were imposed upon the civilian population.

Some people escaped burdensome service, but not everyone could. The laws threatened harsh punishment to the disobedient. An illiterate nobleman could not marry. Beneath the new French fashions and wigs remained the old crude habits. The same disregard for human dignity in one's self and in others lived on, the ugliest example of which was the boisterousness (drunkenness) with which every feast must end. Women were introduced into male society but unshielded by the necessary respect for their sex, for their obligations and pregnancy, and compelled to drink past the point of moderation.

Members of the highest institutions feuded, insulting one another in the crudest manner. Bribery was as prevalent as ever. As before, the weak fell to the strong and, as before, a man supposedly free permitted himself every indulgence when dealing with his peasant, the power of the well-born over the common people.

This is only one side of the picture. Fortunately there is another. The nation was passing through a difficult school. A strict teacher does not hesitate to punish the shiftless and those who violate the statutes, but matters do not end with threats and punishments. The nation indeed was learning, not just arithmetic and geometry, not just in schools only, whether Russian or foreign. The nation was learning civic responsibilities and civic activity. In publishing every important regulation and introducing important reform the legislator explained why he did so, why the new was better than the old.

A Russian received instructions of this kind for the first time. What seem to us now as simple and accessible issues were confronted by our forebears for the first time in the Petrine decrees and manifestos. For the first time the thinking of the Russian individual was aroused, his attention directed to vital questions of the state and social fabric. Whether he was sympathetic or unsympathetic to the words and deeds of the tsar, he nevertheless thought about those words and deeds, and they permanently awakened the Russian individual. What could undo society more completely than a nation incapable of development?

These were the troubling features of the era of reform, the reasons for taking only brief pauses, which strove to develop the forces of a young and strong nation, asleep for so long and in need of a firm push to arouse it. Why study? At the top sat the Governing Senate, the Synod, the ubiquitous collegial structure, the advantage of which was detailed in the Ecclesiastical Statute. The principle of differentiation was everywhere. The industrial estate [that is, merchants and factory owners] was withdrawn from the purview of the military governor and granted administrative autonomy. Peter's entire system was directed against the basic ills from which ancient Russia suffered, namely dispersal of resources, failure to consider matters in their totality, absence of self-reliance, lack of initiative.

These failings also allowed institutions and people to employ force to rise rather easily through ranks which were otherwise closed, to refuse to develop, to evade limitations imposed upon them, to think in everything only of themselves. Earlier the tsar's council suffered from these shortcomings, causing Peter to establish the Senate, to which people swore an oath, and whose decrees must be heeded as were the tsar's. Peter was not jealous of his own authority, nor did he try to limit the Senate. On the contrary, he regularly and unceremoniously demanded that the Senate take advantage of its authority and indeed govern. Peter's reproaches and messages to the Senate related to its slow pace, its inertia, its absence of order, its inability to compel others to execute its decisions in a timely manner.

THE LEGACY OF STATE BUILDING

Previously when a Russian received an order from the government he went straight to the man who wielded the authority. He at first refused to believe the order, then so feared taking even the slightest step that he swaddled himself like a baby in detailed and lengthy instructions. Every new situation not specified in the instruction caused the grown-up baby to demand a written interpolation. This habit of demanding specifics of decrees greatly angered Peter, as we have seen. "Use your own best judgment," wrote Peter to those requesting details of decrees. "How can I show you from so far away?"

Whether he had seen it in the West, or whether recommended by Leibniz, Peter employed collegial organization everywhere as the most potent means of teaching Russian people how to act freely and in common. Institutions moved beyond relying on appointed individuals. Atop them all the edifice of a state was constructed, the real significance of which Russians learned for the first time when they were required to swear an oath to it. We shall not dwell on this picture, as if it were the last. We know very well that both during and after Peter's reign there was strong opposition to his system, that the practice of deferring to certain well-situated notables took precedence, and that the expression *gentlemen of the Senate*[8] soon came to be changed to the *gentlemen senate*.[9]

Nevertheless the idea of a single overarching state structure did not disappear once it was brought to life and assimilated by the institutions, no matter the numerous desires to part from it. Its forms and contents served as constant reminders and it aroused people to demand its return. Even as a temple without worshipers summons one to prayer, so too everything introduced by this single human being stands in his name, and long gave shape to future activities.

There is no need to say very much about the groundlessness of the view that old customs strongly forged in ancient Russia began to disappear simply as a consequence of reform. Powerful habits do not soon give way to even the most powerful contravening forces. It stands to reason they certainly do not yield during times most beneficial to them. Had Russia's commercial elements grown accustomed to acting in concert in ancient Russia they would not have presented such a sorry spectacle in Peter's town assemblies and magistracies. There the rich rode roughshod over the poor, office holders solicited bribes and ignored their responsibilities. This set of practices was rooted in ancient Russia. These ancient customs produced the abuses which evoked such complaints in the towns. They nurtured the behavior that led the guilty to request government protection against their clamorous peasants. Complaints poured forth against the military governors' oppressive behavior.

The government did everything it could by freeing the townsmen from the military governors, granting them administrative autonomy. The government might institute different and better forms, and it did so, but it was unable suddenly to breathe life into municipal administrative autonomy. This could grow only gradually if it did not exist already. It soon was apparent that it did not exist. If the people then asked why industrialists were treated differently than other urban estates let the mayors of Kolomna, with whom other estates got along so well, provide the answer. The possibility of common undertakings among people of varied social circles was influenced favorably by a gradual but permanent evolution of the spirit of Peter the Great's system. This potential could have developed even sooner, had the Russian people followed his system steadfastly.

Peter placed the significance of the state on display. He seemingly compelled the nation to sacrifice notable martyrs to this new deity by offering himself as an example. He took steps to ensure that the nation's character was not undermined while receiving the judicious development it needed. In this respect the education which Peter introduced occupies first place because it familiarized Russia with a development in which other nations outstripped ours.

THE ENDURANCE OF CLANS

We know that pre-Petrine Russia had strong family alliances. Their persistence is explained easily by circumstances in a society unable to offer its members adequate security, which then must be sought in private alliances. These began with the natural blood alliance of members of a single family. The elder, as we know, protected the younger. In return the senior ruled the junior and answered for them to the government.

Everywhere throughout society no Russian ever acted on his own, rather always with his brothers and nephews. The absence of clan or family until very recently was seen as a sign of extreme social vulnerability. It was understood that the family structure inhibited the development of the individual, that the crown could not put personal merit before clan rights. Jealous in the extreme in defending family honor, the ancient Russian was indifferent to personal honor. By the end of the seventeenth century the demands of the crown increased to such an extent that the integral clan could not stand its ground. Moreover elimination of the rule of precedence delivered a strong blow to family alliances among servicemen in the upper strata of society. The Petrine reforms then delivered the final blow by rewarding personal merit in promoting people who thereby rose infinitely higher than their "old parents" (that is, their relatives), and by introducing a large number of foreigners into service. The new men found it profitable to act as if they had no clan, and many quite willingly concealed their foreign origins. A blow was delivered as well to family alliances among the relatively low strata of the population through introduction of the soul tax. The earlier expression "so-and-so with his brothers and nephews" disappeared because every brother and nephew now paid for himself individually as a separate, independent person.

Not only did old clan relations disappear. Even in the immediate family, where children were obliged to defer to their parents, Peter recognized the rights of the individual by prescribing that marriages be entered with the consent of the parties, rather than the arbitrary will of the parents. The right of the individual was recognized even among the serf population because the landlord had to swear not force his peasants into marriage against their will. We have heard the impartial account of a contemporary, a Russian,[10] about the appalling state of our servicemen in the seventeenth and at the beginning of the eighteenth centuries, about their disinterest in honor. They had a shameful saying "Wanting to run away may not be honorable, but it's good for your health." Under Peter these sayings passed away. Peter himself testified that during the second half of the Northern War desertions under fire ceased. Finally, the individuality of women gained recognition as a consequence of their emancipation from the women's quarters.[11]

THE HARSH SCHOOL OF REFORM

Thus were the Russian people reared in the harsh school of reform! The horrific burdens and deprivations all served a purpose. A general program was traced out for very many years to come, traced not on paper but upon the soil, which now was compelled to open its riches to the Russian whose learning granted him right to possess it. On the sea a Russian navy took shape. The rivers now were linked by canals. This program was traced in the state by new institutions and regulations. It was traced upon the nation through education, which broadened its intellectual horizons through the rich storehouse of knowledge the West threw open to it. A new world was established within Russia itself. A large portion of what was accomplished was only preliminary. Other portions existed in rough outline, for much of the rest only materials were readied, only instructions were drafted. Therefore we have termed the activities of the reform era "a program," one which Russia is still fulfilling even now and will continue to fulfill, deviation from which always leads to unhappy consequences.[12]

The proliferation of views and judgements for and against, opinions about how to deal with this or that matter remaining from the reform era, constituted one of the most beneficial consequences of the intellectual awakening which enabled the Russian nation to enter a new life and fulfill the Reformer's program. The potential for this ferment was shaped especially by the numerous and varied elements of progress and related reforms of the state necessary to free itself from the stagnation in which it found itself, a stagnation which provided no means for development. This organism of the state became a unified whole. Once reform was initiated in one organ, its evolution was inevitable in another.

Even had it been possible [to arrest reform] it would have proved extremely harmful. Certainly the historian must acknowledge that these multifarious reforms did bring some harm, which nevertheless was a necessary consequence of the means employed for achieving the reforms. A lack of preparation afflicted both rulers and ruled, beginning with the chief architect, Peter himself, in whom with all due respect for his genius we must be mindful of the man, his substance, his real limitations. We should also acknowledge that Russia was sent at this time a man capable of making hard choices. In particular he opted for a multi-faceted and aggressive reorganization which made the Russian an apprentice to Western Europe, yet simultaneously made him an adult and strong actor in political life overall. This achievement enabled Russia to pursue its own domestic development without fear of foreign intrusions. This was politically significant on the broad historical stage and a necessary condition for development domestically.

A Russian could accept gracefully the importance of his apprenticeship only as a means of achieving rapid success in learning and as a path to sustaining the greatness and strength enveloping Russia and its great tsar. Apprenticeship permitted Russians to continue to have pride and faith in their own nation, which they loved so deeply, and which they would never exchange for any other. Never had one nation carried out a feat of such magnitude as did Russia in the first quarter of the eighteenth century. The nation was little known on the historical stage, poor, weak, a non-participant in the general life of Europe. By incredible effort and frightful sufferings the nation yielded to Peter's demands. It then emerged as a powerful entity without aggressive intentions, once it established the tranquility necessary for the development of its domestic life.

We have every right to call the man who led the nation in achieving this feat the greatest of all historical personages because no other can have greater significance in the history of civilization.

In general, Peter was not a vainglorious conqueror. In this quality he was the perfect representative of his nation, which was not aggressive innately or by the conditions of its historical life. Peter's genius was conveyed in his clear articulation of the state of his nation and of himself as the leader of that nation. He recognized that he was obliged to raise a weak, impoverished, almost unknown nation out of this sorry state by civilizing it. The difficulty of the enterprise became clear to him in all its fullness upon his return from abroad. He could compare what he saw in the West with what he found in a Russia which confronted him with the musketeers' revolt.[13] He was sorely tempted to abandon the whole program of reforms yet overcame this temptation, in full assurance of the moral forces of his own nation. These he never tarried in summoning to a great deed, to endure sufferings and privations of every kind, showing himself as an example in all of this.

Once he saw clearly that Russia must pass through a difficult school Peter did not spare it suffering and a demeaning apprenticeship. At the same time he balanced this disadvantageous status with glory and greatness. Thereby the people became productive, Russia's political importance was established and the means to sustain it created.

A difficult task confronted Peter. To educate Russians it was necessary to summon foreign instructors who quite naturally attempted to dominate their apprentices. This was demeaning to the apprentices, whom Peter wanted to transform into master craftsmen forthwith. Peter resisted the temptation to heed suggestions that his success depended entirely upon experienced and competent men who were foreigners. He wanted his own people, Russians, to acquire practical experience and competence even at the cost of great losses and major inconveniences.

We have noted how he hastened to rid himself of a foreign field marshal.[14] Further we have observed that he appointed Russians to all the highest positions, how he gave only second rank to foreigners. We have observed also how Peter was rewarded for his faith in his own nation, for his devotion to it. Moreover, Peter employed uncommon caution in resolving the delicate task of reorganizing the church by knowing how to stay just inside the necessary boundaries. He eliminated one-man administration and introduced a collegial or conciliar one corresponding fully to the spirit of the Eastern church. One of Peter's main concerns was to improve the Russian clergy through education. Contrary to his strong and understandable aversion for the monastic clergy he did not abolish it as had Henry VIII of England. Rather he tried to lead the monastic clergy into activities corresponding more closely to its character.

ASSESSING PETER THE MAN

From the perspective characterizing our study of the era of reform we ought to be amazed by the moral and physical powers of the Reformer. He cultivated these powers by exercising them. We do not know of another historical personage whose sphere of activity was so broad. Born with a mind uncommonly open to stimulation, sensitive to everything, Peter cultivated this sensitivity to a higher level. From early childhood he paid attention and accustomed himself to life around him, without allowing himself to be influenced or limited by anyone. He was stimulated by a society standing at the brink of upheaval, wavering between two directions, worried already by questions of the old and the new. This was at a time when the vanguard of the West, the Foreign Quarter,[15] was already visible amidst old Moscow. Peter had the nature of an old Russian epic hero,[16] he loved broad vistas and simplicity. Except for his abiding inclination for the sea he displayed no real self-consciousness. The epic heroes of old Rus made their way on the wide steppe, while the new strove on the high seas. He considered land enclosed by mountains disagreeable and ponderous. Thus he complained to his wife about the location of Carlsbad. "This place affords every comfort, nevertheless it is like a luxurious prison because it sits between such high mountains that the sun cannot be seen." In another letter he called Carlsbad a pit.

The pulse of an epic hero was accompanied by Peter's passions, which were not dampened by an overly correct or artificial upbringing. We know how a strong man might become unruly in ancient Russian society by not knowing the limits of his powers. Could the society of Peter's time restrain the passions of a man who stood at its very pinnacle? One observant female contemporary recalled about Peter with complete justification that he was simultaneously a very good and a very bad man. Without rejecting and belittling the dark side of Peter the Great's character, we should not forget the bright side, which overcame the dark and could bind people to him so powerfully. If Peter's anger sometimes lashed out alarmingly against people whom he considered enemies of society, enemies of the common good, nevertheless he was fiercely loyal to people who served society and held to them with equal firmness.

Peter carried out his work with the assistance of capable people, whom he felt he could send anywhere and upon whom he could rely. This pursuit of capable people was not in any sense personal. He considered it unworthy to express his feelings to anyone other than those closest to him because he deemed this unprofitable. But when he sought out capable people he began an aggressive inquiry into their capabilities. Let us listen to one of Peter's fledglings, Nepliuev,[17] known to us for his diplomatic activities in Turkey, about how Peter conducted himself when among people. This story opens up for us the secret of how the great emperor sought out talented people.

Nepliuev studied navigation abroad. Upon his return to Russia he and his companions were presented to Peter, who told General Admiral Count Apraksin "I want to see for myself how they work, so for now assign them to the navy as marine guards." At this point a member of the Admiralty College, Grigory Petrovich Chernyshov, spoke up. "Sovereign! These people were taken at your command away from their families and sent away to foreign lands. In their poverty they have endured hunger and cold, and studied as best they could, wishing to please you. In the foreign land they were already marine guards. Upon returning home they hoped to be rewarded for their service and study, but were sent away with nothing. Instead they find themselves treated like those without such deprivation and experience."

The sovereign assigned them to take an examination at the college in his presence. When he was satisfied with Nepliuev's answers, he promoted him to lieutenant of the naval galley fleet and, after allowing Nepliuev to kiss his hand, said "You see, brothers. I am the tsar, yet my hands are calloused, but it is all from my effort to serve as an example to you. Although they are not old, these are worthy aides who offer their service to the fatherland." Soon after this Peter appointed Nepliuev as the chief judge of the standing naval courts, a responsibility in which he saw Peter nearly every day. The sovereign commented that the little one [that is, Nepliuev] would have a difficult path, but Chernyshov and Admiral Zmaevich set out to teach the little one the art of following the sovereign's way of doing things. "Be correct, be prompt, and speak the truth, save yourself from lying to God, even though what you have to say is bad. He will be angrier if you lie."

Soon Nepliuev passed the examination in this art as well. One time he came to work only to find Peter already there. Nepliuev grew very frightened and his first thought was to run home and claim illness. Then he recalled Chernyshov's advice, and he went over to where the sovereign was sitting. "My friend, I am already here!" Peter said to him. "I am guilty, sovereign," answered Nepliuev. "Yesterday I was visiting someone, and I stayed there a long time, and that is why I am late." Peter grabbed him by the shoulder. Nepliuev winced, thinking that he was in trouble, but the sovereign spoke, saying "Thank you, little one, that you speak the truth. God forgives you! We're all only human after all."[18]

Nepliuev ended up in Constantinople in this manner. During the first days of January 1721 a circular was distributed to all notables and Guards and naval officers explaining why Nepliuev commanded the naval courts. One day, after finishing dinner with his companions, Nepliuev got up from the table and went into a room where the sovereign was still sitting at table. Peter was in a very pleasant mood, and soon started a conversation. "I need a man who knows Italian whom I can send to Constantinople as resident envoy." Golovkin responded that he did not know any such person. "I do," said Fedor Matveevich Apraksin, "a very worthy man, but unfortunately he is very poor." "Poverty is not a hindrance," responded Peter, "it can soon be alleviated. Who is this man?" "Why, he is standing right behind you," said Apraksin. "A lot of people are standing behind me," Peter retorted. "I am referring to your vaunted aide who is standing by the galley,"[19] responded Apraksin.

Peter turned around, gazed upon Nepliuev and said "It is true, Fedor Matveevich, that he is worthy, but I would like him to stay with me." After he thought it over, the sovereign ordered Nepliuev appointed envoy in Constantinople. When Nepliuev approached him to express his gratitude, he fell at Peter's feet, kissed them, and cried. Peter then raised him up and said "Do not bow down, brother. I am God's officer to you. It is my obligation to see that nothing is granted to anyone unworthy, and that nothing is taken from someone who is worthy. By being worthy you will serve not just me, but you will do more good for yourself and for the fatherland. If you are bad, I will call you to account. God demands of me that I give you no quarter to do harm or commit any stupidity. Serve the faith and truth! From the very outset God shall not abandon you and, in his wake, neither shall I."

Peter was deeply conscious of his obligations to God, regularly expressing a profound religious feeling. This faith uplifted his spirit at times of misfortune, restrained his joy in good fortune. During the final year of his life, on August 16, 1724, while composing a program for celebrating the Treaty of Nystadt, Peter wrote "It is appropriate for the first verse to

comment on the victories, and then write for the rest of the celebration
(1) Our inefficiency in all matters. (2) In regard to starting the war which
we entered blindly, unmindful of the strength of the enemy and our own
circumstances (3) Our former opponents always wrote in their own words
and histories as if they did not instigate the war, as if they never brought
it to us. (4) These former enemies interferred in our domestic affairs, even
in the matter of my son, and they influenced the Turks to act against us.
(5) All other nations have a policy of maintaining a balance of power
among their neighbors, in particular that we do not gain access to the light
of reason in all matters, especially in warfare. What they wanted did not
transpire, a fact to which they closed their eyes. This miracle, in truth, is
God's. Here it can be seen that all the minds of humanity amount to
nothing against the will of God. It is fitting to cultivate all of this widely,
but in a reasonable manner."

Let us take into account the man's uncommon greatness combined
with his consciousness of the nothingness of the minds of humanity. Add
to that his firm demand for executing obligations, his strict demand for
truth, his facility for identifying the sharpest opposing views, his remarkable simplicity, conviviality and placidity. These gifts bound the best
people firmly to Peter, those who were close to him. We easily can grasp
the impression that the news of the great emperor's demise had on them.
"In February 1725," Nepliuev wrote, "I received the sorrowful news that
the father of the fatherland, Peter, the first emperor, departed from this
earth. My tears made the paper wet, and out of responsibility towards my
sovereign and the many kindnesses he did me, and of this I do not lie, I
went around for more than a day in a daze, otherwise I would have been
in sin. This monarch brought our fatherland to a level equal to others. He
taught us to recognize that we too are human. In a word, wherever one
glances in Russia, everything has its origin with Peter, and all of our
progress is drawn from this source. For me personally, beyond what I
have just said, the sovereign was also a merciful father, and the Lord now
raises his soul, which troubled itself in so many ways about the general
welfare, with righteousness."

Another man who had been close to Peter, Nartov,[20] said "If at some
time a philosopher happened to decipher the archive of Peter's secret
matters he would recoil in horror at what was done against this monarch.
We, the former servants of this great sovereign, have pined and poured
out tears when we at times heard reproaches about his cruel spirit, when
there was nothing to it. If more people knew what he endured, what he

bore and with what sorrows he was plagued, they would be horrified at how much he made allowances for human weaknesses and how often he forgave crimes undeserving of any mercy. Although Peter the Great is no longer with us, his spirit lives on in our souls. We who had the good fortune of being in the company of this monarch will die remaining faithful to him, taking with us to our graves our fervent love for this earthly God. Without fear we shall proclaim about our father so we all can learn from him noble fearlessness and truth."

APPENDIX

MUSCOVITE RANKS IN THE SEVENTEENTH CENTURY

Below are listed, in descending order of precedence, all ranks (chiny) of
the Muscovite upper and middle service class. All servitors in **A**, **B** and
C held noble status, which entitled them to own land and serfs. No specific duties were linked to these ranks, although office evidently once was
related to function, table attendant for example. Frequently promotion to
a given grade depended on clan status and an individual's seniority within
his own clan, although there were examples of promotion of outsiders on
merit.

Servitors in Grades **A** and **B** were mostly Moscow-based and per-
formed a variety of military, civil and diplomatic duties as required, rang-
ing from the highest military commands and chancellery offices filled
mainly by boyars, of whom there were sixty-three in 1693, to fairly
menial ceremonial duties by the palace attendants, about two thousand of
the younger members of the noble class.

Holders of **C** grades, resident in the provinces, provided the backbone
of junior command in the army. In the 1690s all of these grades coexisted
with the ranks of the "new model" infantry (general, major, lieutenant,
etc.), and civilian ranks such as "councillor," all of which were direct
designations of office.

The older ranks died out with their holders and in 1722 were super-
seded once and for all by Peter's Table of Ranks (see below).

A. The Boyar Council

1. Boyar (boiarin)
2. Lord-in-waiting (okol'nichii)
3. Conciliar noble (dumnyi dvorianin)
4. Conciliar secretary (dumnyi d'iak)

B. Moscow Nobles (non-boyar grade)

1. Table attendant (stol'nik)
2. Crown agent (striapchii)
3. Moscow noble (dvorianin moskovskii)
4. Palace attendant (zhilets)

The addition of the words "privy" or "close" (blizhnii) and "chamber" (komnatnyi) to some of the above grades—blizhnii boiarin, komnatnyi stol'nik—denoted regular attendance on the tsar or other members of the ruling family in person. Young men from the noble class also did duty as chamberlain (spal'nik), gentleman of the bedchamber (postel'nichii), carver (kravchii) and other functions.

C. Provincial Nobles

1. Provincial servitor (dvorianin gorodovoi)
2. Junior boyar (syn boiarskii, plural, deti boiarskie)

Below **A**, **B** and **C** came the lower (sluzhilye liudi po priboru) non-noble service classes: clerks (pod'iachie), musketeers (strel'tsy), infantrymen (soldaty), dragoons (draguny), cavalrymen (reitary), artillerymen (pushkari), postal drivers (yamshchiki), free homesteaders (odnodvortsy) and others.

The English terms listed are those used in the Academic International Press edition of *Soloviev's History*. Scholars have yet to reach a consensus on standard usage. On this and related matters see Richard Hellie, *Enserfment and Military Change in Muscovy* (Chicago, 1971) and R.O. Crummey, *Aristocrats and Servitors. The Boyar Elite in Russia, 1613-1689* (Princeton, N.J., 1983).

TABLE OF RANKS
January 24, 1722

A. NAVAL

I	general-admiral	general admiral
II	admiral	admiral
III	vitse-admiral	vice admiral
IV	kontr-admiral	rear admiral
V	kapitan-komandir	commodore
VI	kapitan pervogo ranga	senior captain
VII	kapitan vtorogo ranga	captain
VIII	kapitan tret'ego ranga	junior captain
IX	kapitan-leitenant	lieutenant captain
X	leitenant	lieutenant

A. NAVAL (cont.)

XI	korabel'nyi sekretar'	naval secretary (later a civil service rank)
XII	michman	midshipman
XIV	michman	warrant officer

B. MILITARY

I	general-fel'dmarshal	field marshal
II	general-anshef	general-in-chief
III	general-poruchik	lieutenant general
	general-leitenant	lieutenant general
IV	general-maior	major general
V	brigadir	brigadier
VI	polkovnik	colonel
VII	podpolkovnik	lieutenant colonel
VIII	prem'er-maior	first major
	maior	major
	voiskovoi starshina	major (cossack)
IX	kapitan	captain
	rotmistr	captain (cavalry)
	esaul	captain (cossack)
X	kapitan-poruchik	lieutenant captain
	shtabs-kapitan	staff captain
	shtabs-rotmistr	staff captain (cavalry)
	pod"esaul	junior captain (cossack)
XI	poruchik	lieutenant
XII	sekund-poruchik	second lieutenant
	unter-leitenant	sublieutenant
	podporuchik	sublieutenant
XIII	praporshchik	ensign
	kornet	cornet
	khorunzhii	ensign
XIV	fendrik	guidon bearer

C. CIVIL SERVICE RANKS

I	kantsler	chancellor
	deistvitel'nyi tainyi sovetnik pervogo klassa	senior privy councillor, first class

C. CIVIL SERVICE RANKS (cont.)

II	deistvitel'nyi tainyi sovetnik	senior privy councillor
III	tainyi sovetnik	privy councillor (from 1724)
IV	tainyi sovetnik	privy councillor (until 1724)
	deistvitel'nyi statskii sovetnik	senior state councillor
V	statskii sovetnik	state councillor
VI	kollezhskii sovetnik	collegiate councillor
VII	nadvornyi sovetnik	court councillor
VIII	kollezhskii assessor	collegiate assessor
IX	tituliarnyi sovetnik	titular councillor
X	kollezhskii sekretar'	collegiate secretary
XI	korabel'nyi sekretar'	naval secretary (originally a naval rank)
	gubernskii sekretar'	regional secretary
XIII	provintsial'nyi sekretar'	provincial secretary
	senatskii registrator	senate registrar
	sinodskii registrator	synodal registrar
	kabinetskii registrator	cabinet registrar
XIV	kollezhskii registrator	collegiate registrar

NOTES

Additional information on personalities and topics found in the text and notes is available in Edward J. Lazzerini, George N. Rhyne and Joseph L. Wieczynski, eds., *The Modern Encyclopedia of Russian, Soviet and Eurasian History* (MERSH, formerly *The Modern Encyclopedia of Russian and Soviet History*); Peter Rollberg, George Gutsche and Harry B. Weber, eds., *The Modern Encyclopedia of East Slavic, Baltic and Eurasian Literatures* (MESBEL, formerly *The Modern Encyclopedia of Russian and Soviet Literatures, Including Non-Russian and Emigré Literatures*); Paul D. Steeves, ed., *The Modern Encyclopedia of Religions in Russia and Eurasia* (MERRE, formerly *The Modern Encyclopedia of Religions in Russia and the Soviet Union*); and David R. Jones, ed., *The Military Encyclopedia of Russia and Eurasia* (MERE, formerly *The Military-Naval Encyclopedia of Russia and the Soviet Union*) all published by Academic International Press.

INTRODUCTION

1. V.I. Ger'e, "Sergei Mikhailovich Solov'ev," *Istoricheskii vestnik. Istoriko-literaturnyi zhurnal* (The Herald of History. A Historical-Literary Journal), Vol. 1, No.1 (1880), p. 80. A very similar assessment can be found in P.V. Bezobrazov, *S.M. Solov'ev. Ego zhizn' i nauchno-literaturnaia deiatel'nost'* (S.M. Soloviev. His Life and Scholarly Career) (St. Petersburg, 1894), pp. 59-61.

2. Bezobrazov, p. 94.

3. On the connection between Ger'e and Vladimir Soloviev see S.M. Luk'ianov, *O Vl. S. Solov'eve v ego molodye gody. Materialy k biografii* (Concerning V.S. Soloviev in his Younger Years. Materials Towards a Biography), Book 2 (Petrograd, 1918), pp. 125-156.

4. P. Miliukov, "Iuridicheskaia shkola v russkoi istoriografii (Solov'ev, Kavelin, Chicherin, Sergeevich) (The Juridical School in Russian Historiography. Soloviev, Kavelin, Chicherin, Sergeevich)," *Russkaia mysl'. Ezhemesiachnoe literaturno-politicheskoe izdanie* (Russian Thought. A Monthly Literary-Political Publication), Vol. 7, No. 6 (1886), pp. 80-92; K.S. Aksakov, *Polnoe sobranie sochinenii Konstantina Sergeevicha Aksakova* (The Complete Works of Konstantin Sergeevich Aksakov), Vol. 1 (Moscow, 1889), p.188 and passim pp. 581-582.

5. Kliuchevsky wrote several essays about Soloviev, mostly eulogies and memorial accounts. Most of these have been reprinted in Volume VII of Kliuchevsky's collected works. Vasilii Osipovich Kliuchevskii, *Sochineniia. Tom VII. Spetsial'nye kursy* (Collected Works, Volume VII. Specialized Courses) (Moscow, 1989), pp. 303-344.

6. V.S. Solov'ev, "Sergei Mikhailovich Solov'ev. Neskol'ko dannykh dlia ego kharakteristiki (Sergei Mikhailovich Soloviev. Some Information Towards a Character Sketch)," *Sobranie sochinenii Vladimira Sergeevicha Solov'eva* (The Collected Works of Vladimir Sergeevich Soloviev), Vol. 6 (St. Petersburg, n.d.), pp. 643-662; M.S. Bezobrazova, "Vospominaniia o brate Vladimire Solov'eve (Reminiscences Concerning My Brother Vladimir Soloviev)," *Minuvshie gody* (Bygone Years), Vol. 5 (1908), pp. 159-161; Poliksena Sergeevna Solov'eva, "Allegro" in F.F. Fidler, ed., *Pervye literturnye shagi. Avtobiografii sovremennykh russkikh pisatelei* (First Literary Steps. Autobiographies of Contemporary Russian Writers) (Moscow, 1911), pp. 91-94. Vsevolod expressed his views in the introduction and conclusion to the edition of his father's memoirs he serialized in *Russkii vestnik* (The Russian Herald) in 1896: "Iz neizdannykh bumag S.M. Solov'eva (From the Unpublished Papers of S.M. Soloviev)," *Russkii vestnik* (The Russian Herald), No. 242 (February, 1896), pp. 1-5; (May, 1896), pp. 145-149.

7. Vl. Solov'ev, *Pis'ma* (Letters) (St. Petersburg, 1923), p. 217.

8. V.S. Solov'ev, "Neskol'ko dannykh...," pp. 643-644.

9. Bezobrazova, "Vospominaniia...," pp. 159-161.

10. V.S. Solov'ev, ed., "Iz neizdannykh bumag...," pp. 1-2.

11. See, for example, Robert F. Byrnes, *V.O. Kliuchevskii. Historian of Russia* (Bloomington, 1995), p. 43.

12. V.O. Kliuchevskii, "Sergei Mikhailovich Solov'ev," *Sochineniia* (Works), Vol. VII, p. 319.

13. Kliuchevskii, "S.M. Solov'ev kak prepodavatel' (S.M. Soloviev as a Teacher)," *Sochineniia*, Vol. VII, pp. 322-23.

14. Kliuchevskii, "Solov'ev kak prepodavatel'," p. 324.

15. Kliuchevskii, "Pamiati S.M. Solov'eva," p. 341.

16. "Iz neizdannykh bumag...," pp. 146-148.

17. S.M. Solov'ev, "Moi zapiski dlia detei moikh, a esli mozhno, i dlia drugikh (My Memoirs for My Children and Possibly for Others as Well)" in *Izbrannye trudy. Zapiski* (Selected Works. Memoirs) (Moscow, 1983), pp. 341-342.

CHAPTER I

1. The Uniates, named after the Union of Brest of 1596, consisted of formerly Orthodox believers who accepted the authority of the Pope and swore their allegiance to Catholicism, but who were permitted to retain most of their old rites and to continue to pray in Church Slavonic. Virtually all Uniates lived in the Ukraine and Belorussia, territories situated in the Polish-Lithuanian Commonwealth and were deeply affected by Polish Catholic culture. See David A. Frick, *Meletij Smotryckyj* (Cambridge, Mass., 1995) and Frank E. Sysyn, *Between Poland and the Ukraine. The Dilemma of Adam Kysil, 1600-1653* (Cambridge, Mass., 1985).

2. Prince Sviatopolk Chetverinsky, the first metropolitan of Kiev, was the Orthodox bishop of Łuck in Poland and subsequently fled to the Left Bank Ukraine, which was under Muscovite control, to avoid Polish pressure to convert to Catholicism. Muscovite church authorities made him something of a *cause célèbre*, a hero of the faith, and by appointing him metropolitan made clear their intentions to use religion as a rallying cry for Orthodox peoples under Polish authority.

3. Swiatzki (or Sviatsky) is identified in various sources as a prominent Polish nobleman.

4. A verst is a linear measure equal to 1,166 yards and slightly more than a kilometer.

5. The Savior monastery (Zaikonospassky) in Moscow at this time had an interesting recent history in the intellectual life of Moscow. In the early 1680s it housed Sylvester Medvedev's school, which taught young boys Latin, Greek and rhetoric. In 1687 Medvedev's enterprise was effectively closed, and replaced by one run by the Likhud brothers which focussed more on Greek. By Peter's reign the school was completely transformed into the Moscow Academy. The otherwise unknown Yustin Rudinsky was presumably a teacher there. See also Chapter IV, Note 8, p. 204.

6. The Treaty of Moscow, or the Treaty of Eternal Peace, of 1686 led to the creation of a "Holy League" with Poland and spoke of Muscovy's special obligation in freeing Orthodox Christian peoples from the "yoke of the infidel" (the Ottoman Turks). Among other things it led to the establishment of the new metropolitanate of Kiev, formally subordinate to Moscow, an act that made Muscovy the de facto protector of the Orthodox within the Polish Commonwealth.

7. Sergei Grigorievich Dolgoruky was the son of Grigory Fedorovich, one of Peter's oldest advisors and heir to one of the old boyar clans. Sergei succeeded his father as ambassador to Warsaw, evidence that Peter continued to rely on the old clans, even with the emphasis on "new men."

8. Augustus II, as Friedrich August I, had been elector of Saxony. He was elected as king of Poland in 1697. An ally of Russia, he brought Poland into the Northern War on the Russian side in 1700. After the defeat of his forces he was deposed in 1704, but ultimately reinstated in 1709.

9. The text here refers to the new title of emperor which Peter was granted by the Senate in 1721 after the victory over Sweden. Prior to that time the highest title accorded to a Russian ruler was "tsar," derived from "Caesar." "Tsar" connoted a line of legitimacy descended from both the Holy Roman emperor, called "tsar" or "tsezar" in Russian, and from the Mongol khan in Saray, also called "tsezar." Ivan IV was the first Russian ruler to have himself crowned as tsar along with grand prince of Moscow and a myriad other patrimonial titles, and over the next century and a half the crowned heads of Europe came to accept that title for Russian rulers. The title "emperor" had no obvious lineage in Russian history although in Peter's mind it linked his realm to the great empires of yore,

Greece, Rome and Egypt. Europe's other crowned heads were reluctant to embrace the new title, especially those who potentially lay in the path of this aggressive new empire.

10. Rzeczpospolita is often translated as "The Polish Republic" or "The Republic of Nobles," though "Commonwealth" is the preferred translation in this series. Earlier it was known as the Confederation of Poland-Lithuania. This is a confusing demarcation because the "republic" and monarchy existed side-by-side, the former referring to the rights of noble families to elect a monarch (in the Sejm), the latter referring to the fact that Poland did in fact have a sitting, albeit an elected, monarch. After the partitions of Poland in the late eighteenth century the myth of an ancient Polish republic became a touchstone of Polish ideas of national independence, a rallying cry which counterpoised its own "republican" past to the absolute monarchies which dismantled it.

11. Augustus II, restored by Peter to the Polish throne in 1709, grew seriously ill in 1722. As elector of Saxony he aspired to put his house on an equal footing with those of the strongest German houses of his day, a goal that required that he be succeeded by his son, Augustus III, as a hereditary rather than elected monarch. Peter was opposed to transforming the Polish monarchy to hereditary rather than elected, and therefore was unwilling to see Augustus pass the crown to his son. Augustus III lived until 1733, at which time Stanisław Leszczyński, the French candidate, was elected, albeit for only a brief time. Russia opposed Leszczyński and sent in troops to prevent him from becoming king. Russia's candidate, paradoxically, was Augustus III, but as an elected monarch.

12. Jacob Heinrich Fleming (or Flemming) was a Saxon count in Polish military service and for a time commanded its armed forces.

13. Jan III (or John) Sobieski (1629-96) was the elected king of Poland from 1674 to 1696. He was a major force behind formation of the Holy League. Born in Lvov, he rose to prominence by leading Polish forces against the Ottomans in 1673-1674 and later routed them from Vienna in 1683.

14. Michał Wiśnowiecki was a noted hetman in Lithuania, and was king, the only one of his line, from 1669 to 1673. He is noted in the literature as ineffective and unduly beholden to the magnates.

15. In December 1721 word reached St. Petersburg that the shah had been overthrown by an Afghan-led revolt. Peter took this as an opening to launch a campaign in the South and especially against Persia, largely in pursuit of land on the Caspian. This campaign began well, and Peter was able to seize Derbent with little difficulty in 1722. The further southeast his detachments went, the more they fell victim to resistance, political turmoil, and disease. In the end he was able to occupy Baku and gain a strip of land on the northern coast of the Caspian, a cession conceded in a treaty signed by Russia and the Ottoman empire, its primary rival in the region, in 1724. See B. H. Sumner, *Peter the Great and the Emergence of Russia* (New York, 1962), pp. 154-157. For a more recent account, see also Lindsey Hughes, *Russia in the Age of Peter the Great* (New Haven, 1998), pp. 57-59.

16. Adam Mikołaj Siniawski was the crown grand hetman of the Ukrainian cossacks in the kingdom of Poland.

17. Chervontsy (pl.) here translated as "ducats," were gold coins used during the eighteenth century worth approximately three rubles.

18. Here and in several other passages throughout the text Soloviev invents these hyperbolic quotes to signify irrational and overly emotional responses of which he seems to disapprove. In particular, when discussing the ways in which people employ religion to demarcate distinctions between themselves and others, he seems to emphasize their irrationality in their superimposing of antimonies of good and evil on these distinctions. In this particular passage Soloviev appears to disapprove of the Catholics in Pinsk for their exaggerated hostility to Orthodox, who, in this made-up quote, were worse than "Jews and Muslims," that is, worse than infidels, the very definition of inassimilable aliens. Interestingly Soloviev shows considerably more restraint when describing the responses of Orthodox populations to Old Believers and non-believers.

19. The Sokoliński family were old Polish-Lithuanian magnates. It is not known which member of the family Soloviev is discussing here.

20. Orsha is a town in Belorussia on the upper Dnieper, about forty miles north of Mogilev.

21. These letters of benediction, "blagoslavitel'nye gramoty" in Russian, were messages of blessings and prayer sent by the religious authorities, in this case bishops, to the laity. Such pronouncements were in themselves common forms of conveying the church's blessings on the faithful, but bishops were constrained to restrict their blessings to their own dioceses. Letters sent across diocesan boundaries implicitly challenged the authority of the local bishop, and in this case the problem was compounded by the fact that the letters were crossing international boundaries as well.

22. In the Roman Catholic church the Thursday after Trinity Sunday is observed as the feast of Corpus Christi. This feast is not observed in the Orthodox church, which is why they refused to ring the bells.

23. The reference here is to Prince Vasily Lukich Dolgoruky, one of Russia's most experienced and well-traveled diplomats. He studied in France for twelve years and had diplomatic postings in Warsaw and Copenhagen earlier in Peter's reign.

24. Nakhimovsky and Orlik were Ukrainian cossack leaders who turned against Peter during the Northern War, much like Mazepa. Little is known about either of them, though Orlik at one point claimed for himself the title of hetman of Zaporozhie.

25. Ivan Mazepa was hetman of the Left Bank Ukraine and in that capacity led an unsuccessful campaign against Russian rule in the area in autumn 1708. Peter's erstwhile devoted ally, Mazepa had come to the conclusion that Peter's forces would be defeated by Sweden's army, and he switched sides, offering his support to Karl XII. This gamble proved disastrous, as Peter soon gained the upper hand, and Mazepa was forced to withdraw along with Karl from the Left Bank Ukraine. Filipp Orlik served as Mazepa's chief scribe, and ultimately

succeeded him as hetman. He was forced into exile because of his support of Karl XII of Sweden in 1712 and 1713. Soloviev's treatment of Mazepa follows something of a nationalist line which, until very recently, was the view espoused by virtually every Russian specialist. In his book *The Reforms of Peter the Great*, Anisimov adopts a more nuanced view, arguing that the relations between hetmen and the Russian state were complicated and confused, and marked by betrayals and broken promises on both sides. Thus for Anisimov, Mazepa is a somewhat sympathetic figure, albeit one who made a disastrous strategic error. See Volume 26 in this series, pp. 66 and ff.; Evgenii V. Anisimov, *The Reforms of Peter the Great* (Armonk, New York, 1993), pp. 111-21; N. I. Pavlenko, *Petr Velikii* (Peter the Great), (Moscow, 1990), pp. 260-91.

26. Courland was a German-speaking duchy on the Baltic Sea, contiguous to Poland. As Soloviev makes clear, competition over influence in Courland was fierce, and typically ran through Warsaw. During Peter's reign, again as Soloviev describes, Russia's influence in Courland grew. Anna, the daughter of Peter's half brother Tsar Ivan V, was married to Duke Friedrich of Courland, and after his death remained there as duchess. During this time representatives from Russia actively bought up estates that were heavily mortgaged by Courland's nobility, as a result of which Russia was a major property owner in the duchy. When Anna became empress of Russia in 1730 she kept her status as duchess of Courland and further cemented Russia's influence there. Finally, during the third partition of Poland in 1795, Courland was formally incorporated into the Russian empire.

27. The Polish Sejm, or diet, operated according to the principle of *liberum veto* whereby all representatives must agree to a given decision before it could become law. The purpose of this system was to defend the rights of weaker clans and alliances against more powerful lords who, as Soloviev amply shows, otherwise could use their resources to shape policy. If unanimity were not reached conflicts were to be resolved literally on horseback, the dissenting party essentially declaring war on the rest, the winner gaining the right to set policy. This dire mode of conflict resolution placed a premium on compromise and private understandings, an arrangement that worked reasonably well for several generations. In the eighteenth century party conflicts grew more difficult to resolve, in large measure because of the growing influence of foreign powers within the Sejm. Hence, the risk of a "Sejm on horseback" loomed large during the time which Soloviev is discussing.

28. The term used here, dessidenty, is obscure. It probably refers to Russian Old Believers who had fled across the border into Poland to avoid religious persecution over the previous thirty years.

CHAPTER II

1. Savva Vladislavich Raguzinsky was a merchant from Ragusa on the Dalmatian coast who resided at Venice at this time. He was an informer to the court

in St. Petersburg through Peter Tolstoy for some time, and was entrusted by Peter with stirring revolt in the Balkans. See B.H. Sumner, *Peter the Great and the Emergence of Russia* (New York, 1962), p. 72.

2. Clement VII served as Pope from 1700 to 1721. Although his relations with Peter were uneven, since 1717 there was an effort on both sides to improve relations. As Soloviev indicates, these moves towards détente temporarily ended on the death of Clement.

3. Russia maintained an uneasy relationship with the Jesuits (Society of Jesus) since the late sixteenth century. In 1684 a Jesuit mission opened in Moscow, sponsored by the Holy Roman empire. It had some support at court and succeeded in ministering to the Catholic population of Moscow. They were expelled in 1689, shortly after Peter took full control of the throne. Peter allowed Jesuits to return to Russia in 1698, and they gained grudging permission to serve Catholic populations in several cities and even to construct a few stone churches. The deteriorating relationships between Russia and Austria led to a second expulsion in 1719. Jesuits in Beijing continued to play an important diplomatic role in Russian-Chinese relations, and this petition to cross Siberia resulted from that ongoing relationship. See Daniel L. Schlafly, Jr., "The Jesuits in Russia," *The Modern Encyclopedia of Russian and Soviet History*, ed. by Joseph L. Wieczynski (Gulf Breeze, Fla., 1976-), Volume 15, pp. 128-136. Hereafter MERSH.

4. Cardinal Pietro Ottoboni was the patron of the Accademia Fisic-matematico in Rome, a position which won him broad respect and recognition in the capitals of Europe. At this time he was acting as the Pope's Protector of the French Crown. As the passage makes clear, Ottoboni was entrusted with securing the safe entry of Catholic orders into areas of the Russian empire with significant Catholic populations.

5. Cardinal Niccolò Spinoli was the papal nuncio in Poland.

6. Gavrila Ivanovich Golovkin (1660-1734), a descendant of an old and distinguished boyar family, was head of Peter's College of Foreign Affairs and was given the new title of state chancellor in 1709. According to Lindsey Hughes (*Russia in the Age*, p. 421), he had no particular qualifications for his position and knew no languages other than Russian.

7. Anna Ivanovna was the daughter of Peter the Great's half brother, Ivan Alekseevich, who served as co-tsar with Peter between 1682 and 1689. The real power was their half sister, Sophia, who served unofficially as regent during this time. When Peter became sole ruler in 1689 Ivan's line was removed from positions of influence and Sophia was cloistered in the New convent in Moscow. Anna ultimately was sent to Courland and was married to the duke. After the death of Peter II in 1730 she was invited by the nobility to return to Russia to rule as empress. This invitation set off a complex succession crisis that set several elite families who dominated the Supreme Privy Council against the larger body of service nobles (shliakhetstvo, as Peter termed them). For a short time it appeared that the Privy Council would succeed in imposing formal conditions on the terms of Anna's rule, but their endeavor was opposed and ultimately defeated by the shliakhetstvo. Anna

thus ruled with no formal limitations, and during her ten-year reign effectively alienated most of the leading families at court, who denounced her privately as a slave of the Germans with whom she surrounded herself. See Lindsey Hughes, *Sophia. Regent of Russia, 1657-1704* (New Haven, Conn., 1990) and Brenda Meehan-Waters, *Autocracy and Aristocracy. The Russian Service Elite of 1730* (New Brunswick, N.J., 1973).

8. The Land of Schwedt-Vierraden was inherited in 1670 by the electress Sophia Dorothea and elevated to the rank of a margravate. She brought in Dutch and Huguenot settlers to cultivate tobacco. It was granted to Philipp Wilhelm (1669-1711), the eldest son of the Great Elector's second marriage to Dorothea of Holstein-Glücksberg. This cadet line of the Hohenzollerns ruled the magravate until 1788, when it reverted to the Prussian crown. There seems to be some confusion as to the names of Anna's suitors, both by Soloviev and subsequent historians. Philipp Wilhelm's son Friedrich, born in 1700, was margrave from 1711 to 1771. Therefore his cousin Karl (1705-1762) was not actually the margrave, as Soloviev styles him, though he was of the margravial family. The original aspirant to the hand of the widowed duchess of Courland was Johann Adolf of Sachsen-Weissenfels, a relative of the Polish king, who failed to ratify the match within the specified time. The tsar broke off the negotiations and entertained the proposal of King Frederick William that Anna marry Margrave Friedrich, who already had some claims to Courland. The king had designs on Courland himself and was delighted when the margrave stated that, although he would submit to the king's will, he would rather marry one of the king's daughters. A new contract involving Karl, another cousin from the same princely house, was signed in December 1723, but this plan also fell by the wayside. See Eugene Schuyler, *Peter the Great* (New York, 1884), Volume II, p. 416.

9. Tsaritsa Praskovia Fedorovna (Saltykova, 1664-1723) was married to Tsar Ivan V, Peter's half-brother, in 1684. She is described as a traditionalist who nevertheless made sufficient concessions to the new order so as to remain influential at the Petrine court.

10. Andrei Artomonovich Matveev (1666-1728) was the son of Artamon Sergeevich Matveev, the former guardian of Tsaritsa Natalia. The elder Matveev was murdered in 1682 by the Moscow musketeers (streltsy), an experience which left Andrei with a life-long antipathy to Regent Sophia and the traditionalists at court. Because of his outlook and his facility with foreign languages Peter held him in high regard and made him, at various times, ambassador to the Dutch republic and Austria, as well as special representative to France and England.

11. Probably a reference to Prince Ivan Lvov, who was posted as a chamberlain to various imperial households at different times. Many Lvovs served during Peter's time, and this passage does not specify which one this was.

12. Count Ludwik Lanczyński was the Russian ambassador at the imperial court in Vienna during much of Peter's reign. His dispatches to St. Petersburg provide an extensive commentary on Viennese court politics and on official attitudes towards Russia. After the Treaty of Nystadt he provided extensive commentary on Vienna's reaction to Peter's wish to adopt the imperial title.

13. Count Friedrich Schönborn was the Austrian vice-chancellor who served as an intermediary between Tsarevich Alexis Petrovich and both the Austrian and Russian governments during the period when Alexis unsuccessfully sought to be granted asylum in the Habsburg lands.

14. Probably referring to Prince Johann Adolf of Sachsen-Weissenfels. See Note 8, above.

15. At the conclusion of the Northern War Peter dispatched Yaguzhinsky on special diplomatic missions to Sweden and Austria, largely to facilitate the terms of the Treaty of Nystadt. Austria was concerned lest Yaguzhinsky's visit to Prussia indicate a warming of relations between the two powers.

16. Prince Eugene of Savoy gained a reputation as a brilliant field officer for the Holy Roman empire in battles against the Turks in 1697 and against the French in 1701-1706. The establishment of an Anglo-French alliance in 1712 greatly strengthened France's position, and in 1714 Eugene and his French counterpart, Villars, negotiated a treaty at Rastatt which ceded Alsace to France but none of its conquests east of the Rhine. See John B. Wolf, *The Emergence of the Great Powers, 1685-1715* (New York, 1951), pp. 50, 65 ff.

17. On the Polish succession, see Chapter I, Note 8 and 11, above. Peter did in fact sound out Prussia about working together in Poland so as to prevent the monarchy from becoming hereditary. This fanciful ruler implied that Peter hoped to marry one of his daughters or nieces to the son of the French regent who, as the elected king of Poland, would have a marriage link to Peter. Such a link would have raised the possibility of a French-Russian alliance in Poland, an arrangement which would have isolated Austria.

18. Franz Ludwig von Zinzendorf was Austrian vice-chancellor and special ambassador attached to the Swedish high command during much of the Northern War.

19. Peter's involvement in Mecklenburg dated back to 1712 when his troops entered the duchy in pursuit of the Swedish army. Peter exerted considerable pressure on Duke Karl Leopold of Mecklenburg to accept a marriage to Peter's niece Catherine Ivanovna, to which he finally acceded in 1716. By acquiescing the duke generated considerable opposition among his own nobility, whose revolt was crushed by Peter's troops. As the duke's armed patron Peter was able to play a decisive role in Mecklenburg's politics and to use his armed presence there to influence the delicate relations among the German states, and hence to set off the so-called "Mecklenburg affair" within European diplomatic circles.

20. A thaler was a Prussian coin equal approximately to a ruble.

21. Heinrich Rüdiger von Ilgen was a Prussian minister, sometimes termed the "chief minister" in Berlin, charged with overseeing diplomacy, in which capacity he played an influential role in relations with Russia.

22. Count Alexander Gavrilovich Golovkin was the Russian ambassador to Prussia at this time.

23. The Treaty of Vienna of 1719 forged a temporary alliance between Hanover, Saxony and Austria that aimed to limit Russian advances in the region.

24. Andreas Gottlieb von Bernstorff (or Bernsdorf) was a British minister of state whom George I brought with him from Hanover. Because of his extensive holdings in Mecklenburg Bernstorff was thought to be in favor of an anti-Russian policy in the Northern War. Nevertheless, George I came to rely on his advice less and less and to leave him in Hanover rather than London. See Penfield Roberts, *The Quest for Security, 1715-1740. The Rise of Modern Europe Series,* ed., William L. Langer (New York, 1947), p. 49.

25. Sir Charles Whitworth was a British diplomat in Russia for much of Peter's reign. His diplomatic dispatches to London constitute one of the richest sources available on the course of the Northern War and public opinion in the Russian capital. Based on his experiences Whitworth authored a book entitled *An Account of Russia as it Was in the Year 1710.*

26. Frederick William I was king of Prussia from 1713 to 1740. As the passage makes clear, his primary concern in the wake of Russia's victory over Sweden was to limit Russia's expansion on the Baltic and the Gulf of Finland without undoing the alliance made between the two powers during the Northern War.

27. The duke of Holstein, Karl Friedrich, was obliged to surrender to Denmark his possessions in Schleswig. Because the duke had Russian support, and was soon to marry Peter's daughter Anna, Prussia was loath to endorse the transfer publicly, by guaranteeing Schleswig's security, without first gaining assurances that Russia did not object.

28. See Note 8, above.

29. Otto von Schwerin came from an old Prussian noble family, one that provided several important ministers to the court in Berlin.

30. Soloviev discusses this gambit in the previous volume. Briefly, in 1720 two people representing Augustus II approached the Prussian king in Berlin with a suggestion for dividing Poland. If the king of Prussia helped Augustus become an autocratic ruler, he (the king) would receive Polish Prussia and Warmia in return. In the end the plan was rejected.

31. Who would inherit the Swedish throne after Karl XII proved to be a complicated affair. Karl was childless and one of the strongest contenders was the duke of Holstein, son of his deceased elder sister. In the end the duke lost out and the crown went to Karl's other sister, Ulrika Eleonora, in 1719.

32. Alexis Petrovich Bestuzhev, son of Peter Mikhailovich, served as Peter's diplomatic representative in Denmark.

33. Soloviev apparently is referring to the events of 1713 when Denmark invaded Schleswig-Holstein and occupied that part of Holstein which stood adjacent to Danish-held Schleswig. At that point Sweden proved too weakened by the Northern War to offer significant resistance to this seizure despite its offer of armed assistance.

34. Vice Admiral Thomas Gordon was the Russian-born son of Patrick Gordon (1635-1699), a Scottish soldier of fortune who entered Russian service in 1661.

35. Mikhail Petrovich Bestuzhev-Riumin (1688-1760) was the brother of Alexis Petrovich (see Note 37, above). He was a life-long ambassador, beginning his career abroad in 1720 as Russia's resident minister in London. Expelled for protesting the Anglo-Swedish alliance he was reassigned as resident ambassador in Sweden from 1721 to 1726.

36. Count Arvid Bernard Horn was the president of the Swedish College of Foreign Affairs. Carl Gustav Duecker, Count de la Gardie, and Nicodemus Tessin were Swedish senators.

37. Karl XII's wars devastated the Swedish economy and after his death in Norway in 1718 the leading nobility imposed governmental changes, establishing a ruling council largely controlled by the nobility. They further established an all-estate council, in this case a quasi-parliament which met in secret session. This reform effectively limited the ability of Swedish kings to make war by subjecting their powers of taxation to the approval of the council.

38. The Union of Kalmar in 1397 joined Denmark, Sweden and Norway into a single political union headed by the ruling family of Denmark. It survived, in increasingly weakened form, until the sixteenth century, when Gustav Vasa declared himself king of an independent Sweden.

39. Baron Akel Axelson Sparre was a general lieutenant in the Swedish army and Swedish ambassador to England.

40. Friedrich of Hesse-Cassel was married to Ulrika Eleonora, a Swedish princess and sister of Karl XII. When Karl died in 1718 the pair was chosen to reign as king and queen of Sweden.

41. Martin Neugebauer was a German hired as the tsarevich's tutor in 1701 only to be dismissed a year later. Years later he appeared in Constantinople in the service of Karl XII.

42. Tsarevich Alexis Petrovich (1690-1718), the deceased son of Peter the Great and his first wife Evdokia Lopukhina, was the heir apparent until he was implicated in a conspiracy intending to bring him to power and to restore the seemingly lost Muscovite order. Although not an active participant in these machinations, he had become estranged from his father, who had decided that Alexis would not succeed him. In October 1715 Alexis agreed to renounce his claim and subsequently agreed to enter a monastery. Instead, he fled to Austria and returned to Russia with great reluctance in early 1718. Although freed, he was subject to investigation, and in summer 1718 accused of treason and imprisoned, where he died unexpectedly on June 26. Three years later Peter issued a new decree on succession which empowered the reigning monarch to select his heir. Unfortunately, Peter died without doing so. See Anisimov, pp. 269-276, and Volume 30 of this series.

43. Jean Jacques Campredon, French ambassador to Russia.

44. Henning (or Heinrich) Friedrich Bassewitz was a count of Holstein who in 1715 attempted to forge a marriage alliance between Russia and Holstein, wherein Peter's elder daughter, Anna Petrovna, would marry Charles Friedrich, the duke and the nephew of Karl XII, as a way of mitigating Sweden's influence in the duchy.

45. The Pacta Conventa refers to a series of pacts with the Sejm signed by the king of Poland in 1573 which imposed specific constitutional limits on his authority.

46. Baron Schleinitz was the Russian ambassador in Hanover and a noteworthy political opponent of Prince Boris Kurakin.

47. Soloviev uses the term *ministry*, but this is clearly anachronistic in the pre-1802 context.

48. Konstantin (or Konstanty) Sobieski was the younger son of Jan. Upon his death in 1696 his mother, Marysienka, pushed for him to succeed to the Polish throne. See Andrzej Sulima Kamiński, *Republic vs. Autocracy. Poland-Lithuania and Russia, 1696-1697* (Cambridge, Mass., 1993), p. 261. At the same time Karl XII backed Konstantin's elder brother Jakub. Neither succeeded.

49. Prior to his death in 1714 Louis established a regency on behalf of the child Louis XV. He appointed the duke of Orleans, the nephew of Louis XIV and a potential claimant to the French throne, as its chairman. According to Roberts, the duke was obliged to make considerable concessions both to the Parlements and to the various estates. Soloviev, however, suggests that he succeeded in garnering significant authority over foreign affairs. Roberts, pp. 6-7.

50. Until his death in 1723 Abbé Dubois had virtual prime ministerial authority as chief advisor to the regent. He and Lord Stanhope of Great Britain worked jointly to establish an alliance between the two states as a way of mediating the competing claims to succession in Spain and Italy. This alliance came to be directed against Russian claims at the conclusion of the Northern War. Roberts, pp. 18-20.

51. Ferencz Rákóczi (1679-1735) was an early Hungarian national figure and leader of a rebellion against Habsburg suzerainty. At one point Peter contemplated backing Rákóczi for the Polish throne. See Sumner, p. 61; also C.A. Macartney, *Hungary. A Short History* (Edinburgh, 1962), pp. 92-96.

52. Louis-Pierre, comte de la Marck, was the French ambassador to Sweden during the last years of the Northern War. In 1717 and 1718 de la Marck mediated between George I of Britain and Karl XII. Simultaneously, he was circulating exaggerated claims of Russia's military prowess so as to demoralize French public opinion. See R. M. Hatton, *Charles XII of Sweden* (New York, 1968), pp. 449 ff.

53. Elizabeth Petrovna was Peter's middle daughter, between Anna and Natalia.

54. Praskovia Ivanovna was the only one of Peter's nieces not to marry a foreigner, choosing instead the Russian nobleman Peter Ilich Mamonov. Since the duke of Bourbon was regent to the young king Louis XV, the proposed marriage to him would have given Peter a close family tie to the most powerful man in France.

55. Alexander Borisovich Kurakin (1697-1749) was one of the first Russian noblemen educated abroad, largely thanks to his father's many years of service

as ambassador in various capitals. Between 1722 and 1724 he was Russia's resident minister in France, albeit under his father's supervision.

56. Boris Ivanovich Kurakin (1626-1727), Alexander's father, was Peter's brother-in-law, married to Evdokia Lopukhina's sister Ksenia. He served prominently in Peter's campaigns and diplomatic corps in various European capitals, among them Paris, London, The Hague, and Stockholm. Like many of Peter's oldest associates Kurakin had a reputation for a sharp tongue and strong opinions. In his case, the opinions were directed against many of the new men who occupied positions of prominence in the Senate. Prudence demanded that he be kept abroad, where his talents could be put to good use and there his rivalries might not prove deadly for him.

57. The passage here refers to the so-called "pragmatic sanction" of 1713 which established a permanent law of succession for the Austrian domains of the Habsburgs. The emperor, Charles VI, had no male heirs, and the sanction established that the domains pass in toto to his daughter Maria Theresa. It required the sanction of all those Habsburg lands in which formal estates still existed. See Max Beloff, *The Age of Absolutism, 1660-1815* (New York, 1962), p. 117.

58. King Gustav Adolf of Sweden (reigned 1611-1632) is credited with building Sweden into a great power, thus paving the way for the more aggressive and imperial policies of Karl XII. The reference here presumably is to Sweden's participation in the Thirty Years War, and its alliance with France that enabled the French king to make gains against Protestant territories.

59. Marshal Tessé of France had a relationship with Russia dating back to Peter's second trip to Europe in 1717. Tessé was sent by the regent to accompany the tsar to Paris and to attend to his needs. From that time forward Tessé acted as confidant to Russian officials and advised the French crown on Russian affairs.

60. During the minority of Louis XV the duke of Orleans was regent and Dubois the virtual prime minister. Louis reached his majority in February of that year (1723), thus obviating the need for a regency. For the next three years the duke of Bourbon acted as chief minister but without the title of prime minister. His successor Fleury followed the same course.

61. Cardinal Fleury was minister of state under Louis XV until his death in 1743. The former bishop of Fréjus, Fleury proved to be highly influential with the king, whom he had tutored, and for a time he functioned as de facto prime minister of France. During the mid-1720s orders from Fleury carried the same authority as those which emanated from the king. See Roberts, pp. 39, 213-216 and passim.

62. The reference here is to "James III" (James Francis Edward, 1688-1766) the Stuart (hence Catholic) pretender to the British throne and son of King James II. Exiled in France, the Stuarts made an effort to regain the throne during the failed Jacobite uprising of 1715-1716.

63. The duke of Orleans, Philippe, was the nephew of the late Louis XIV of France and arguably legal heir to the throne. So determined was he to become the next king of France that he renounced his claims to the Spanish throne. Instead

Louis XIV established a Regency Council until Louis XV came of age, with the duke as chairman. The boy's sickly constitution gave the duke continued hope to gain the crown and led him to establish close ties with England as a way to counterbalance the Spanish connection cultivate by his rivals. Similarly the ministry of the duke of Bourbon under the still young king Louis XV gave rise to speculation that the duke himself wished to be king, an illusion that Kurakin wished to cultivate to Russia's advantage.

64. As Soloviev explains George I, who became the Hanoverian king of England in 1714, also was the elector of Hanover since 1698. In the aftermath of Sweden's defeat in the Northern War he directed England's foreign policy so as to limit Russia's absorption of formerly Swedish territories. As elector of Hanover he gained the bishoprics of Bremen and Verden, which the Treaty of Westphalia had granted to Sweden. Britain also was concerned at the specter of Russian naval power on the Baltic, even though the Treaty of Greifswald in 1715 obliged George to guarantee Russia's Baltic conquests in exchange for Russia's endorsement of Hanover's rights to Bremen and Verden.

65. Sergei Dmitrievich Golitsyn was the son of Dmitry Mikhailovich Golitsyn.

CHAPTER III

1. Statements such as these are very revealing of Soloviev's outlook and concerns. For him, Russia's place in Europe was of primary importance, both to situate the heritage of the nation in the geographic center of historical development, and to give Russia a separate identity within that setting. This passage makes Russia stand for "the eastern half of Europe" and depicts European men of state as showing concern over what this all might mean. The fact that much of Russia's recent expansion took place outside of Europe is acknowledged, but given rather little interpretive importance in this scheme.

2. The suggestion that domestic policy came before foreign affairs is curious in light of the fact that the state was at war virtually the entire time that Peter was tsar and that in some years the state diverted up to ninety percent of its revenues to the armed forces. Soloviev seems to be arguing that diplomacy and warfare served to strengthen and secure the nation, to drag it out of backwardness and obscurantism and into the light of modernity. All of this makes sense in a Hegelian and juridical light since, from that perspective, it was the nation which experienced various historical phases of development, and the state, ruler, and law were the midwives, or agencies, that pushed Russian history forward. Hence, foreign policy, no matter how preoccupying, derived its meaning from the evolution of state and nation.

3. The distinction between senior privy councillor (deistvitel'nyi tainyi sovetnik) and privy councillor (tainyi sovetnik) was one of grade. Both were important officials, but the former received a rank of two on the Table of Ranks and the latter one of three.

4. In 1708 Peter decreed that Russia be divided into eight sprawling territorial units, each of which was supposed to be administered by a gubernator (civil governor) and a voevoda (military governor). Military governors were familiar figures in Russian law and politics, and they often were granted broad authority to employ the force of the state to maintain order. During the eighteenth century Russia endeavored to enhance the authority of the civil authorities and not rely so extensively on physical force, as a result of which the term voevoda lost its specific connection to military power and came increasingly to refer vaguely to a regional or provincial authority. For detailed discussion of the background to these reforms, as well as a delineation of the new offices and institutions, see Hughes, *Russia in the Age of Peter the Great*, pp. 114-130.

5. A college or collegiate councillor was a high-ranking official in one of the newly-established colleges, assigned a rank of six in the Table of Ranks.

6. The Russian term used here, "striapchii," had a reasonably precise meaning in the Muscovite period but, like so many expressions, it was used in a far looser sense by Peter and his immediate heirs. Originally meaning a strirrupper, in the Muscovite system of precedence a striapchii evolved into a title given to a middle servitor, or dvorianin, to fulfill a specific guards role at court. Precedence was abolished in 1682, however, and Peter was using the term to mean something akin to "watchdog" or "guardian." The term continued to evolve during the eighteenth and nineteenth centuries, coming ultimately to refer to a legal practitioner, someone familiar with the laws and competant to compose formal petitions, who had not completed the juridical faculty of a university.

7. Fiskaly were a cadre of governmental inspectors established by Peter in 1711 to combat corruption and abuses of position. They were assigned to all governmental offices and military commands. Universally despised, the office was abolished in 1730.

8. The office of master of heraldry (gerol'dmeister) was established in 1722, as the passage shows, to keep accurate lists of men in service and their families. This office also compiled information on noble family lineage, coats of arms and previous service by family members. Although the Code of Precedence (mestnichestvo) was abolished in 1682, now replaced by the new Table of Ranks, lineage and family honor still had a place in Russian service. Former boyar families were allowed to register their previous rank, although the term "boyar" no longer had any legal meaning. Moreover, all things being equal, Peter's statutes stipulated giving preference to serving men from older noble families over others. Subsequent research has shown that the old families not only registered with the master of heraldry, they used their clan identities effectively to dominate the highest offices until well into the reign of Catherine the Great.

9. The Russian here is "grazhdanstvo," meaning something like "the civil sphere." Peter is making the point that the society overall must continue to produce candidates for important military service, and he employs the word grazhdanstvo as a contrast to the military.

10. The Russian term here is general reketmeister, a position established by Peter in 1720 to oversee that administration of justice in the colleges. It was his responsibility to hear complaints of collegial injustice and present them to the Senate.

11. The Russian here is druzhinniki (pl.), an old and familiar Russian term dating at least to Kievan times. Its original meaning was something akin to military retinue, which stood closest to the prince in status and authority. By the late seventeenth century the term had lost most of its juridical content, but it still was employed informally to refer to armed or military entourages.

12. The Russian here is chinovniki (pl.), a term which soon came to refer to petty bureaucrats. This decree employs the word in its literal sense, meaning people who hold specific ranks or grades (chiny, pl.) in Russian service.

13. Grigory Grigorievich Skorniakov-Pisarev was one of the cadre of students whom Peter sent abroad to learn mathematics and navigation. In the 1720s he was charged with revising the curriculum of the navigational academy as well as setting up a network of arithmetic classes, known as cipher schools

14. Derbent is a town at the head of the Caspian Sea.

15. Peter Shafirov (1669-1739) received the title "baron" in 1710. As the many relevant passages in this and previous volumes reveal, Shafirov was one of Peter's closest confrères, in many ways rivaling Menshikov as the parvenu most likely to succeed.

16. Ivan Ilich Skoropadsky was hetman of the Don Cossacks who was appointed by Peter after the desertion of Mazepa and Chechel. As Peter's ally he played an important role in mobilizing cossack regiments against Sweden during the Northern War.

17. The battle of Poltava (1709) on the lower Dnieper river is often considered the decisive battle of the Northern War. Russian forces defeated the alliance of Sweden, the Crimean Tatars under Devlet-Girey, and the rebel hetman Mazepa. Peter's cavalry forced his enemies to surrender, while Karl XII and Mazepa barely escaped to the Turkish town of Bender.

18. Soloviev uses stats-kontora, or Bureau of State Accounts, actually the newly-formed College of State Accounts, as close to a College of Finances as the collegial system ever got.

19. Menshikov's origins are obscure, but they certainly were humble. As his fortunes improved he invented a lengthy ancestry for himself dating back to Riurik in the ninth century. Eventually he granted himself a lengthy series of exalted titles, beginning with "Illustrious Prince of the Holy Roman Empire and Russia." For a fuller discussion, see Hughes, *Russia in the Age of Peter the Great*, pp. 432-441.

20. The Vinius family came to Russia from Holland in the 1640s to establish foundries in the town of Tula, about a hundred miles south of Moscow. The father and son mentioned in this quote are Andrei Denisovich Vinius, the founder, and Andrei Andreevich (1641-1717), born in Russia and a close confidant of Peter. See Soloviev, Volume 26 in this series, p. 50 ff.

21. The municipal court (nadvornyi sud) was established in ten major cities in 1719. It proved unworkable and was abolished in 1727.

22. The project to build a canal on Lake Ladoga was begun in 1719 and completed in 1730. It connected the Neva river, the central waterway of the new capital, with the Volkhov river on the other side of the lake. One hundred and four versts in length, it was the first leg of an extensive network of canals that brought goods from the interior to St. Petersburg, either for consumption or for export. See Arcadius Kahan, *The Plow, the Hammer, and the Knout. An Economic History of Eighteenth-Century Russia* (Chicago, 1985), p. 247.

23. The Russian here is posadskii chelovek, someone registered to a town, or posad. Although a product of Muscovy, posadskii chelovek continued to be widely used as a legal status well into the eighteenth century, overlapping with meshchanin, tsekhovyi chelovek, and other terms employed to define juridically the urban lower classes.

24. The division of the realm into eight large geographic units, or "governments" (gubernii), in 1708 included provisions for a series of regional and local courts, all of which were incorporated into the College of Justice when it was founded a few years later. As Soloviev notes, these courts functioned largely in the breach.

25. The word sutiaga means litigation in Russian.

26. A grivna was a coin worth twenty dengas, or slightly more than a ruble.

27. On Mazepa see Chapter I, Note 11, above. Dmitry Chechel was a colonel and commander for Hetman Baturin.

28. These formulaic expressions by Menshikov echo the popular saying "God is on high and the tsar is far away."

29. In 1709 Peter changed the basis of direct taxation from a household-based tax to a poll, or "soul," tax (podushnaia podat'). The tax was based upon a count of the male population, excluding only those groups who were specifically exempted from paying direct tax. The first census was conducted in 1707, according to which the adult population declined significantly. He ordered periodic recounts, or revisions, of which the 1722 revision is summarized by Soloviev. See V.M. Kabuzan, *Narodonaselenie Rossii v XVIII-pervoi polovine XIX v.* (The Population of Russia in the Eighteenth and First Half of the Nineteenth Centuries) (Moscow, 1963).

30. The Russian word for urban lower classes here is meshchanstvo, a difficult and ambiguous category that had both juridical and informal contents. Officially, the meshchanstvo included people registered in towns and engaged in petty trade, handicrafts, or lower-level service activities. In practice, many members of the meshchanstvo lived outside of towns and hired themselves out in a wide variety of trades. As a term of everyday speech meshchanstvo referred to this ill-defined mass of urban poor, with no specific designation of trade or skill.

31. The Russian term employed here, izba, literally means hut, but for census and tax-paying purposes refers to peasant households.

32. All official and legal transactions had to be composed on stamped paper, a government monopoly.

33. The reference is to Peter (Pierre) Lefort, the nephew of Peter the Great's comrade in arms François Lefort, who died in 1699.

34. The Russian here is slobody (pl.), usually meaning urban neighborhoods. In this context it refers simply to a cluster of housing.

35. The expression "Little Russian" was used during the eighteenth and nineteenth centuries as a synonym for "Ukrainian." For the Russian state the term had specific territorial and administrative meaning, differentiating "Little Russia" from "Great Russia," rather than a cultural or linguistic one. Ukrainian was not officially acknowledged either as an ethnicity or a language, let alone a nationality, a perspective that to a considerable degree Soloviev seems to have shared.

36. Sloboda or "Settlement" Ukraine refers to a portion of Eastern Ukraine formed in the late seventeenth century in parts of what later became Kharkov, Kursk and Voronezh provinces. It was so named because of the large number of peasants who fled there from other parts of the Ukraine to avoid bloodshed, and who were permitted by the tsar to establish their own settlements, or slobody (pl.).

37. As their name implies, patriarchal nobles were literally nobles who served and received their service lands from the patriarch in a manner approximately equivalent to princely or tsar's servitors. Upon abolition of the patriarchate in 1721 these nobles were transferred to state rank.

38. Efimoks were foreign coins, thalers, worth approximately a ruble.

39. Kasha is usually buckwheat porridge, but also was a generic term for any cooked processed grain.

40. The reference here is to General Count Burkhard Münnich, vice-president of the War College and earlier a commander of Russian troops in Poland during the Northern War.

41. The Russian term used here is derdivel'.

42. The following section details Peter's efforts to refashion town government by making the urban merchantry responsible for maintaining public spaces, civil order and keeping accurate records of the town residents. The agencies created for this purpose were the magistracies, whose functions and experiences Soloviev delineates. As readers of earlier volumes in this series will recall, this type of service was nominally voluntary, in that the individuals so chosen did not receive payment and thus were reluctant to take on the additional responsibilities. They also were not authorized to impose urban taxes, instead having to rely on the authority of the central government or on "voluntary" levies. Caught between an officialdom which commanded these functions to be carried out and an urban population none to willing to cooperate, the magistracies were in a difficult position and often resorted to coercion and graft to meet their responsibilities. By contrast the old military governors (or voevodas), who de facto exercised these responsibilities earlier, had the force of arms behind them. Although ruthless and often unchecked, their orders carried considerable authority. In fact, as Soloviev shows, military governors still exerted considerable power at this time, and they often disregarded the town magistracies, to act as they pleased. The problem of disorderly and insufficient local administration continued in Russia right up until the zemstvo reforms of 1864.

43. Both the word for peasant (muzhik) and the word for man (muzh or muzhchina) come from a common root. "Men" in this context refers to free men, specifically men who owned landed property. "Peasants" here implicitly refers to serf males, who were subordinated to "men" in spite of their common humanity, a point that Soloviev seems to be underscoring in his choice of words, since he could easily have chosen alternative terms to describe the same categories.

44. Burgomasters (burmistry) were urban officials in the magistracy, often functioning as city managers or mayors. Ratmany (pl.) were members of the town council (Rat) established by the magistracy, usually consisting of four people.

45. Because much of the tax was collected in kind, principally grain or produce, tax collection required extensive storage areas to hold what was collected.

46. Until the eighteenth century Russia's merchants were organized into specific status and economic groups, the most powerful being the gosti who occupied a central place in urban and international trade, as well as in urban administration. The next most prominent group were the gostinnaia sotnia (Merchants' Hundred), the term that Soloviev uses here. Although the term lost most of its juridical meaning during Peter's reign it was still widely employed to refer to prosperous merchants of the second tier.

47. Here Soloviev is referring to an episode which he discusses in Volume 16 (Book VIII, p. 489 in the 1962 edition). The tsarevna had participated in a scheme by which coachmen were paid large sums to bring these supposed hay stokers to the chambers of the tsarevna. Under her protection these stokers and coachmen carried on an extensive and highly lucrative trade in Moscow.

48. Trading peasants. The Russian for a tax-exempt person is belomestets, plural belomesttsy. These typically were people from the lower classes, even peasants, who were exempted from paying tax in exchange for performing a specific service or function in the towns. See the following clauses in the Law Code (Ulozhenie) of 1649: Chapter 19, parts 13, 18 and 39.

49. This somewhat opaque passage reflects the difficulties of establishing clear juridical distinctions between the multiple urban groups engaged in trade along with other activities. Peasants traded and worked the land, merchants traded and bought land in villages, courtiers served at court and traded on the side. The regulations endeavored, unsuccessfully, to differentiate these categories and functions by forbidding merchants from working the land. The goal was to get them to focus on their designated economic activity rather than seek protection and economic favors at court. It did not work.

50. The serving men/traders are making a familiar argument here, one based on lineage, past service and the principle of precedence. They now served at the duchess's court, yet the traders whom they are ordered to survey had a similar patronage-based relationship with the court in the past, a lineage which put them on a social par with the serving men. They also imply that the reasoning behind the new ruling could apply to them as well, thus jeopardizing their own ability to trade and serve simultaneously.

51. The term "eminent man" (imenityi or imianityi chelovek) refers to an urban magnate, typically a prosperous merchant, who was granted this title in recognition for his service in a non-salaried position in urban government. During the eighteenth and nineteenth centuries the term for these figures changed at times, as did the specific privileges ascribed to them.

52. Guriev is arguing that his status ought to entitle him to exemption from physical labor. His case is based on lineage, namely the fact that his father belonged to the gostinnye sotni (Merchants' Hundreds), the second highest ranking for wealthy merchants in Muscovy, entitling one to considerable privileges. He also endeavors to show that his income is sufficient to support him and to provide taxes for the state, enough so that he will not become a burden. In short, he wants to be treated like a nobleman, as did the majority of wealthy merchants in seventeenth and eighteenth-century Russia.

53. Russian has many ways of distinguishing between ordained clergy (priests) and unordained clergy. This particular text uses the word prichetniki, which subsumes virtually all unordained parish clergy.

54. The terms in Russian are zavod and fabrika. In Russian law the distinction corresponds approximately to the English words "factory" and "workshop." They were subject to somewhat different regulations and different modes of taxation. For a fuller explanation of this distinction see Reginald E. Zelnik, *Law and Disorder on the Narova River. The Kreenholm Strike of 1872* (Berkeley, 1995), p. 17.

55. Friedrich Wilhelm von Bergholz's diary was published in Russian in the mid-nineteenth century under the title *Dnevnik kameriunkera Berkhgol'tsa, vvedenyi im v Rossii v tsarstvovanie Petra Velikogo s 1721-1725 gg.* (Diary of Chamberlain Bergolz Kept by Him in Russia During the Reign of Peter the Great, from 1721 to 1725) (Moscow, 1857-1860). Berholz kept detailed and meticulous notes of the duke's affairs in Russia and his diary provides considerable insight into the behind-the-scenes deliberations over the duke's political fate, as well as his economic activities.

56. The term employed here, kolomniki, refers to thin strips of woolen fabric typically woven in household workshops.

57. An arshin equals approximately 28 inches.

58. A pud was a measure of weight equal to about 36 pounds.

59. The Russian terms are shakhty (pl.) and shtolaty (pl.). Shtolaty were open-faced or secondary mines, considered to be less rich or productive than major mines, or shakhty.

60. The notary general (general'nyi pisar') is described as a high governmental rank in the Ukrainian hetmanate of the Russian empire. His exact responsibilities are not clear, but the position was ultimately included in the Table of Ranks, and the incumbent was considered an agent of the state rather than a servant of the hetman. See *Slovar' russkogo iazyka XVIII veka* (Dictionary of the Russian Language in the Eighteenth Century) (Leningrad, 1991), Vol. 6, p. 115.

61. See Note 36, above.

62. The Russian is zakladchiki, a legal term referring to individuals who literally sold themselves into a form of indentured servitude, in return for which they received the protection of someone more powerful. See Richard Hellie, "The Stratification of Muscovite Society," *Russian History,* Vol. 6, No. 2 (1979), pp. 133-209.

63. The Russian term zakhrebetniki (pl.), from the word khrebet, or spine, referred to poor but free peasants and workers who were dependent upon ("rested on the back of") other peasants for work. It is not clear whether the term had a specific juridical meaning, but its usage as an expression referring to free dependent peasants dates back at least as far as medieval Novgorod. They may have been sharecroppers, and, according to some scholars, they did not pay taxes, but these usages are specifically mentioned or implied in the legislative passage to which Soloviev refers. In the late seventeenth century zakhrebetniki appear frequently in tax records and land surveys. For examples see *Akty pistsovogo dela* (Census and Tax Documents) (Moscow, 1990), pp. 291-293.

64. The Russian term here is podlye liudi, an expression with no specific juridical meaning, here referring to the poorer classes in general, or the downtrodden.

65. The Russian term for elder is starosta, from the word staryi, or "old." There were many variants of the word staryi which denoted seniority, authority, and respect, as much as they denoted age. Starosta usually referred to the village or community elder, the figure endowed with senior authority to mobilize others to make decisions and carry out tasks. This is the sense in which the law employed the term in discussing merchant guilds. The elder was expected to preside over the guild's institutional responsibilities and represent the guild to higher authorities.

66. Tensmen (desiatskie) were minor police officials in towns and villages. The term has a military derivation, much like hundredmen or centurions. *Slovar' russkogo izayka XVIII v.*, Vol. 6, p. 115

67. The tasks of these officials went beyond assessment. They had a responsibility much like village elders to make sure (in theory anyway) that people were cared for.

68. Soloviev uses the term khlebopashtsy, a common but formalistic term for peasants, those who toil on the land. In this passage he distinguishes between peasants (plowmen) who legally belong to the land and work it with their family and village, and runaways, who may find themselves on the land but have no legal standing in the locality and no claim to the ploughlands

69. Polovniki, from the Russian word polovina, or "half," were independent or sharecropping peasants who, according to tradition, gave over half of what they harvested or produced to the people who owned their land, in exchange for working the fields. Later in the century they were subsumed under the larger category of black-plow peasants.

70. Here the text uses the word pomeshchiki (pl.), a word whose juridical meaning was undergoing considerable change in the late seventeenth and early

eighteenth centuries. During the sixteenth and much of the seventeenth century a pomeshchik was a servitor who held only lifetime, rather than patrimonial tenure over his land. By contrast, votchiniki (pl.) owned patrimonial land which they could pass on independently of service. As a practical matter, the distinctions between the two became increasingly blurred, and Peter abolished them completely, making all landed tenure patrimonial. Oddly, the word that came to denote these landed and ennobled servitors was pomeshchiki. Elsewhere in this passage Peter employed the word zemlevladel'tsy (pl.), a more neutral expression that includes all individuals who owned their own land.

71. This curious expression, "led them to the cross and gospels" (privodil k krestu i evangeliiu), does not appear in reference works of Russian religious phraseology and terminology. From the context it is clear that Gerasim was conducting the peasants in some sort of procession and obliging them to swear an oath, presumably by kissing the cross and placing their hand or forehead on the gospels, that they would present truthful information to the census-takers.

72. The Russian term is odnodvortsy, a legal category referring to free men who owned their land but had no serfs. It is often argued that odnodvortsy were former noblemen whose status had declined to the point where they were indistinguishable from free peasants. In fact the term was elastic enough to include free non-noble homesteaders.

73. Fedor Polikarpov replaced Larion Istomin as director of the Printing Office in 1701, in part because Peter believed that Istomin had not produced a sufficient number of "useful" books. Polikarpov presided over the press for over two decades until 1727, overseeing its transformation into the Moscow Press, whose primary responsibility was church publications. At one point Peter turned to him with a request to assemble materials for a history of Russia, but little came of it.

74. *Stepennaia kniga*, The Book of Degrees, was a genealogy of the ruling family in Russia beginning with Riurik. It also included extensive narratives about saints, important events, and historical personages. The khronograf (chronograph) was a similar type of Muscovite text, written in the form of a chronicle narrative. See Paul Bushkovitch, *Religion and Society in Russia. The Sixteenth and Seventeenth Centuries* (New York, 1992), pp. 106-107.

75. Feofan Prokopovich (1681-1736), archbishop of Novgorod and first vice-president of the Holy Synod, was Peter's most important ideological defender (see Chapter IV, Notes 4, 8, below). As the text suggests, this history was not published during Peter's day. In 1773, M.M. Shcherbatov published it under the title *Istoriia imperatorskogo Petra Velikogo, ot rozhdeniia ego do Poltavskoi batalii* (A History of Emperor Peter the Great, from His Birth Until the Battle of Poltava) (St. Petersburg, 1773).

76. The Russian terms for chancellery clerks are podiache and prikaznye liudi. Peter was using the term in a slightly anachronistic way here since the chancelleries were essentially abolished by the time this decree was published, soon to be replaced by the new colleges. Both terms were widely recognized well into the

eighteenth century as denoting the entire category of employees in civil administration, including most important scribes. This cadre of perhaps three thousand men was obliged by profession to possess sufficient literacy either to keep accounting books or to transcribe manuscripts, and hence were considered to be among the most likely groups to send their offspring to school.

77. Soloviev is contrasting the new Academy of Sciences in St. Petersburg with the Slavonic-Greek-Latin (or simply Slavonic) Academy in Moscow. Begun in 1687, the Slavonic Academy taught mostly classical languages, rhetoric, logic and physical sciences. By 1689 it enrolled nearly two hundred students, a mixture of clerical and lay children, and its graduates went into ecclesiastical and state service. It remained Russia's foremost institution of higher learning until the establishment of Moscow University in 1755. Soloviev's point here is that the Moscow Academy continued with its scholastic and faith-based curriculum, whereas the Academy of Sciences taught science.

78. Peter here is referring to a book published in 1601 entitled *Il regno degli Slavi hoggi* by Mauro Orbini Ravseo. It described the various Slavic peoples in Central and Eastern Europe, emphasizing their military abilities. It was translated into Russian and published in 1722 under the title *Kniga istoriografiia imeni slavy i razshireniia naroda slavianskogo*. See P. P. Pekarskii, *Nauka i literatura v Rossii pri Petre Velikom* (Science and Literature in Russia During the Reign of Peter the Great) (St. Petersburg, 1862), Vol. 2, No. 525, pp. 575-576.

79. Although the text suggests otherwise, this book by Dmitry Cantemir was in fact published in 1722 under the title *Kniga sistima ili sostoianie mukhamedanskiia religii* (The Book of the System or Composition of the Muslim Religion). See T.A. Bykova and M.M. Gurevich, *Opisanie izdanii grazhdanskoi pechati, 1708-ianvar' 1725 g.* (A Description of Civil-Type Publications, 1708-1725) (Moscow, 1955), No. 715.

80. Peter here is apparently referring to Samuel Pufendorf's *Introductio ad Historiam Europaeam* (Introduction to European History), which was translated into Russian under the title *Vvedenie v gistoriiu evropeiskuiu* and published twice during Peter's reign, in 1718 and 1723. See Bykova and Gurevich, No. 320, 744.

81. Psalm 42:3

82. The primers sent probably were those written by Fedor Polikarpov, an instructor at the Slavonic Academy in Moscow and the director of Moscow's printing office (pechatnyi dvor). Polikarpov composed a massive three-language (Slavonic, Greek, Latin) primer and published it in 1701, nominally for use in church schools. A year later he published an equally massive three-language lexicon as a companion volume. Although individual copies of these two texts did show up in church and monastic libraries, Polikarpov's primer was little used in Russia, as a result of which it never went into a second edition. In the Balkan states, Polikarpov's text found a ready audience in those seminaries whose courses of instruction corresponded more closely to what Polikarpov had composed. The four hundred copies mentioned here constituted by far the largest

market for either of Polikarpov's volumes. The grammar book to which Soloviev refers is most likely Melety Smotritsky's *Grammatika iazyka slavenska* (A Grammar of the Slavic Language), a highly formalistic, but widely-used grammar of Slavonic throughout the East Slavic world.

CHAPTER IV

1. See Chapter III, Note 10, above.

2. Stefan Yavorsky (1658-1722) was the metropolitan of Riazan and Murom dioceses, 1700-1722. When the last patriarch of the Russian Orthodox church, Adrian, died in 1700, Peter chose not to replace him. Instead he revived the old Monastyrskii prikaz (Monasterial Chancellery), which had been dormant for several years, and put it in charge of church administration. He appointed Yavorsky as the head of this chancellery, in essence making him the chief administrator of the Orthodox church. When Peter finally abolished the patriarchate and established the Synod he made Yavorsky the first president of the Synod. Yavorsky was opposed to much of Peter's church reforms, but he swore an oath to them anyway and agreed to serve. See James Cracraft, *The Church Reform of Peter the Great* (London, 1971), pp. 104-124, 163-167.

3. This is a very curious statement. The title of metropolitan, in fact, was not eliminated, even though there were far fewer archbishops elevated to the title after Peter's reign than before. Neither the Ecclesiastical Regulations nor the supplement to it contains such an order, neither could I find any individual decree in the published sources that eliminate the title. As a practical matter eighteenth-century metropolitans had no more authority than other archbishops, and their primary responsibilities consisted of managing the dioceses. Yet the title did connote higher respect and authority, and some of the century's leading churchmen employed it widely.

4. The term employed here is lazaretnyi, meaning a small hospital or infirmary. The word derives from St. Lazarus (Lazar') who cured the infirm.

5. The term used here is tsaredvortsev, literally those guarding the tsar's palace.

6. Kozyr', literally "trump card."

7. Peter's convoluted formulation of paternal authority seems to refer to the ambiguous position of parish clergy within communities, and Peter's intention to turn the village priests into respected agents of both church and state. The Ecclesiastical Regulations commanded priests to keep official records of births, deaths and marriages, and to read aloud in church any official decrees sent from the capital. These responsibilities required priests to be literate, no small problem in the early eighteenth century, and it expected them to have sufficient standing in the community so that they would be perceived as an extension of officialdom. Unfortunately village priests drew no salaries from the church and they depended

on donations of food, land and cash to sustain themselves. Their economic dependency on local peasants created severe tensions and seriously impeded the clergy's attempt to establish moral authority over individual peasant households.

8. The monastery dedicated to the Miracles of St. Michael was founded in 1365 by Metropolitan Alexis, and for more than five hundred years was the most important monastery in the Moscow Kremlin. During the Time of Troubles the monastery played a very important role. Grishka Otrepiev, who later surfaced as False Dmitry I, formerly was a monk there. His patriarch, Ignaty, was imprisoned there from 1606 to 1611, and within its walls Patriarch Hermogen was starved to death. During the reign of Michael a school for translating works from Greek and Latin was established. During the 1930s the Miracles monastery and the adjoining Ascension convent were demolished to make way for the School of Red Commanders.

9. Like many of Peter's historical and biblical allusions, the reference to "certain Greek emperors" is opaque. Presumably he is referring to the Byzantine emperors in the period just before the fall of Constantinople in 1453. His comments on Byzantine monasteries and blasphemous behavior remain unclear.

10. Acts 16:3. Paul rejected the rite of circumcision for Gentiles. Timothy was the son of a Greek father but had a Jewish mother, and therefore was considered a Jew rather than a Gentile.

11. The Ecclesiastical Statute (Dukhovnyi Reglament) was written by Feofan Prokopovich and published in 1721 to enumerate the new organization and responsibilities of the clergy at all levels in the wake of the abolition of the patriarchate and its replacement by the Holy Synod. See *The Spiritual Regulation of Peter the Great*. Translated and edited by Alexander V. Muller (Seattle, 1972).

12. An altyn was worth 6 dengas, or 3 copecks.

13. A chetvert was a measure of grain equal to about 8 bushels.

14. The closure of the monasteries initiated a long-term assault on the economic order of the ecclesiastical and monastic side of the Russian Orthodox church, the black clergy. Closing most of the monasteries and convents sent literally thousands of monastic residents out onto the streets to fend for themselves, thus creating a fluid mass of itinerant preachers and wanderers who came to be known as tserkovnye liudi (church people). Peter, as we see in this section, also closed off many other sources of monastic income, such as charging fees for certain services or benedictions. Left untouched were the massive lands held by several monasteries and the church peasants who lived and worked on them. The last foundation of the monastic economy finally was surrendered in 1762 when Peter III ordered the state to take over all church lands, whether monastic, synodal or diocesan.

15. The Synod was organized on the same collegial model as the colleges of the Senate. The chancellery served at the behest of the Synod collectively and coordinated all day-to-day business that fell within the Synod's responsibility.

16. The Old Believers were subjected to double taxation as the price of a modicum of toleration.

17. The Viaznikovo community in Settlement Ukraine was considered a hotbed of Old Believer activity, and was a center of inquisitorial investigations in the early eighteenth century.

18. Peter's former wife Evdokia was forcibly tonsured and confined to the Intercession convent in Suzdal, where she died in 1731.

19. Lefort here refers to François (or Franz) Lefort (1655-1699), a Swiss national who was one of Peter's first "fledglings," a friend from the old days in the Foreign Quarter of Moscow (see earlier volumes in this series). Lefort initially entered Russian service in the mid-1670s and was a close drinking companion of Peter's until his death. Their shared pleasure in debauchery in the Foreign Quarter gave rise to numerous rumors of illegitimate children, switched parentage and the like.

20. The term "junior boyars" (deti boiarskie) is employed somewhat anachronistically here. In the system of precedence that Russia had employed until 1682 the highest ranking aristocratic office was that of boyar, a position that allowed its holder to sit in the Boyar Council and advise the tsar. The junior boyars, on the other hand, were of relatively lowly standing, roughly on par with the service gentry (dvoriane). See entry by Robert D. Givens, MERSH, Volume 9, pp. 101-103.

21. Shortly before the publication of the Ecclesiastical Statute an order was circulated to the parish clergy to cease reading selections from Ephraim the Syrian and the *Sobornik* (Miscellaneous Readings, mostly historical tales and saints' lives) the traditional and previously approved sources of non-scriptural texts to be read aloud in the service. They were to substitute passages from A Student's First Lesson (Pervoe uchenie otrokom), a catechistic primer recently composed by Feofan Prokopovich. Since the non-scriptural texts mostly were memorized, rather than read from the written page, it is unlikely that the substitution was made quickly or easily. Nevertheless each parish church was required to have a copy of Feofan's primer, and it became the basis of periodic examinations of the preparedness of parish clergy.

22. Imperator is, of course, the Russian word for emperor. The speaker is playing with words here, since the verb imperet' means to crush or grind down. Hence, Peter would be "the crusher" rather than an emperor.

23. The Vyg community is the subject of a superb study by Robert O. Crummey, *The Old Believer and the World of Antichrist. The Vyg Community and the Russian State, 1694-1855* (Princeton, N.J., 1983).

24. Here Soloviev is recounting various strains of folk religion in a decidedly patronizing way. Thus we can make nothing more than an educated guess regarding these references. Elias probably was a reference to the Old Testament prophet Elijah, and Enoch could be either the father of Methusaleh or the fabled "Ethiopic Enoch" who is thought to have authored a book of revelations on the Old Testament, revealing such mysteries as Gehenna and the nature of paradise.

25. The Russian word used is bogatyr, used to describe the heroes of many medieval epics.

26. In this case even guesswork fails. The reference could be to the early church historian Eusebius, to the Jewish historian Josephus, or to any one of a number of other figures from early Christian times.

27. Stoglav, or Council of a Hundred Chapters, was the product of a deliberation in Moscow in 1550 of the leading Muscovite clerics. In addition to codifying a good deal of church law, the Council commonly is seen as a proclamation by Tsar Ivan IV of the ascendancy of the Russian church within Eastern Orthodoxy.

28. The Bogomils were a sect which flourished in what is now Bulgaria, originating in the eighth or ninth century. Bogomils believed that all of the physical world was evil, created by Satan, and that only the soul was created by God. They strove to renounce marriage, possessions, wine, meat and any other ties to the physical universe. Their creed proved popular in Southeastern Europe, and proliferated well into the fifteenth century.

29. The Russian here is strannopriimnitsy (pl.) , an imprecise word that seems to refer to blasphemers, heretics, and other categories suspected of following strange practices in the guise of Russian Orthodoxy. In earlier legal texts, from the tenth to the fifteenth centuries at least, the term referred more specifically to religious wanderers or pilgrims. Here the text is too vague to determine whether it had such a precise meaning.

30. Yurodivye (holy fools) were a familiar presence in Russian popular religion and culture, permitted to mock authority and ritual. Because their behavior bordered on the sacrilegious sometimes they were accused of sacrilege and blasphemy. During the eighteenth century the church's efforts to establish greater controls over popular worship and to stamp out alternative rituals and appeals to supernaturalism put the phenomenon of holy fools closer to the margin of sanctioned behavior. See D.S. Likhachev and A.I. Panchenko, "Smekh v drevnei Rusi" (Laughter in Ancient Russia) in D.S. Likhachev, *Izbrannye raboty v trekh tomakh* (Selected Works in Three Volumes), Vol. 2 (Leningrad, 1987), pp. 343-417.

31. The Russian here is dvoeperstnoe slozhenie, referring probably to the two-fingered sign of the cross. The two-fingered cross was outlawed in the seventeenth century during the patriarchate of Nikon in favor of the three-fingered cross deemed by the church to be the only correct form. This change in ritual was one of the principal matters of contention in the church schism.

32. Feofan Prokopovich's book referred to in the preceding paragraph contained nine blessings.

33. See Note 21, above.

CHAPTER V

1. Ivan Ilich Skoropadsky was hetman of the Ukraine from the time he replaced Mazepa in 1708 until his death in 1723. Although approved by Peter, Skoropadsky was widely distrusted by both the emperor and the court.

2. Bogdan Khmelnitsky was hetman of the Ukrainian cossacks who led a decisive uprising against Polish and especially Catholic rule in 1648. In the wake of the rebellion Moscow agreed to become protector of the Ukrainian cossacks, and in 1654 the two sides signed the Pereiaslav Act of Union, in which the cossacks agreed to merge themselves into Muscovy. The union was rejected by Poland, leading to war with Muscovy, a war which Sweden entered on the Polish side. Khmelnitsky died in 1657 and his replacement, Ivan Vygovsky, renounced the union, leading to several more years of warfare, ultimately resolved by the Truce of Andrusovo (1667) which formally ceded the Ukrainian cossack lands, including Kiev, to Muscovy. Khmelnitsky has a complicated reputation in the lore of the region. For some he represents a religious martyr, for others a Ukrainian patriot. For the non-Ukrainian peoples living within the hetmanate, he has a uniformly negative reputation. This is particularly true within Jewish history, which focuses on the widespread anti-Jewish violence associated with his rule.

3. Russian law employed a specific term, universaly (pl.), to refer to orders or decrees issued by local authorities in the Ukraine.

4. The expression here is general'naia starshina, referring to the totality of local officials in the Ukraine.

5. In 1719 Peter ordered the construction of a canal to link the Neva river, which flowed through St. Petersburg, and the Volkhov river. This canal ran through the south shore of Lake Ladoga and, when completed in 1730, constituted the capital's lifeline to the outside world. Through the rest of the eighteenth century the Ladoga canal was the empire's primary artery for the import and export of agricultural products and other commodities. See Kahan, *The Plow, the Hammer and the Knout*, p. 247, also Chapter III, Note 22, above.

6. The Holy Cross fortress was begun at the onset of the Persian campaign, north of the Caspian Sea, at the intersection of the Sulaka and Agrahan rivers.

7. The Voinskie artikuly (Articles of War) were issued in 1716 as a code of conduct for the armed forces. In the absence of an updated civil or criminal code of law it tended to be applied much more broadly, serving as the legal basis for a wide variety of crimes and punishments in civilian society as well.

8. The Russian term polchanin is an approximate synonym for polk, or regiment.

9. The word for authority here is derzhavstvo denoting great power and individual command.

10. The Russian term is sotniki (pl.), hundredsmen or centurions, commanders of cossack formations, equivalent in rank to a lieutenant in the regular army.

11. A znachkovyi cossack, sometimes znachkovyi tovarishch, was a member of a Ukrainian cossack regiment who carried out police responsibilities at the local level.

12. Pavel Polubotok was tried in St. Petersburg and found guilty of deliberately disregarding the sovereign's orders. He was sent with his family to Siberia and deprived of his property. Catherine I brought them back to St. Petersburg

with the proviso that he never leave the city. In St. Petersburg he killed a milk-maid and was given the death sentence. The verdict was revised and he was ex-iled to hard labor at Rogervik, where he died. Ivan Chernysh, implicated in the same affair, also was sent to Siberia. Catherine brought him back as well, and allowed him to return to the Ukraine in 1726.

Paragraph 3, page 147 ("Peter's attendance..."), which in the Moscow edition of 1959-1966 apparently in error appeared after the sentences "The murza ad-vised..." and "The khan refused...," has been shifted to this position for conti-nuity and clarity.

13. Kondraty Bulavin, a Don Cossack hetman, led a rebellion in October 1707 against Russian rule. The upper Don region was deeply affected by the Northern War, and experienced extensive in-migration from peasants fleeing the fighting. The Don Cossacks looked upon this disruption as a further encroachment by Moscow on their traditional autonomy from Russian rule, a controversy that was building since the middle of the seventeenth century. Bulavin hoped to unite cossacks from the Don, Zaporozhie the and Kuban in a massive rebellion but failed to generate sufficient support, and himself died in July 1708. The rebellions outlived him, and in the autumn of 1708 cossack detachments overran several southern towns as far East as the Volga. See Anisimov, pp. 83-86.

14. The Russian here is batko, a diminutive of batushka, itself a diminutive of the word for father, otets. When employed in this manner it connotes affec-tion and respect, as in "dear loving father."

15. The Russian term arba refers to a particular kind of wagon used to cart people or goods. It was drawn by a horse or other draught animal, and it usually had two wheels.

16. The term for non-Russians here is inorodtsy (pl.), meaning literally "people of another clan or non-natives," from the root "rod" meaning "clan," "ex-tended family," or "native". Eighteenth-century Russia had many additional terms to denote others, some of which denoted non-Orthodox, others denoted non-Russian speakers, still others denoted people from a different territory or home-land.

17. Extending a practice begun in the seventeenth century, Peter often sent convicted felons to a form of internal exile in remote regions as a cheaper alter-native to building prisons. Criminals in those areas typically lived in assigned villages, but generally were free to wander in public and intermingle with the local population. The Bashkir territories east of the Volga were a common stag-ing area for convicts, then as Siberia was incorporated into the empire the gov-ernment began sending them further north and east. As this passage makes clear, the Bashkirs were unhappy with this arrangement, one that treated them as a depository of the empire's problems while importing dangerous and alien indi-viduals into their midst.

18. A newly-baptized person, presumably of Bashkir or other Turkic origin, was deemed more reliable by Russian authorities because he had accepted Russian Orthodoxy, and thereby separated himself from the faith of his ethnic

community. In this case the boundary dividing identify could shift from inorodtsy to inovertsy (people of other faiths).

19. Gottfried Wilhelm von Leibniz, the great German philosopher and scientist, conducted an active correspondence with Peter the Great, offering advice on a wide range of subjects, including education, science and the Academy of Sciences. Many of those scientists initially recruited for the Academy of Sciences were recommended by Leibniz, even though personally he never visited Russia. See Alexander Vucinich, *Science in Russian Culture. A History to 1860* (Stanford, Cal., 1963), pp. 43-48.

20. Vitus Bering, after whom the straits are named, was a Lithuanian sea captain employed by Peter to undertake the exploration of eastern Siberia, the so-called first Kamchatka expedition, specifically to determine whether there was a Northwest Passage, or a land link between northern Siberia and America. Commissioned before Peter's death, the expedition did not begin until 1727.

CHAPTER VI

1. Peter II, the sixth child of Peter's second marriage, was born October 28, 1714 and died April 25, 1719. Another son, Paul, died in infancy in January 1717.

2. Absalom was the rebellious son of King David in the Old Testament (see 2 Samuel 13-19). Anointed by David to be his heir, Absalom ultimately took up arms against his father and was defeated and killed. In Peter's mind he himself was the aggrieved David, and Alexis was Absalom.

3. This probably referred to the disinheritance of Ivan III's grandson by his first marriage, Dmitry Ivanovich, in favor of the eldest son of his second marriage, Vasily III.

4. *Pravda voli monarshei* (The Right of the Monarch's Will) was published in August 1722 in a voluminous press run and was widely distributed to dioceses and monasteries. Employing arguments from several schools of thought, the treatise emphasizes the unity of God's law and the monarch's will: the faithful must obey the word of the monarch or else they are in sin. Coming from the most visible clerical figure of Peter's reign, *The Right of the Monarch's Will* constituted a powerful ideological defense of the Petrine reforms. Most scholars, like Soloviev, have accepted the attribution of the text to Prokopovich. Recently, James Cracraft has argued against this attribution. See James Cracraft, "Did Feofan Prokopovich Really Write *Pravda voli monarshei?*" *Slavic Review,* Vol. 40, No. 2 (Summer, 1981), pp. 173-193.

5. The origins of the future Catherine I are obscure. In all probability she was the daughter of a Lithuanian peasant, but she was also briefly married in 1701 to a Swedish dragoon called Johan Raabe, who disappeared from the historical scene when the Swedish garrison was swept by the Russians under Sheremetev out of the fortress of Marienburg. This may be why here she is called the "Swedish woman."

6. Soloviev is referring to Peter's two daughters, Anna and Elizabeth. The term "tsarevna" means literally "daughter of the tsar" and it continued in official usage even after the declaration of empire in 1721. Thus Russia never adopted a term for "daughter of the emperor," though later on in this paragraph Soloviev uses the awkward neologism "tsesarevna." The heir apparent also in later times was referred to as "tsesarevich." With the demise of the one-time heir Alexis and the absence of a clear line of succession, widespread attention, both at the Russian and foreign courts, was focused on these two young women, either of whom might well have succeeded Peter.

7. Tsarevich Alexis Petrovich's wife Princess Charlotte of Brunswick-Wolfenbüttel (1694-1715) was sister to Elisabeth Christine (1691-1750), wife of Charles VI, born 1685, titular king of Spain 1703-1711, Holy Roman emperor 1711-1740.

8. Alexander Lvovich Naryshkin was Peter's cousin through Peter's mother Natalia Naryshkina, and one of the earliest graduates of the Navigation Academy who transformed its curriculum in the 1720s. One of the most ancient boyar clans, the Naryshkins were deeply enmeshed in court politics and frequently advanced candidates for intermarriage with the ruling family.

9. Duke Karl Friedrich preferred to marry Anna, but Peter wanted him initially to marry Elizabeth. He hoped he could marry Anna to Louis XV of France. Catherine quietly interceded on the duke's behalf while Peter was fighting by the Caspian and made certain there would be no public betrothal between Elizabeth (who in the end never married) and the duke. Eventually Anna married the duke and, although she died in 1728, she gave birth to a son, the future Peter III.

10. This compromise was discussed in the previous volume. George I, the Hanoverian king of England, made a secret agreement in 1719 whereby in exchange for Hanover receiving Bremen and Verden, which was under Swedish rule since the Treaty of Westphalia, he would support the Swedish side against Russia to lead Prussia to break its Russian alliance. In particular it would push for a return of Baltic territories which Sweden had lost to Russia.

11. Ulrika Eleonora's husband who eventually reigned as Fredrik I (1719-1751).

12. See Note 10, above.

13. Bassewitz is being metaphorical, saying that it would not take much to use the duke of Holstein to effect a Swedish alliance.

14. In Russia the feast day of St. Catherine of Alexandria is celebrated on November 24. In the West it is celebrated a day later.

15. Despite this proviso, the son of this marriage, born in 1728, reigned briefly as Emperor Peter III (1761-1762).

16. Kleinody (or kleinoty), from the German "Kleinod" meaning something precious. It generally referred to insignia of authority, such as a banner or coat of arms, employed by a Ukrainian hetman.

17. The original text employs two words, pridanie and veno, both of which translate as dowry. The latter term could also refer to bride price, the sum paid by the groom's family to the bride's, but that is not the meaning intended here.

18. Probably a reference to the Germanic custom of Morgengab, a gift made by the groom to the bride on the morrow of the wedding, presumably in token of consummation of the marriage.

19. The Secret Chancellery of Investigated Affairs was established by Peter to investigate Grand Duke Alexis, but its duties later expanded to include other allegations of treason. Peter Tolstoy headed the Secret Chancellery and is widely credited with bringing the grand duke back to Russia. See Anisimov, *The Reforms of Peter the Great*, pp. 275-285.

20. A reference to the fate of the "Brunswick family" during the reign of Elizabeth, and the murder of Ivan VI in 1764.

21. Blagorodstvo is the term used in the original.

22. blagovernye.

23. Conveying the precise English equivalents for Russian terms denoting authority and sovereignty is extraordinarily difficult and controversial. Here the text employs the term samovlastie, a word which later in the century comes close to the English word "tyrant." However in this context it seems to mean approximately "autocratic." The other contemporary terms denoting the power of the ruler were gosudar', usually translated as "sovereign," and samoderzhets, a word whose meaning is a highly contested among scholars. Isabel de Madariaga has insisted that it too meant "sovereign," at least until the very end of the eighteenth century, when it acquired the properties of "autocrat." Others see Peter's own use of the term as denoting "autocrat" and "autocracy." As Soloviev's text makes clear, Peter and his court were struggling with this terminology in pursuit of a fitting way of conveying the greater authority of the Russian ruler as emperor than as tsar. In the end the meanings of these words have to be conveyed in specific context, since it is highly doubtful that contemporaries had a clear and unanimous understanding of what they expressed. Isabel de Madariaga, "Autocracy and Sovereignty," *Canadian American Slavic Studies*, Vol. 16 (1982), pp. 369-387.

24. Anna Mons was the daughter of a German wine merchant in the foreign quarter of Moscow who was Peter's mistress in the 1690s until 1703. See Volume 26 of this series, Chapter V, Note 11, p. 299.

25. The Russian here is nadvornyi sud. See Chapter III, Note 16, above.

CHAPTER VII

1. Soloviev is being very Hegelian here. Geist (spirit) is the cornerstone of history and national development.

2. Soloviev is using the language of religion, specifically Christianity, quite deliberately. He could not say so explicitly, but Peter's hagiographers, mostly churchmen, cast him as Christ-like. Yaguzhinsky and Prokopovich were quite shameless in this regard.

3. Ivan Ivanovich Golikov (1734-1801) was a tax farmer and prominent late eighteenth-century writer who composed numerous volumes recounting the life and times of Peter the Great. Soloviev presumably is referring to Golikov's

twelve-volume *Deianiia Petra Velikogo* (Deeds of Peter the Great) (Moscow, 1788-1789). Golikov also wrote *Anekdoty, kasaiushchiesia do gosudaria Imperatora Petra Velikogo* (Anecdotes about Peter the Great) (Moscow, 1798) and *Dopolnenie k deianiiam Petra Velikogo* (An Addendum to The Deeds of Peter the Great), 18 vols. (Moscow, 1790-1797). Ivan Nikitich Boltin (1735-1792) was an early historian of Russia and essayist of the late eighteenth century. Boltin wrote two prominent works of history in which he defended both his era and his nation against what he perceived to be verbal assaults from others. See especially *Primechaniia na istoriiu drevniia i nyneshniia Rossii g. Leklerka* (A Commentary on the History of Ancient and Modern Russia by Mr. Leclerc), 2 vols. (St. Petersburg, 1788).

4. Soloviev is being very cautious here relative to national minorities. This is one point where overt references to modern nationalism would not pass the censor.

5. Soloviev is referring here to Nikolay Mikhailovich Karamzin, whose multi-volume *History of the Russian State* is generally credited as being one of the earliest attempts to write a scholarly history of Russia. Karamzin was noted for linking the history of the nation with the development of the central state, arguing that the state was the historic agency of Russia's greatness and independence from invaders. Karamzin also composed a book-length essay, *A Memoir on Ancient and Modern Russia*, in which he openly advised the emperor, Alexander I, not to impose a constitution on Russia for fear of opening the door to chaos. A devotee of Montesquieu, Karamzin embraced the idea that each nation had its own "climate," meaning traditions and historical development, that made a particular form of government more appropriate than any other. Russia, he insisted, required autocracy and serfdom as the primary bulwarks of the nation's strength and safeguards against internal disorder. N.M. Karamzin, *A Memoir on Ancient and Modern Russia*. Ed. and trans. by Richard Pipes (Cambridge, Mass., 1959).

6. Soloviev offers a particularly severe judgment of the slavophiles, an important group of nineteenth-century intellectuals who argued that Russia was fundamentally different from the West. Russia's fate, they insisted, lay not in adapting western ideas or institutions but with following their own true national values, based as they saw it on the spirituality of Russian Christianity, a spirituality still retained in the repartitional peasant commune. As Soloviev notes, many leading slavophiles, including Alexis Khomiakov and Ivan Kireevsky, held deeply negative views of the Petrine era, believing that Peter's turn to the West constituted a tragic misdirection of Russia's fate. For more on the slavophiles, see Nicholas V. Riasanovsky, *Russia and the West in the Teaching of the Slavophiles* (Cambridge, Mass., 1952).

7. Soloviev here is making reference to the anecdote concerning the gift of tall soldiers recounted earlier in this volume.

8. Gospoda Senat.

9. Gospoda senaty. Soloviev is implying that this shift in case endings signified a more important shift in relations of authority, away from the institution itself as an anonymous agency of state, and toward the more traditional private authority of families and their scions who occupied seats in the Senate.

10. The reference is unclear, possibly Pososhkov or Peter Tolstoy.

11. The terem was an institution of cloistering women, mostly from the elite social groups, in Muscovite Russia. The terem could mean a separate building, or a separate series of rooms in a residence in which women were hidden away from public exposure as a way of protecting their honor. In the second half of the seventeenth century boyar women increasingly abandoned the strict observation of cloistering, even appearing at public events and at court. During Peter's reign the practice was abandoned, as upper-class women were expected to appear in public, albeit under specific and fairly formalistic settings, such as the assembly. See Nancy Shields Kollmann, "Women's Honor in Early Modern Russia" in *Russia's Women. Accommodation, Resistance, Transformation.* Barbara Evans Clements, Barbara Alpern Engel, and Christine D. Worobec, eds. (Berkeley, Cal., 1991), pp. 60-73, and Kollmann, "The Seclusion of Elite Muscovite Women," *Russian History,* Vol. 10, No. 2 (1983), pp. 170-187.

12. See the Introduction to this volume for an elaboration of Soloviev's views on the politics of his own time.

13. This is a reference to the musketeer revolt of 1698. The strel'tsy (musketeers) formed one of the oldest networks of standing regiments in Muscovite society. Unlike many other regiments, it consisted largely of Russians. By the beginning of Peter's reign there were several thousand musketeers located in fortresses and outposts throughout the realm. The largest contingent was stationed in Moscow and, discontented with Peter's early forms of modernization and Europeanization, they drew close to the party of his cloistered half-sister, Sophia. Many of them also appear to have been sympathetic to the Old Belief. This combination of affinities led them to engage in several revolts during the 1690s. The greatest of these took place in Moscow in 1698 while Peter was still abroad on his Grand Embassy, causing Peter to hurry back, quell the revolt and execute the guilty. A stone chopping block on Moscow's Red Square marks the place where the executions took place. See Volume 26 in this series, pp. 161-185.

14. Soloviev here is referring to the fate of Field Marshal George Ogilvie, a Scotsman who served in the Habsburg armies for many years and who at age sixty commanded Russian troops at Narva in 1705. He led the successful evacuation of Russian troops from the fort of Grodno, but fell afoul of the Russian commanders in the area, especially Menshikov. In frustration he requested that he be relieved of his commission. Peter accepted Ogilvie's resignation in 1706. See Volume 27 of this series.

15. The Foreign Quarter (nemetskaia sloboda), was the neighborhood of Moscow where foreign residents tended to live. During the seventeenth century, as an increasing number of foreign merchants, artisans, and mercenaries came to work in Muscovy, this settlement became a center of European culture and influence, noted for its inns and taverns, and a periodic object of anti-foreign violence by the domestic population. In modern Russian "nemetskii" refers specifically to Germans, but it originally denoted all foreigners. Its root is the word "nemoi," or "mute," meaning those who were unable to speak in the native

language. By the seventeenth century "nemetskii" referred specifically to Northern Europeans. By the late eighteenth century it began to take on its current meaning.

16. The Russian word "bogatyr" is used in the original. See also Chapter IV, Note 25, above.

17. Ivan Ivanovich Nepliuev (169-1773) was one of the more prominent men who came of age during the reign of Peter. Referred to as Peter's "ptentsy" (fledglings), these were individuals specifically chosen by Peter for important careers. Nepliuev, for example, was sent abroad for four years to study, leaving behind a wife and family. He later became ambassador in Constantinople and wrote one of the most revealing memoirs of the late Petrine era, *Zapiski Ivana Ivanovicha Nepliueva (1693-1773)* (St. Petersburg, 1893).

18. Literally "Who is not a grandson to a grandmother?

19. "u galernogo stroeniia." It is uncertain whether he means the kitchen or a ship.

20. Andrei Konstantinovich Nartov was a mechanic who became close to Peter and later played a prominent role in the Academy of Sciences. He is the source of many of the anecdotes about Peter that Soloviev recounts. See L.N. Nartov, *Rasskazy Nartova o Petre Velikom* (Nartov's Tales about Peter the Great) (St. Petersburg, 1891).

INDEX

THE EDITOR AND TRANSLATOR

Gary Marker is Professor of Russian History and head of the Department of History at the State University of New York at Stony Brook. He received his Ph. D. from the University of California, Berkeley, in 1977 under the supervision of Nicholas Riasanovsky. Prior to teaching at Stony Brook he taught for one year at Oberlin College and one year at Berkeley. The author of numerous articles and books, Professor Marker's primary scholarship has focused on the history of printing, education, literacy, and reading in Russia from mid-seventeenth through the end of the eighteenth centuries. In addition to the present work Professor Marker's principal publications include *Publishing, Printing, and the Origins of Intellectual Life in Russia, 1700-1800* (Princeton, N.J., 1985), *Reinterpreting Russian History* (with Daniel Kaiser) (Oxford, 1994), and *Ideas, Ideology, and Intellectuals in Russian History. A Festschrift in Honor of Nicholas Riasanovsky* (Charles Schlacks Jr., Publisher, 1993). He is preparing a translation and interpretation of the diary and memoir of Anna Labzina, an eighteenth-century noblewoman, and a lengthy study entitled *Literacy and Reading in Russia, 1649-1800*. Professor Marker is the principal organizer of the Eighteenth-Century Russian Studies Association, an affiliate society of the American Association for the Advancement of Slavic Studies, in 1994, and of its annual series of summer workshops at the University of Illinois. He is married and has one child.

FROM ACADEMIC INTERNATIONAL PRESS*

*Request catalogs. Sample pages, tables of contents, more on line at www.ai-press.com